mustsees
Andalucia

Olvera, one of the Pueblos Blancos/Matt Trommer/Shutterstock.com

MICHELIN

mustsees **Andalucia**

Editorial Director	Cynthia Clayton Ochterbeck
Production Manager and Additional Layout	Natasha G. George
Texts, Photo Editing, Layout	Buysschaert&Malerba, Milan
	Aaron Maines (principal writer), Giacomo Serra (editor),
	Martine Buysschaert, Francesca Malerba
	(photo editing and layout)
Cartography	Cartographie Michelin Paris
Interior Design	Chris Bell, cbdesign
Cover Design	Chris Bell, cbdesign, Natasha G. George

Contact Us

Michelin Travel and Lifestyle North America
One Parkway South
Greenville, SC 29615, USA
travel.lifestyle@us.michelin.com
www.michelintravel.com

Michelin Travel Partner
Hannay House
39 Clarendon Road
Watford, Herts WD17 1JA, UK
www.ViaMichelin.com
travelpubsales@uk.michelin.com

Special Sales

For information regarding bulk sales, customized
editions and premium sales, please contact us at:
travel.lifestyle@us.michelin.com
www.michelintravel.com

Michelin Travel Partner

Société par actions simplifiées au capital de 11 288 880 EUR
27 cours de l'Ile Seguin - 92100 Boulogne Billancourt (France)
R.C.S. Nanterre 433 677 721

© Michelin Travel Partner
ISBN 978-2-067188-78-5
Printed: November 2013
Printed and bound in Italy

MIX
Paper from
responsible sources
FSC® C015829

Note to the reader:
While every effort is made to ensure that all information printed in this guide is correct
and up-to-date, Michelin Travel Partner accepts no liability for any direct, indirect or
consequential losses howsoever caused so far as such can be excluded by law. Admission
prices listed for sights in this guide are for a single adult, unless otherwise specified.

Welcome to Andalucía

The Lion Courtyard in the Alhambra in Granada

p 101

Must Do

Must Eat

Must Stay

Must Know

TABLE OF CONTENTS

★★★ ATTRACTIONS

Unmissable historic, cultural and natural sights

Sevilla p 26

© Pedro Salaverría/Shutterstock.com

Córdoba p 154

© Cam/Shutterstock.com

Costa del Cabo de Gata p 141

© SueC/Shutterstock.com

MUST KNOW

Olvera, one of the typical *pueblos blancos* p 111

© Matt Trommer/Shutterstock.com

Granada p 116

© Kutlayev Dmitry/Shutterstock.com

The Sierra Nevada and the villages of Las Alpujarras p 132

E.Loudier/Hemis.fr

STAR ATTRACTIONS

★★★ ATTRACTIONS

Unmissable historic, cultural and natural sights

For over 75 years people have used Michelin stars to take the guesswork out of travel. Our star-rating system helps you make the best decision on where to go, what to do, and what to see.

★★★	Unmissable
★★	Worth a trip
★	Worth a detour
No star	Recommended

★★★Three Star

Córdoba *p 154*
Corta Atalaya (Parque Minero de Riotinto) *p 58*
Gibraltar *p 88*
Granada *p 116*
Gruta de las Maravillas (Aracena) *p 55*
Parque Nacional de Doñana *p 67*
Parque Natural de las Sierras de Cazorla, Segura y Las Villas *p 150*
Sevilla *p 26*

★★Two Star

Las Alpujarras *p 135*
Arcos de la Frontera *p 111*
Baeza *p 148*
Cádiz *p 78*
Carmona *p 52*
Castillo de Almodóvar del Río *p 169*
Cueva de Nerja *p 102*
Desfiladero de los Gaitanes *p 115*
Jerez de la Frontera *p 70*
Medina Azahara *p 168*
Minas de Riotinto *p 57*
Osuna *p 113*
Pampaneira *p 136*
Paraje Natural de las Marismas del Odiel *p 64*
Parque Natural de Cabo de Gata-Níjar *p 141*
Parque Natural de El Torcal *p 115*
Parque Natural de la Sierra de Aracena y Picos de Aroche *p 55*
Puerto de la Ragua *p 136*
Ronda *p 106*
Setenil *p 111*
Úbeda *p 146*
Valle del Guadalhorce *p 114*

★One Star

(Among others)

Alájar *p 56*
Almonaster La Real *p 56*
Las Alpujarras *p 135*
Andújar *p 152*
Aracena *p 55*
Ayamonte *p 66*
La Calahorra *p 135*
Casares *p 92*
Estepona *p 94*
Frigiliana *p 101*
Guadix *p 134*
Huelva *p 64*
Itálica *p 52*
Jaén *p 144*
Laguna de la Fuente de Piedra *p 114*
Málaga *p 96*
Marbella *p 94*
Mijas *p 95*
Mojácar *p 142*
Nerja *p 101*
Palos de la Frontera *p 66*
Parque Natural de Despeñaperros *p 152*
Parque Natural de la Sierra de Andújar *p 152*
Parque Natural de los Alcornocales *p 91*
Parque Natural La Breña y Marismas de Barbate *p 91*
Ruinas Romanas de Baelo Claudia *p 90*
Salobreña *p 102*
Sanlúcar de Barrameda *p 75*
Setenil *p 111*
Sierra Nevada *p 132*
Valle del Lecrín *p 135*
Vejer de la Frontera *p 91*
Zahara de la Sierra *p 111*

MUST KNOW

ACTIVITIES

Unmissable activities, entertainment, restaurants and hotels

From Arab baths to boat trips, we've compiled a list of things to do and places to go that will enrich anyone's visit to Andalucía. While we recommend every activity we've included in this guide, the Michelin Man logo highlights our top picks.

STAR ATTRACTIONS

IDEAS AND TOURS

Looking for a change? Had your fill of church ogling and museums? This chapter will help you explore the wide range of alternative activities and adventures available in Andalucía. Whether you'd like to crisscross the countryside on horseback, visit a world-renowned vineyard or windsurf the wild waters in Tarifa, the region offers a host of interesting alternatives to the traditional tourist's vacation.

ART AND NATURE

Andalucía means having your cake and eating it too: you can enjoy the cultural and artistic attractions of its big cities as well as the natural beauty of its open countryside, all in a single trip. From **Sevilla★★★**, famous for its folklore, myths and myriad attractions, you can head west toward the beaches of **Huelva Coast★**, making a short side trip north into the vast forests punctuated by slender peaks of the **Sierra de Aracena y Picos de Aroche Nature Park★★**. Or you can travel southwest to the medieval heart of elegant **Jerez de la Frontera★★**, and the ancient city of **Cádiz★★**, where you'll find a fascinating mix of elegant Baroque and Neoclassical buildings; then you can move north to explore the marvelous wetlands of **Doñana National Park★★★**, one of Europe's largest wilderness sites.

From the magnificent city of **Córdoba★★★**, flush with art and history, you can head out to explore delightful towns like **Baeza★★** and **Úbeda★★**, then wind your way up into mountainous landscapes amid the rivers and gorges of the **Sierras de Cazorla, Segura y las Villas Nature Park★★★**.

From **Granada★★★** and its **Alhambra★★★**, respectively the capital of the former Nasrid kingdom and one of the world's most breathtaking monuments, you can travel through the **Sierra Nevada★** and the gentle slopes of the **Alpujarras★★** on you way to the enchanting beaches of **Cabo de Gata★★**, on the **Almería Coast★**! Andalucía has two national parks, 20 nature parks and a number of protected areas covering 18 percent of the region (for further information visit www.andalucia. org, click on "What We Offer You" and choose "Nature").

Wine and Sherry tours

© R.Mattes/Hemis.fr

COAST TO COAST

Andalucía has the geographical advantage of bordering both the Atlantic and the Mediterranean. The **Atlantic coast**, also known as the **Costa de la Luz** (Coast of Light), extends a total of 330km/206mi from the Portuguese border to the Straits of Gibraltar, through the provinces of Huelva and Cádiz. In general, its beaches are popular with Spanish visitors, particularly families. Days are hot, while ocean breezes provide cooler evenings. Sea temperatures are lower than in the Mediterranean. The 15 beaches in **Huelva province** are characterized by golden sand, clear water, surf, sand dunes and pine forests. The **Cádiz coast**, the most southerly in Spain, stretches 200km/125mi. Its beaches of fine, golden sand are lined by some of Spain's most historic towns and cities, such as **Sanlúcar de Barrameda★**, **El Puerto de Santa María★** and **Cádiz★★**. The only drawbacks for sun-worshippers are the strong winds, which attract thousands of windsurfers every year.

The **Mediterranean coast** includes areas with differing geographical characteristics, but all share a similar hot, dry climate. The waters of the Mediterranean are generally calm, warm and crystal clear. The western section of the **Costa del Sol** (Sun Coast), from Gibraltar to Málaga, contains over half of all hotel accommodation along the Andalusian coasts. Paradoxically, the majority of the beaches here are pebbly. The high-rise resorts in this area have embraced mass tourism for better and for worse. Exclusive **Marbella★** is at the top end of the spectrum. East of

Málaga★, as far as **Nerja★**, tourist development is less pronounced. The shores of Granada province are known as the **Costa Tropical**, and enjoy a sub-tropical climate thanks to protection afforded by the Sierra Nevada. The beaches along this stretch range from coves protected by high cliffs to enormous beaches like those in **Salobreña★**.

The **Costa de Almería★** between **Adra** and **Aguadulce** features the immense sandy beaches of Balanegra and Balerma, while to the east of Almería the Mediterranean is bordered by the **Parque Natural de Cabo de Gata★★**, where you'll find superb beaches like **Playa de los Genoveses★**.

🍷 WINE AND SHERRY

Andalucía has almost 90,000ha/222,000 acres of vineyards, and its wines enjoy a superb global reputation. Wine production throughout this region is classified and protected through certified designations of origin. Four *denominaciones de origen* (D.O.) currently govern the quality of Andalusian wines: Jerez, Montilla-Moriles, Condado de Huelva and Málaga. Sherries produced in the **Jerez de la Frontera area** (*see also p 77*), including the famous *finos* and *manzanillas*, are Andalucía's best-known and most prestigious wines. Montilla-Moriles are excellent wines produced in the area **south of Córdoba**, toward Antequera.

MORE ON MOORS

The **Moorish Legacy** (El Legado andalusí) initiative has been developed by the

Junta de Andalucía and the Spanish government to provide information about Moorish art and culture for visitors to the Iberian peninsula. This includes a series of exhibitions and the creation of official tourist routes through al-Andalus (Andalucía, Murcia, Portugal and North Africa). Designated tourist routes (all well signposted) deliberately explore areas outside the well-trodden tourist centers, offering an in-depth look at the historical and artistic heritage of one of the most brilliant civilizations in history.

The **Route of the Caliphate** links the two main cities of Moorish Spain, Córdoba and Granada, and is around 180km/112mi long.

The **Washington Irving Route** follows the itinerary American Romantic writer Washington Irving took in 1829, during which Irving was struck by the exuberant and exotic nature of the Moorish monuments in Andalucía. Linking the towns of Sevilla and Granada, this historical route once served as an important communication channel between the Nasrid kingdom and Christian authorities.

The **Nasrid Route**, straddling the provinces of Jaén and Granada, is dedicated to the last chapter of Moorish history in Spain. In 1212 in Las Navas de Tolosa, near Despeñaperros, the battle that led to the Christian reconquest of Andalucía took place, setting in motion conflicts that culminated in the capture of Granada in 1492.

The **Route of the Alpujarras** (*see also p 137*) links Almería and Granada via a series of mountain passes. It stretches north to the peaks of Sierra Nevada and south to the Mediterranean.

For detailed information: Fundación El Legado andalusí, Avenida de la Ciencia, Granada, 958 22 59 95, www.legadoandalusi.es.

GOLFING

Golfers flock to Andalucía year-round for the region's superb golfing conditions and the high quality of the roughly 100 courses scattered around the region, ranging from 9-hole courses for beginners to elite championship golf greens. The majority are along the Costa del Sol, although excellent courses can also be found near Sevilla, Huelva, Cádiz, Granada Jaén, Córdoba and Almería. Details on the specific aspects of each course are listed in a golf brochure published by the Andalusian Tourist Board. You can also visit www.andalucia.org/en/golf.

HORSE RIDING

For those who like to saddle up to sightsee, Andalucía offers excellent options, including cross-country treks lasting several days that include stays in horse farms, country houses and rural hotels; as well as courses on breaking in horses and equestrian techniques. Visit www.andalucia.org for

Costa de Almería, Mini Hollywood

information on the many operators present across Andalucía.

If you are vacationing in the Tarifa area and would like ride horseback across on the sands, visit www. aventuraecuestre.com.

⚓ WATER SPORTS

From sailing to scuba diving and water-skiing to windsurfing, Andalucía offers a range of sporting options for water sports enthusiasts of all levels. There are operators on most beaches and at marinas. Most are reputable, but you should still try to establish their professional qualifications before you sign up for anything and note their approach (or lack thereof!) to safety.

Tarifa is the windsurfing capital of Spain, though beginners and less experienced boardsailors should build up their confidence and abilities elsewhere before taking on this gusty coastline. You'll find the best surfing in the region around this area, on the **Costa de la Luz** between Tarifa and Cádiz.

⚓ SPAS

You'll find details and information on the National Spa Association's website (www.balnearios.org), or at www.andalucia.org.

© J-P Degas/Hemis.fr

Quick Trips
Stuck for ideas? Try these:

Alcazabas *25, 97, 102, 123, 134, 140*

Arab/Moorish baths *25, 38, 61, 73, 76, 88, 108, 123, 127, 140, 146, 151, 162, 172*

Botanical gardens *74, 100, 101, 173*

Caves *15, 55, 90, 102, 111, 115, 130, 134, 143, 150*

Contemporary art *30, 55, 95, 100*

Entertainment parks *63, 129, 138, 142, 143, 173*

Fine Art *35, 42, 46, 50, 86, 100, 113, 123, 126, 167*

Fishing ports *65, 66, 138*

Food specialties *54, 55, 58, 73, 92, 100, 111, 114, 131, 136, 153*

Marinas *65, 67, 88, 93, 94, 96, 105, 138, 142*

Markets *61, 76, 87, 100, 126, 131, 141, 151, 153, 164, 173*

Mountain views *54, 55, 56, 106, 115, 145, 151, 152, 170*

Music and dance *15, 55, 57, 60, 61, 62, 63, 74, 80, 101, 102, 124, 130, 131, 172, 173*

Nature parks *9, 53, 55, 67, 91, 115, 132, 137, 141, 143, 150, 152, 153*

Panoramic roads *58, 69, 90, 91, 94, 101, 110, 114, 115, 134, 135, 136, 139, 142, 151, 152, 170*

Patios *15, 33, 35, 36, 37, 38, 47, 48, 53, 80, 82, 85, 91, 109, 121, 122, 123, 124, 126, 127, 128, 134, 135, 146, 149, 159, 162, 163, 165, 172, 173*

Pilgrimages *14, 15, 63, 131*

Popular arts and traditions *45, 51, 87, 100, 131, 134, 141, 150, 151, 163, 173*

Roman history *24, 26, 47, 48, 51, 52, 53, 57, 73, 78, 82, 90, 91, 95, 96, 97, 106, 111, 113, 114, 116, 129, 138, 151, 154, 162, 164, 166*

Sand dunes *11, 65, 68, 90, 139*

Shopping *48, 61, 76, 87, 96, 112, 131, 137, 141, 153, 173*

CALENDAR OF EVENTS

Here you'll find a selection of Andalucía's most popular annual events. Be sure to doublecheck dates, which may vary from year to year. You can also consult Fiesta & Events in Sevilla (p 62–63), Córdoba (p 173), Granada (p 131) and the Costa del Sol (p 105). For information on these and other Andalusian festivals, contact the local tourism offices you'll find listed in each section or visit www.andalucia.org.

January

Fiesta de la Toma

Granada, *958 24 71 28, www.turgranada.es.*
Commemoration of the capture of Granada (Jan 2).

February

Candlemas processions

Many towns and cities.
The faithful carry candles during a solemn procession celebrating the presentation of young Jesus in the temple.

February/March

Carnival

Cádiz, *956 25 04 26, www.carnavaldecadiz.com; and other cities.*
Cádiz hosts the biggest carnival *(see also p 85)*, but exciting parades are also held in Alhama de Granada, Bornos, Carmona, Chipiona, Isla Cristina, Úbeda and throughout Andalucía.

Holy Week

Semana Santa celebrations

Throughout Andalucía.
Processions, particularly in Sevilla, Córdoba, Granada, Huelva, Jaén and Málaga (last week before Easter).

April

Feria de abril de Sevilla

Sevilla, *902 19 48 97, www.visitasevilla.es.*
Two weeks after Holy Week, Sevilla holds its spring fair.

Virgen de la Cabeza pilgrimage

Andújar, *953 50 49 59.*
One of Andalucía's principal pilgrimage destinations, especially on the last Sunday in April.

May: El Rocío pilgrimage

© P. Wysocki/Hemis.fr

May

Horse Fair
Jerez de la Frontera, *956 14 98 65, www.turismojerez.com.*
Horse parades and competitions, a fun fair, plus plenty of Fino sherry and flamenco. Dates vary (late April to mid-May).

Manzanilla Fair
Sanlúcar de Barrameda, *956 36 61 10, www.sanlucar debarrameda.es.*
Celebrating the sherry-like drink *manzanilla* in its hometown (19–24 May).

Events in Córdoba
Córdoba, *957 35 51 79, www.turismodecordoba.org.*
Throughout May: May crosses; patio competition; annual fair; national flamenco contest (held every three years, next in 2016).

Whitsunday

El Rocío pilgrimage
Almonte, *959 44 38 08, www.almonte.es.*
Most pilgrims, known as *rocieros*, approach the 13th-century statue of the Virgen del Rocio crossing the Doñana National park (May or June).

June/July

Granada International Music and Dance Festival
Granada, *958 24 71 28, www.granadafestival.org.*

Nerja Cave International Music and Dance Festival
Nerja, *952 52 15 31, www.cuevadenerja.es.*
Internationally-renowned musicians and dancers perform in the extraordinary Nerja Cave.

Seafaring processions
Several towns and villages along the Mediterranean, particularly Almería.
16 July (Virgen del Carmen).

August

Horse races on the beach
Sanlúcar de Barrameda, *956 36 61 10, www.sanlucar debarrameda.es.*

Málaga Fair
Málaga, *951 92 72 05, www.malagaturismo.com.*

Virgin del Mar Fair and Festival
Almería, *950 21 05 38, www.turismodealmeria.org.*

September/October

Pedro Romero Fair and Festival
Ronda, *952 18 71 19, www.turismoderonda.es.*
Theater performances, a parade, the Flamenco singing festival, sports competitions and more (8–10 September).

Wine Harvest and Horse Week
Jerez de la Frontera, *956 14 98 65, www.turismojerez.com.*
The second fortnight in Sept. and first fortnight in Oct.

October

St Luke's Fair
Jaén, *953 19 04 55, www.turjaen.org.*
Corridas, music, culture and sports.

December

Los Verdiales Music Festival
Málaga, *951 92 72 05, www.malagaturismo.com.*
Various groups challenge one another in performances of Verdiales flamenco, a form of the dance first developed in the Los Verdiales olive-growing region north of Málaga.

PRACTICAL INFORMATION

WHEN TO GO

Spring and **autumn** are the best seasons for touring inland Andalucía, as temperatures can exceed 40°C/104°F in **summer**. **Winters** are generally mild, although temperatures can dip dramatically at higher altitudes. Coastal resorts along the Mediterranean enjoy mild temperatures and plentiful sunshine even in winter. Generally speaking Andalucía enjoys a **Mediterranean** climate, with dry summers and relatively mild winters, during which the region receives the majority of its somewhat scarce and irregular precipitation. Because of the size of Andalucía and the presence of high mountain ranges skirting an extensive stretch of coastline along two huge bodies of water, closer analysis of the Andalusian climate shows **significant differences** between areas. As an example, although the Guadalquivir Valley has a climate that could be described as typically Mediterranean, neighboring mountain areas are much colder and receive far greater precipitation. Along the coast, there is a marked contrast between the **beaches** of the Mediterranean, with its calm, warm waters, and those of the more open Atlantic coast, characterized by colder waters and frequent strong winds, particularly around Tarifa on the Straits of Gibraltar, a paradise for windsurfers.

Specific areas clearly demonstrate the region's climatic differences: the region's coldest temperatures have been recorded in the Sierra Nevada, where **snow** remains year-round on the highest peaks and where ski slopes stay open until May; in complete contrast, the startling Campo de Níjar area in the province of Almería is arid, volcanic and **desert-like**, with temperatures to match.

For up-to-date information on weather in Andalucía visit the Spanish Meteorological Office website at www.inm.es.

Temperature chart (min/max temperatures)				
	Jan	**Apr**	**Jul**	**Oct**
Almería	8/16°C	12/20°C	21/29°C	16/23°C
Cádiz	8/15°C	12/21°C	20/29°C	16/23°C
Córdoba	4/14°C	10/23°C	19/36°C	13/24°C
Granada	1/12°C	7/20°C	17/34°C	9/22°C
Huelva	6/16°C	11/22°C	18/32°C	14/25°C
Jaén	5/12°C	10/20°C	21/34°C	13/22°C
Málaga	8/16°C	11/21°C	20/30°C	15/24°C
Sevilla	6/15°C	11/23°C	20/36°C	14/26°C

MUST KNOW

Sevilla

© F. Rodriguez/Age Fotostock

KNOW BEFORE YOU GO
Useful Websites

www.andalucia.org –
The Andalusian Tourist Board
presents destinations subdivided
by province, including information
useful for organizing a visit and
contact info for many operators:
accommodations, cultural visits,
events, sport activities, nature
areas, beaches, information
services.

www.spain.info – The official
visitors' information site for tourism
in Spain.

www.andalucia.com – A
unofficial long-running site with a
wealth of detail and much useful
information.

www.visitacostadelsol.com –
A good source of information
covering the Costa del Sol and its
inland villages.

www.state.gov – American
visitors should check the US State
Department website for worldwide
travel advice.

Tourism Offices

Local tourist offices provide
information about things like
accommodations, entertainment,
festivals and recreation free of
charge. See *Practical Information*
in the Must See section for the
addresses, telephone numbers and
websites of major visitor centers
throughout the region.

International Visitors
Foreign Embassies and
Consulates in Spain

Australia – **Embassy:** Torre
Espacio, Paseo de la Castellana
259D, 28046 Madrid; 913 53 66 00;
www.spain.embassy.gov.au

Canada – **Embassy:** Torre Espacio,
Paseo de la Castellana 259D,
28046 Madrid; 913 82 84 00;
www.canadainternational.gc.ca

Ireland – **Embassy:** Paseo de la
Castellana 46-4, 28046 Madrid,
914 36 40 93; www.embassyof
ireland.es.

UK – **Embassy:** Torre Espacio,
Paseo de la Castellana 259D, 28046
Madrid; 917 14 63 00; www.gov.
uk/government/world/spain.
Consulate: Calle Mauricio Moro
Pareto 2, 29006 Málaga; 902 10 93
56 (in Spain), 913 34 21 94 (outside
Spain); Info.Consulate@fco.gov.uk.

USA – Embassy: Calle de Serrano 75, 28006 Madrid; 915 87 22 00; madrid.usembassy. gov. **Consulates:** Consular agencies in Sevilla (Plaza Nueva 8-8 duplicado, 41001 Sevilla; 954 21 87 51; sevillecons@telefonica. net) and Fuengirola (Avenida Juan Gómez "Juanito" 8, 29640 Fuengirola, Málaga; 952 47 48 91; conagencymalaga@telefonica.net).

Spanish Embassies and Consulates Abroad

For a complete list of Spanish embassies and consulates abroad, visit the Spain Ministry of Foreign Affairs and Cooperation online at www.exteriores.gob.es (Citizen services section).

Entry Requirements

In Spain, no visas are required for stays of less than 90 days over a six month period for citizens of Australia, New Zealand, Canada and the US. Travelers must be in possession of a valid national passport. Citizens of European Union countries, Switzerland, Norway, Iceland and Liechtenstein only require a national identity card or passport. All travel documents must be valid for at least three months beyond the period of stay. Others, and those planning to stay longer than 90 days, should inquire at a Spanish consulate.
US citizens should visit http:// travel.state.gov for futher general information on visas, customs regulations, and more.

Customs Regulations

Travelers are permitted to enter Spain with their personal baggage, which may contain items for personal or family use, or to be given as presents. These may not necessarily be considered commercial goods, depending on the quantity or type of goods. This evaluation will be made by the customs services on arrival. Currently, travelers over 18 are authorized to carry 200 cigarettes, or 100 mini-cigars, or 50 cigars, or 250 grams of rolling tobacco. Visitors are allowed to bring one liter of an alcoholic drink (over 22% alc. by volume), or two liters (under 22% alc. by volume). Perfumes are limited to 50 grams of perfume and 0.25 liters of eau de toilette.
For more information about what you can bring into Spain, depending on your nationality, visit:

Australia – Australian Customs Service: 1300 36 32 63, www.customs.gov.au.
Canada – Canada Border Services Agency: 800 461 99 99 in Canada, or 204 983 35 00; www.cbsa-asfc. gc.ca.
Ireland – Revenue, Irish Tax and Customs: www.revenue.ie.
UK – HM Customs and Excise: 0845 010 90 00; www.hmrc.gov.uk.
USA – US Customs and Border Protection: 877 CBP-5511 in the US, or 202 325 80 00; www.cbp.gov. *Know Before You Go* is available as a downloadable PDF from www. cbp.gov (click on "Travel," then on "Know Before You Go.")

Health

Always verify whether or not your insurance covers health care and emergencies abroad. If not, it's wise to purchase optional coverage. If you come from an EU member state, the **European Health Insurance Card** (EHIC) gives you access to medically necessary, state-provided healthcare during a temporary stay under the same conditions and at the same costs as Spanish citizens. You will have to pay any hospital, medical or pharmaceutical bills in advance, and then seek reimbursement from the relevant organization in your country of origin, providing all receipts. All visitors should also be insured for uncovered medical expenses (such as a return flight to your home country), lost luggage, theft, etc.

Generally speaking, Spain has excellent healthcare. There are several private care organizations with links to US and UK private healthcare organizations as well.

GETTING THERE
By Air

A number of Spanish and international airlines operate scheduled services to airports in Andalucía.

These include **Iberia** (*902 40 05 00, www.iberia.com*), **British Airways** (*902 11 13 33, www.britishairways. com*), **American Airlines** (*www. aa.com*), **Delta** (*www.delta.com*), **United** (*www.united.com*), **TAP Portugal** (*www.flytap.com*), **KLM** (*www.klm.com*).

The following low-cost airlines also offer inexpensive flights to Andalucía from the UK: **Easyjet** (*www.easyjet.com*); **Flybe** (*www.flybe.com*); **Monarch** (*www.monarch.co.uk*); **Thomson** (*flights.thomson.co.uk*). From Ireland: **Aerlingus** (*www.aerlingus.com*); **Ryanair** (*www.ryanair.com*).

You can land at any of the following airports in Andalucía: **Sevilla**, **Almería**, **Granada–Jaén**, **Jerez de la Frontera**, **Málaga–Costa del Sol**, or the airport at **Gibraltar**. For information on airport facilities, as well as connections to various cities, see *Practical Information* in the Must See section, and visit www.aena.es.

By Ship (and Car)

Brittany Ferries (*0871 244 07 44; www.brittany-ferries.com*) operates services to northern Spain from the UK: Plymouth to Santander; Portsmouth to Bilbao or Santander.

By Train

Eurostar (*08432 18 61 86; www.eurostar.com*) operates high-speed passenger trains from the new London terminal of St Pancras to Paris, where overnight train services depart for Madrid, with connections to destinations across Andalucía. Services can be booked through the Spanish State Railway Network's (**RENFE**) UK agent, the Spanish Rail Service (*+44 203 137 44 64; www.spanish-rail.co.uk*). Alternatively, visit www.renfe.es.

Getting There and Around

You'll find more detailed information about the main destinations in Andalucía on the Practical Information pages in each chapter of the Must See section: Sevilla (*p 27*), Costa de Huelva (*p 65*), Jerez de la Frontera (*p 71*), Cádiz (*p 79*), Strait of Gibraltar (*p 89*), Costa del Sol (*p 93*), Ronda and Pueblos Blancos (*p 107*), Granada (*p 117*), Sierra Nevada (*p 133*), Costa de Almería (*p 138*), Northeast Andalucía (*p 145*) and Córdoba (*p 155*).

PRACTICAL INFORMATION

By Train and Car

From the UK, the high-speed Channel Tunnel rail link ferries motorists and their cars beneath the channel in around 35min on specially designed double-decker carriages. For information and bookings contact **Eurotunnel** (*08443 35 35 35; www.eurotunnel. com*). The Calais terminal is linked to the French highway network (Madrid is roughly 1,600km/just under 1,000mi from France, and Sevilla or Málaga are an additional 550km/344mi further).

Visit **www.ViaMichelin.com** for driving routes from 43 European countries to Spain.

By Bus

Regular long-distance bus services operate from London to major towns and cities in Andalucía. For information, contact **Eurolines** (*08717 81 81 78; www.eurolines.co.uk*).

GETTING AROUND
By Train

Spain's rail network is operated by **RENFE** (Spanish State Railways). Information is available 24hr a day; reservations can be made from 5:30am to 11:50pm; 902 32 03 20; www.renfe.com.

Interrail

An Interrail pass will give you unlimited travel on European trains (in second class), for a price calculated based on the countries you intend to visit. The **InterRail Global Pass** covers travel within 24 European countries, or you can choose a **Select Pass** (3, 4 or 5 countries) or a **Regional Pass** (2 countries). The **InterRail Spain Pass** covers travel all over Spain through tickets valid for 3-, 4-, 6- or 8-day voyages (either consecutive or separate) within a single 1-month period. Prices are discounted roughly 30% for travelers under 26. Visit **www. eurail.com** or **www.interrail.eu** for additional information.

By Car

Andalucía has a good network of highways (*autopistas*), roadways (*autovías*) and other roads of varying categories.

Drivers usually need only a current driving license from their home country and vehicle documentation and insurance to drive in Spain. In certain situations an International Driving Permit is required. Check with the AA or RAC (UK), the AAA (US) or CAA (Canada). Bear in mind that Spain's highway naming system is currently being overhauled, and some numbers may have changed by the time you visit.

Rental Cars

You can rent a car in Andalucía through the offices of all major car rental companies around the world. Alternatively, cars can be rented at major airports, train stations and large hotels around Andalucía. Most companies will only rent to drivers over the age of 21.

Car Rental Companies

- **Avis** – 902 18 08 54, www.avis.com.
- **Enterprise Atesa** – 902 10 01 01, www.enterprise.com.
- **Europcar** – 902 50 30 10, www.europcar.com.
- **Goldcar** – 902 11 97 26, www.goldcar.com.
- **Hertz** – www.hertz.com (online only).

MUST KNOW

- **Record Go** – 964 34 36 26, www.recordrentacar.com.
- **Sixt** – 902 49 16 16, www.sixt.com.

Rules of the Road

A driving license, car document and insurance (your rental car company will automatically provide these) must be carried at all times. Maximum speed limits in Spain are: 120kph/75mph on highways and dual roadways; 100kph/62mph on national roads; 90kph/56mph on minor roads; 50kph/31mph in built-up areas. Traffic violations are punished with on-the-spot fines for non-residents. Here's a look at some important rules:

- Drive on the right side of the road and give way to the right.
- Priority is given to traffic already on a roundabout.
- Seat belts must be worn in front and back seats at all times.
- Children under 12 must sit in the back seat of a car.
- Do not drink any alcohol; the limit here can be exceeded after consuming just one glass of wine or beer.
- You must have a hands-free device to use a mobile phone while driving.
- Helmets are required for mopeds and motorcycles.

In Case of Accident

Two warning triangles and reflective vests (your rental car company will automatically provide these) must be in your vehicle at all times, and used in case of accident or car problems. Drivers are required to aid accident victims if they are the first on the scene.

RACE (Spanish Royal Automobile Club) offers roadside assistance: 902 40 45 45; www.race.es.

By Coach/Bus

Traveling by bus is an inexpensive way of getting around the region, and often the only form of transport between small villages. Main intercity connections and the contact details of major bus companies are listed in *Practical Information* in the Must See section of this guide. You can also visit **www.movelia.es**.

© R. Harding/Hemis.fr

Bicycle renting in Sevilla

ACCESSIBILITY
Disabled Travelers

Visit **www.spain.info** and click on "Practical Information" and "Accessible Tourism" to find information and downloadable PDF guides to accessibility for monuments, museums, restaurants, accommodations, activities in nature areas and leisure activities. The **Tarjeta Dorada** (Golden Ticket) offers persons over 60 and people with a 65% or more disability a 40% discount on rail travel. Companions of the disabled traveler will also receive the discount. www.renfe.es.

BASIC INFORMATION
Accommodations

For suggested lodgings and information about hotel and parador rates and reservations, see Hotels.
In addition to the selection included in this guide, you can contact large hotel chains, which often offer reduced rates on weekends. These include: **Meliá Hotels International** (www.solmelia.com); **NH Hoteles** (www.nh-hoteles.es).

Paradores

This state-run network of luxury hotels is most famous for its accommodation in restored historic monuments, such as castles, palaces, monasteries, etc.
While in the recent past the sense of history pervading paradores was matched by a lack of modern facilities, today you can usually enjoy Wi-Fi while sprawled in a four-poster bed used by ancient kings. For more information, contact **Paradores de Turismo**: calle Requena 3, 902 54 79 79; www.parador.es.

Bed and Breakfasts

Normally a B&B offers a cozier atmosphere than a hotel. Various websites offer B&B listings, including the popular www.bedandbreakfast.com.

Hostels

The **Inturjoven** organization (902 51 00 00; www.inturjoven.com) manages a large network of youth hostels, located at strategic centers in cities, along the coast and in the mountains across Andalucía.
A hosteling card, obtainable from any hostel or from the Inturjoven reservations center, is required to stay in any of the hostels within the network. Cards issued by members of the IYHF (International Youth Hostel Federation) are also accepted.

Campsites

There are numerous campsites in Andalucía, especially along the coasts. Visit www.guiacampingfecc.com or www.campingsandalucia.es for additional information.

Discounts

Students, children and senior citizens often get discounts at museums and attractions, as well as on public transportation.

Business Hours
Banks

Banks are generally open 8:30am–2pm, Monday to Saturday, and closed on Saturdays in summer.

Attractions

Hours for individual attractions are given in each entry. Closing dates vary; note that most sights and attractions are closed Jan 1, May 1 and Dec 25, and many are closed on major holidays. October 12 is a national holiday in Spain.

Shops

Traditional shops are open mornings to 2pm, closed for lunch and siesta, then reopen 5pm–8pm or 8:30pm. Larger stores and shops in tourist resorts may not close for lunch. Most shops close on Sundays, as well as a few on Saturday afternoon. Those in tourist resorts may stay open longer hours and on Sundays.

Pharmacies

Hours vary: they may be similar to shop hours or remain open

MUST KNOW

nonstop from 8am to the late evening. In large cities you will also find pharmacies open 24 hours a day.

Electricity
220v/50Hz (110v/60Hz in some older establishments). Plugs are two-pin.

Emergencies
Emergency Services: 112.

Internet
Many hotels provide internet access to guests, and you'll find internet cafés in the more touristic areas in Andalucía. Wi-Fi hotspots are still relatively rare, but are increasing every year: visit **www.andaluciaviveconectada.es** to find the one closest to you.

Mail
Post offices are generally open Mon–Fri 8:30am–2:30pm, Sat 9:30am–2pm. Stamps (*sellos*) can also be purchased at tobacco stores (*estancos*).

Money/Currency
Euro are issued in notes (€5, €10, €20, €50, €100, €200 and €500) and coins (1 cent, 2 cents, 5 cents, 10 cents, 20 cents, 50 cents, €1 and €2).

Credit Cards
Most shops, hotels and restaurants accept major credit cards.

Currency Exchange
If you exchange traveler's cheques or cash at banks and exchange offices (*cambios*) you will usually get a good rate of exchange, but you may have to pay a transaction charge (so it is best to exchange

one or two large sums, rather than keep returning). It is much easier and probably just as cheap to obtain euros from cash machines (ATMs) using credit or debit cards, but do check with your bank before you go, as charges can vary dramatically.

Smoking
Smoking is officially banned in all public places, bars and restaurants.

Tipping
If service is not included, it is customary to leave up to a ten percent tip in restaurants and hotels when you consider the service satisfactory. Passengers are also expected to leave a small tip for taxi-drivers.

Telephones
For calls within Spain, dial the full 9-digit number; from abroad, dial the international access code (00), then 34 for Spain, then the full 9-digit number.
Public telephones accept coins or phonecards (*tarjetas telefónicas*), sold at tobacco shops and post offices.

Temperature and Measurement
In Spain, temperatures are measured in degrees Celsius, and measurements are expressed according to the International System of Units of weights and measures (meter, kilogram, second, liter, ton…).

Time Zone
Spain is one hour ahead of the UK, 6 hours ahead of Eastern Standard Time and 9 hours ahead of Pacific Standard Time.

ANDALUCÍA IN HISTORY

From the kingdom of Tartessus through a long period of splendor dominated by the al-Andalus civilization, to its slow, inexorable destruction during the Reconquest and the golden age of New World discoveries... Enjoy a brief overview of the history of Andalucía.

From Phoenicians to the Romans and Visigoths

Ever since navigators from the far east of the Mediterranean first landed toward the end of the second millennium BC, modern day Andalucía has hosted numerous different civilizations: it was a **Phoenician colony** and a territory in the **Kingdom of Tartessus** (c. 13C–6C BC), which later came to be identified with the biblical Tarsis and whose legendary status is equal to that of Atlantis (modern archaeologists have discovered numerous remains in Huelva, Sevilla and Córdoba). The **Carthaginians** (6C–4C) settled here before they were forced to abandon the region by the **Romans** in the wake of the two **Punic Wars** (264–241 and 218–201 BC). During Roman domination, Andalucía became

The Royal Chapel of Granada

Baetica, a province of the Roman Empire, with important cities like Corduba (the capital), Gadir (Cádiz), Hispalis (Sevilla) and Itálica. Quickly adopting Roman habits and customs, the region enjoyed a period of peace spanning several centuries. The philosopher **Seneca** (4 BC–65 AD) was born in Córdoba, as was his nephew **Lucan** (b. 39); two future Roman Emperors, **Trajan** (53–117 AD) and **Hadrian** (76–138 AD), were born in Itálica. In the 3C Rome moved its commercial axis to the east and Hispania began a slow decline. In the 5C the region was conquered by the Visigoths.

Al-Andalus

At the beginning of the 8C the Umayyad Caliphate from Damascus conquered the Berber lands of North Africa. The dominant tribes adhered to the Islamic faith, joining together with powerful Muslim forces. In 711 an army under the command of the Berber **Tarik-ibn-Ziyad** crossed the straits and conquered the Visigothic kingdom, marking the beginning of Muslim domination in Spain. Halfway through the 8C the al-Andalus kingdom, populated by Arabs and Berbers, was created. Eventually Al-Andalus expanded to include almost the entire Iberian Peninsula. Over centuries, various different Arab dynasties took power in Andalucía. During the Caliphate of Córdoba ruled by **Abd ar-**

Al-Andalus cities

Andalusian cities of the period were equipped with sewage systems, public lighting and various communal services. In fact, they were blessed with far more amenities than their contemporary Christian counterparts. The interior of the **medina** (the walled center of the city) housed markets now known in Spanish as *zocos* (from the Arabic suq), public baths (*hamam*), mosques and restaurants. Larger towns and cities generally had a university or *madrasa* as well. Civil and military authorities, the army and their families all lived in the **alcazaba**, an independent walled fortress equipped with its own services. Public baths (it is said that Córdoba had over 600) satisfied the population's need for water, especially the Islamic obligations of spiritual and bodily cleanliness. Boasting hygiene centers with specialized staff, baths also acted as a place where people could meet and relax.

Rahman III (912–61), the kingdom became the most powerful in the West and its court the most cultured and refined; Spain regained its commercial impetus in the Mediterranean.

Though plagued by internal conflicts and battles against nearby Christian kingdoms, for almost eight centuries Al-Andalus remained the backdrop for the cohabitation of two completely contrasting religious, architectural and cultural worlds: Islam and Christianity. It was also an extraordinary center of artistic and scientific culture that produced progress in many different fields: alchemy, medicine, physics, botany, mathematics (including the introduction of so-called Arabic numerals), astronomy, philosophy and more. Inventions considered revolutionary were produced here: from astrolabes and quadrants to refrigeration systems; lighting effects created with bowls of mercury; and water clocks.

The Reconquest

Catholic Monarchs reconquered the territories governed by Arabs rather slowly, over the course of three centuries (12C–15C). The decisive offensive against the Nasrid kingdom of Granada took place from 1482 to 1492.

The Golden Age

Christopher Columbus set sail from the port of Palos de la Frontera on 3 August 1492. On 12 October he arrived at Guanahani Island (Bahamas).

Trade with America brought wealth to Sevilla and the surrounding region, including Córdoba and Málaga. Sevilla, which benefited from the monopoly, was transformed into a major Spanish city and a paradise for powerful merchants and adventurers. But the situation in the rest of Andalucía was different. The arrival of new products from the Indies (cochineal, indigo) had an effect on the region's traditional textile industry, while Granada's silk industry, which produced satin, velvet and damask, suffered from the austere clothing policy imposed on the Spanish Empire by the Habsburgs. However, Córdoba began to specialize in the production of harnesses and cordovans made from American leather.

SEVILLA★★★

Aware they live in a metropolis filled with extraordinary art and rich in history, *Sevillanos* are confident about their city's charms and happy to display them to others. You'll find citizens who are passionate about their hometown and enjoy extolling their city's virtues. They'll tell you Sevilla is more than a city: it is a way of embracing life to the full that is exuberant, festive and particularly passionate. You'll enjoy Velázquez, Murillo, Don Juan and Carmen; the scent of orange blossoms; the world famous Semana Santa (Holy Week) celebrations and the Feria de Abril, or April Fair; dancing *sevillanas* in the street and, like it or not, the blood and drama of the corrida.

A Bit of History

From its earliest days Sevilla's fate has been determined by its role as a **river port**. Although its precise origins remain unclear, the city was probably founded by Iberians. It became in turn a Greek, Phoenician and Carthaginian colony that was overrun by the Romans in 205 BC following a long siege.

From Romans to Moors

At first, Roman occupation was marked by factional disputes. **Julius Caesar** seized the city in 42 BC and fortified it, transforming Sevilla into one of the main cities in Baetica. In the 5C Vandals invaded the region; they were expelled by the **Visigoths**, who made the city their capital until the court was transferred to Toledo.

Beginning in 712, **Moorish conquest** of Sevilla heralded a long period of Arab domination. During the Caliphate, the city came under the control of Córdoba; then a taifa kingdom in 1031. Sevilla experienced great cultural development during the reign of Al Mutamid, but difficult relations with the Christian king, Alfonso VI, obliged Al Mutamid to seek aid from the Almoravids who subsequently seized the kingdom in 1091. In the 12C, the Almohads took control from the Almoravids and began a period of urban transformation that included construction of both the Giralda

Plaza de España

© Pedro Salaverría/Shutterstock.com

Practical Information

Location
Sevilla is an inland port city on the Guadalquivir river, located in west-central Andalucía.

Population
706,365.

Getting There
♦ **By Air** – **San Pablo international airport** (902 40 47 04, www.aena.es) is located 8km/5mi northeast of the city center, along the A 4 toward Madrid. **Buses** run direct to the city center and Santa Justa rail station (5:20am–1:15am to Sevilla; 4:30am–0:30am to the airport; €4, or €6 roundtrip; www.tussam.es). **Taxis** charge a flat fee for travel to and from the airport. (€21.89 Mon–Fri 7am–9pm; €24.41 Mon–Fri 9pm–7am, Sat–Sun and public holidays).

♦ **By Car** – The A 4–E 5 highway connects with Cádiz to the south and Córdoba to the northeast. The E-1 runs toward Huelva and Portugal to the west.

♦ **Parking** – It is difficult to find parking downtown, and the best solution is to leave your car in one of the numerous parking garages: in plaza Nueva (calle Albareda); paseo de Colón; calle Cano y Cueto (a list of available parking garages can be consulted at www.visitasevilla.es).

♦ **By Train** – Trains arrive in Sevilla's **Estación de Santa Justa** (avenida Kansas City) train station from all the other main Andalusian cities (Jaén, Cádiz, Jerez, Huelva, Málaga, Osuna, etc.), as well as from all over Spain. The AVE high-speed train connects Sevilla with Madrid in just 2hr 25min; Córdoba in 45min. The AVANT Málaga–Córdoba–Sevilla train is the best bargain (for information and reservations, 902 320 320, www.renfe.com).

♦ **By Bus** – Inter-city buses run from **Estación Plaza de Armas** (avenida Cristo de la Expiración, 902 45 05 50, www.autobusesplazadearmas.es) to Sevilla province, Huelva, elsewhere in Spain, and Europe.

Getting Around
♦ **On foot** – Sevilla's historical center is pedestrians-only.

♦ **By Public transportation** – For information on routes, timetables and prices for public transportation, visit: www.consorciotransportes-sevilla.com, or 902 45 99 54, www.tussam.es (autobus e tram); 954 03 21 00, www.metro-sevilla.es (metro).

♦ **By Bicycle** – **SEVici** is Sevilla's bike sharing service. You can rent a bike using your credit card in one of the 250 stations set up around the city. Rentals are for min. 7 days (first 30 mins. free; €12.30 for one week; for further information, 902 01 10 32, www.sevici.es).

♦ **By Taxi** – Radio Taxi (954 58 00 00); Tele Taxi (954 62 22 22); Taxi Giralda (954 99 80 70).

Visitor Information
The following tourist offices (**Oficina de turismo de Sevilla**) will answer all your questions: Calle Arjona 28, 902 19 48 97; plaza de San Francisco 19, 954 59 52 88. Info Point stations are open in the airport and train station, or by visiting www.visitasevilla.es.

SEVILLA

MUST SEE SEVILLA

Map of Sevilla

PI. de la Concordia
PI. Duque de la Victoria
POL.

Alfonso
A. Gordillo
San V
de la Iglesia
XII
PI. de Armas

MUSEO DE BELLAS ARTES
PI. del Museo

Monsalves
San Roque
Eloy
O'Donnel
San
Murillo
Rioja

Pedro del Toro
S. Pedro Mártir
Gravina
Canalejas
Bailén
Méndez
Núñez

Puente del Cachorro

La Cartuja
Av. Cristo de la Expiración

PI. Legión

LA MAGDALENA

Julio César
San Pablo
Zaragoza
Bilbao

Paradas
Arjona
Reyes Católicos
EL ARENAL
Doña Guiomar

El Patrocinio

Pastor y Landero
Castelar
Harinas

Paseo
La Real Maestranza
Adriano
Díaz

Nuestra Señora de la O
Castilla
PI. Callao
El Carmen

Puente Isabel II o de Triana

Pas.
Alcalde
Ant.
G.ª
Castaños
Dos de May

Cristóbal
Colón

S. Jorge
Antillano
Campos
Jacinto
PI. del Altozano

Capilla de los Marineros
PUERTO
PUERTO
Marqués
de Contadero

San
Rodrigo
Pureza
TRIANA

Pagés

Sta Ana
Betis

Leiria
Evangelista
Triana
del
TORRE DEL ORO

Troya

Febo

Farmacéutico E. Murillo Herrera

Martínez Trabajo
M. Champagnat
Ardila
Salado
Corro

Puente de San Telm

Sánchez Arjona
Argentina
PI. de Cuba

Salado
Avenida
República
Niebla
Arcos
Virgen
Asunción

Virgen de Fátima

Niebla
Virgen de África
Miño
Turia

Virgen
Juan Ramón Jiménez
Valle
Monte
Turia

LOS REMEDIOS

Turia
Virgen
Padre Damián
Virgen
de
de
Loreto
Carmelo
Elcano

Santa Fe
Virgen del Águila

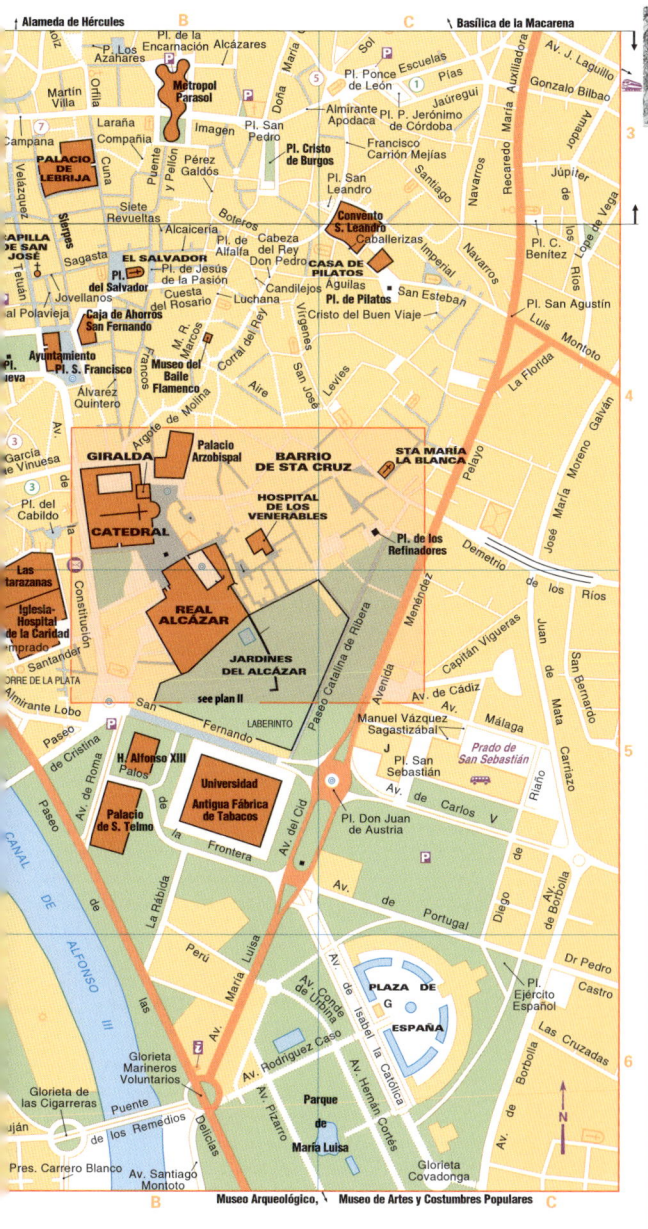

and the *mezquita* (mosque), on the site now occupied by the cathedral.

Reconquest

On 23 November 1248, Fernando III (the Saint) reconquered Sevilla and established his court in the city. He was followed by Alfonso X the Wise and then Pedro I, who restored the Alcázar and took up residence there.

16C: The Golden Age

After America was discovered in 1492, Sevilla held a monopoly on trade with the New World and became the departure and arrival point for every expedition to the Americas. Among those who sailed from Sevilla were Amerigo Vespucci and Magellan, who set out in 1519 and was the first to circumnavigate the globe. In 1503 the **Casa de Contratación** was founded, a body established to encourage, inspect and control trade with the Americas.

Sevilla began to amass great wealth, and foreign merchants and bankers were drawn to the city, where they built new palaces and established new industries. But the smell of money attracted hustlers, villains and people from all walks of life; so much so that Sevilla's population nearly doubled during the 16C, rising to some 200,000 inhabitants.

Decline

The city entered a period of decline following the plague of 1649, exacerbated by the transfer of the Casa de Contratación to Cádiz in 1717.

20C

During the 20C Sevilla hosted two major international exhibitions:

Touring Tip

Sevilla's two most important monuments, the **cathedral** and the **Alcázar**, as well as its famous **Santa Cruz quarter**, are located in the city center.

A **Sevilla Card** (*www.sevillacard. es*) allows you to skip the line at the cathedral entrance, and provides discounts in restaurants, shops and hotspots, as well as a number of other perks depending on the kind of card you buy: 24 hr (admission to two museums and a Guadalquivir river cruise, €33); 48 hr (admission to all participating museums and your choice of a river cruise or tour bus ride, €53); 72 hr (all museums, river cruise, tour bus ride and admission to Isla Mágica, €71; 120 hr €77).

the 1929 **Ibero-American Exhibition** and **Expo'92**, both of which had a significant effect on the city's layout. A number of large projects were completed for Expo'92, in particular the **Isla de la Cartuja**, where the fair was held. The **Isla Mágica** theme park and the **Centro Andaluz de Arte Contemporáneo** (*955 03 70 70; www.caac.es*) are now located on the Isla de la Cartuja.

CATHEDRAL AND THE GIRALDA★★★

Maps p33 and p39.

Open Jul-Aug Mon 9:30am–2:30pm, Tue–Sat 9:30am–4pm, Sun 2:30pm–6pm; rest of the year Mon 11am–3:30pm, Tue–Sat 11am–5pm, Sun 2:30pm–6pm. €8. 902 09 96 92. www.catedraldesevilla.es.

Cathedral★★★

"Let us build a cathedral that will make them think us mad," the chapter is said to have declared in 1401 when it ordered men to demolish the mosque. The cathedral is enormous; considered the third largest in floor space in the Christian world after St Peter's in the Vatican and St Paul's in London. One of the last Gothic cathedrals built in Spain, it shows obvious Renaissance influence. The Cristóbal (or Príncipe), Asunción and Concepción (in the Patio de los Naranjos) doorways are modern (19C and 20C), yet respect the style as a whole. The Puerta del Nacimiento and Puerta del Bautismo, which open out onto the Avenida de la Constitución, include beautiful sculptures by Mercadante de Bretaña (1460). At the east end, admire the rounded Chapel Royal (*Capilla Real* – 1575), decorated with coats of arms and, on either side, the Gothic Puerta de Palos and Puerta de las Campanillas with Renaissance-style tympana in which you can appreciate Miguel Perrin's use of perspective.

Interior

This universe of stone, stained glass and grilles bewilders visitors with its size and richness. The ground plan consists of five aisles – the central nave is wider and higher – with chapels in the side aisles. The column shafts support simple Flamboyant Gothic pointed vaults. The vault of the transept rises 56m/184ft above the floor. A mirror **(1)** located on the floor provides a striking view.

High Altar

The richly decorated **high altar** (*capilla mayor*) is enclosed by a splendid 16C Plateresque **grille★★** by Fray Francisco de Salamanca. The immense Flemish **altarpiece★★★** (1482–1525), the largest in Spain, is profusely and delicately carved with colorful scenes from the lives of Christ and the Virgin Mary (except the predella, decorated with saints).

The Cathedral

SEVILLA

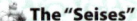
The Seises are a group of twelve brightly dressed choir boys who perpetuate a tradition dating back to the 16C, singing and dancing in front of the cathedral's high altar during the eight days following Corpus Christi (*generally in May and June, though dates may change depending on when Easter occurs each year*) and the Feast of the Immaculate Conception (December 8). Initially the group consisted of six (*seis*) *niños*, hence the name. They also accompany the **Corpus Christi** procession when it stops in the plaza del Ayuntamiento and the plaza del Salvador.

Chancel

In the main nave, partly hidden by a 16C grille, you'll find the *coro*, with fine 15C–16C choir stalls. The majestic organs are from the 18C. The **trascoro** (chancel screen) of multi-colored marble, jasper and bronze, is 17C.

Treasury

The treasury in the 16C **Sacristía de los Cálices** (Chalice Sacristy) is surmounted by a fine vault. Interesting paintings on display include *Santa Justa* and *Santa Rufina* by Goya, a Zurbarán, a triptych by Alejo Fernández and several canvases by Valdés Leal. The anteroom of the sacristy houses the **Tenebrario**, a 7.80m/25ft, fifteen-branch Plateresque candelabrum used during Holy Week processions.

The main **sacristy** (*sacristía mayor*) contains the impressive Renaissance silver **monstrance** (*custodia*) by Juan de Arfe, measuring 3.90m/13ft and weighing 475kg/1,045lb. A *Santa Teresa* by Zurbarán and *The Martyrdom of San Lorenzo* by Lucas Jordán can be seen on the rear wall.

Chapter house

The 16C Renaissance chapter house (*sala capitular*) has an elliptical dome and a characteristic *Immaculate Conception* by Murillo.

Capilla Real★★

The monumental Plateresque Chapel Royal was built during the reign of Charles V over an earlier chapel. It is covered by an elegant, richly ornamented coffered dome with carved busts and contains a small apse covered by a decorated scallop shell.

A wooden carving of the **Virgen de los Reyes**, patron saint of Sevilla, decorates the altar. Behind it, a silver urn houses the remains of Fernando III the Saint. The Capilla Real is enclosed by a majestic grille dating from 1771.

Chapels and Altars

Once you have seen the cathedral's major works, take time to admire the numerous works of art on display in its chapels:

- **Altar de Nuestra Señora de Belén (2)**: north side, to the left of the Puerta de la Concepción. Fine portrayal of the Virgin Mary by Alonso Cano.
- **Capilla de San Antonio (3)**: this chapel contains several interesting canvases dominated by **Murillo**'s *Vision of St Anthony of Padua*, on the right-hand wall. Also worthy of

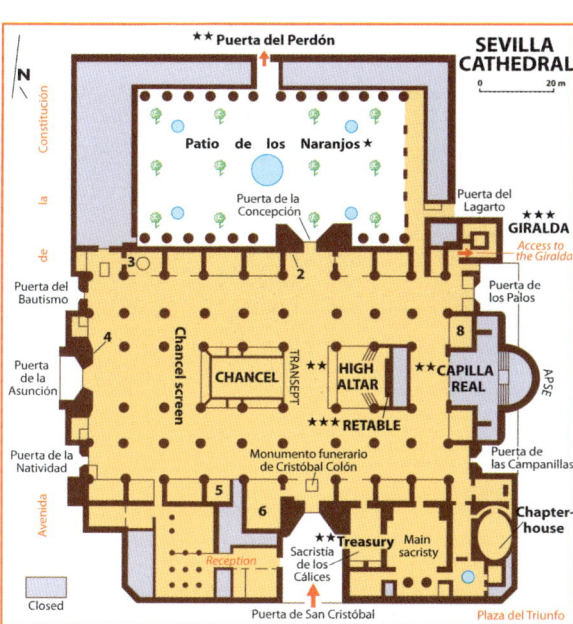

note are Murillo's *The Baptism of Christ*, and two paintings of St Peter by Valdés Leal.

- **Altar del Santo Ángel (4)** (at the foot of the cathedral, to the left of the Puerta Mayor): this altar is dominated by a fine *Guardian Angel* by Murillo.
- **Capilla de San Hermenegildo (5)** (next to the Capilla de San José): the 15C alabaster tomb of Cardinal Cervantes sculpted by Lorenzo Mercadante.
- **Capilla de la Virgen de la Antigua (6)** (the next chapel): larger than the others and covered with an elevated vault. A fine 14C fresco of the Virgin adorns the altar.
- 19C funerary monument to **Christopher Columbus (7)**: the explorer's coffin is borne by four pallbearers bearing

the symbols of Castilla, León, Navarra and Aragón.

- **Capilla de San Pedro (8)**: the walls of this chapel are hung with a superb series of paintings by **Zurbarán** illustrating the life of St Peter.

Patio de los Naranjos

This exceptional rectangular patio is planted with orange trees (*naranjos*) and was used for ritual ablutions in the former mosque.

Puerta del Perdón

The Almohad arch and the door leaves from the original mosque survive on this majestic portal. The impressive sculptures and the relief, representing the Expulsion of the Money Changers from the Temple, are from the 16C.

View from the Giralda

Giralda★★★

The Giralda can be accessed from inside the cathedral. See below.
Elegant and lofty, the Giralda is the symbol of Sevilla. Built at the end of the 12C, this brick minaret (96m/315ft), part of the mosque (*mezquita*), was once surmounted by three gilded spheres, which sadly fell off during an earthquake that struck in 14C. The belfry, three superimposed stages and balconies are 16C additions by Córdoban architect Hernán Ruiz. These were crowned with an enormous weather vane, the Statue of Faith, known as the Giraldillo (from *girar*: to turn), which inspired the tower's name. The tower is a masterpiece of Almohad art, delicate yet restrained. This purist dynasty shunned ostentation, yet managed to create a harmonious style of beauty and simplicity. The decoration on each side is organized into three vertical registers with sebka panels.

Climbing the Giralda

A segmented ramp inside the cathedral will take you up to the tower belfry (70m/230ft). The ascent is not particularly difficult; take your time to admire views of the Patio de los Naranjos, the gargoyles and pinnacles of the cathedral and the Alcázar. Your efforts will be well rewarded at the top with a magnificent **panorama★★★** over the city.

Palacio Arzobispal

The residence of the Archbishop of Sevilla is in the attractive **plaza de la Virgen de los Reyes**, with its monumental lantern (and numerous horse-drawn carriages), and elegant, late-Baroque, early 18C façade.

Plaza de Santa Marta

Take the narrow callejón de Santa Marta, opposite the Palacio Arzobispal.
The alleyway offers the only access to this delightful small square of whitewashed façades, simple wrought-iron grilles and a small stone cross shaded by orange trees where you can enjoy a charming, hushed atmosphere.

Archivo General de Indias

Open Mon–Fri 8am–3pm (mid Jun–mid Sept, 2:30pm). 954 50 05 28. www.mcu.es/archivos/MC/AGI/index.html.

This sober, Renaissance-style building houses archives relating to the Spanish conquest and colonization of the Americas, including documents that boast the signatures of Columbus, Magellan, Hernán Cortés, Juan Sebastián Elcano and others. Note the building's sumptuous 18C pink and black marble staircase. Visitors are only allowed access to the upper floor, characterized by large rooms topped with elegant vaults.

Plaza del Triunfo

Some of Sevilla's most impressive buildings look out onto this square. In the center stands a "triumph" (*triunfo*) to the Immaculate Conception. Along the sides you'll see the Archivo General de Indias; the cathedral (south side); the Alcázar; and the former Hospital del Rey, now the Casa de la Provincia.

REAL ALCÁZAR★★★
Maps p36 and p39.

Open Apr–Sept daily 9:30am–7pm, Oct–Mar daily 9:30am–5pm. Closed 1, 6 Jan, Good Fri and 25 Dec. €8.75. Night visits available only by reservation via Internet (Apr–Sept 9pm–10:30pm, Oct–Mar 7:30pm–9pm, €12). 954 50 23 24. www.alcazarsevilla.org.

This magnificent palace is the result of several phases of construction that took place from the 10C onwards in a variety of architectural styles. All that remains of the 12C Alcázar of the

Almohads are the Patio del Yeso and fortified arches separating the Patio de la Montería from the Patio del León. In the 13C Alfonso X (the Wise) built the Gothic-style apartments known as the Salones de Carlos V. The nucleus of the palace was built by Pedro I (the Cruel) in 1362. This Mudéjar masterpiece was built by masons from Granada who were highly influenced by the Alhambra (*see GRANADA*), which dates from the same period. Modifications were made by Juan II, the Catholic Monarchs, Charles V and Felipe II.

Cuarto del Almirante
To the right of the Patio de la Montería.

Isabel the Catholic founded the Casa de Contratación in the Admiral's Apartments in 1503. The Sala de Audiencias (Audience Hall) has an altarpiece, the **Virgin of the Navigators**★ (1531–36), by Alejo Fernández.

Sala de la Justicia and Patio del Yeso
To the left of the Patio de la Montería.

The Sala de la Justicia (Justice Chamber) was built in the 14C

© Massimiliano Pieraccini/Shutterstock.com

Real Alcázar

over the remains of the Almohad palace. Note the finely sculpted plasterwork *(yesería)* and magnificent cupola.

Palacio de Pedro el Cruel★★★

The façade of Pedro the Cruel's Palace is reminiscent of the Patio del Cuarto Dorado in Granada's Alhambra, with *sebka* decoration, fragile multifoiled arches and a large epigraphic frieze beneath a carved wood overhang.

A small hallway leads left from the entry to the **Patio de las Doncellas**. Note the exquisite *yesería* decoration over a gallery of foliated arches above paired columns; and magnificent 14C *azulejo* panels. The Italian upper storey was added under Charles V. A number of Mudéjar rooms open onto this patio: **the Salón del techo del Carlos V (1)** (Carlos V's Room), the palace's former chapel, with a splendid Renaissance ceiling with polygon caissons; the **Dormitorio de los Reyes Moros (2)** (Bedroom of the Moorish Kings), two rooms with blue-toned stucco and artesonado ceilings;

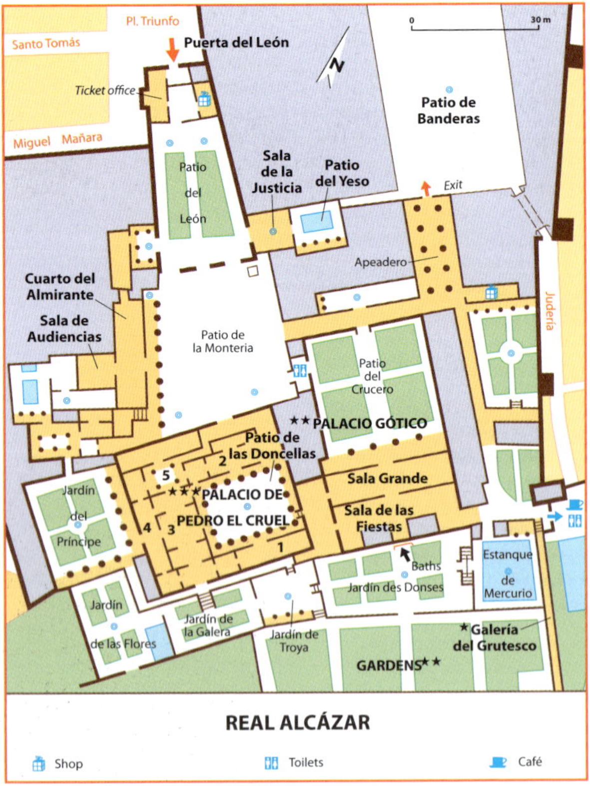

REAL ALCÁZAR

Map labels:
- Pl. Triunfo
- Santo Tomás
- **Puerta del León**
- Ticket office
- Miguel Mañara
- **Patio de Banderas**
- Patio del León
- **Sala de la Justicia**
- **Patio del Yeso**
- Exit
- **Cuarto del Almirante**
- **Sala de Audiencias**
- Apeadero
- Patio de la Montería
- Judería
- Patio del Crucero
- **★★ PALACIO GÓTICO**
- **Patio de las Doncellas**
- 2
- 5
- **★★ PALACIO DE PEDRO EL CRUEL**
- 4 3
- 1
- **Sala Grande**
- **Sala de las Fiestas**
- Jardín del Príncipe
- Baths
- Jardín des Donses
- Estanque de Mercurio
- Jardín
- de las Flores
- Jardín de la Galera
- Jardín de Troya
- **GARDENS★★**
- **★ Galería del Grutesco**
- 0 — 30 m

Legend:
- Shop
- Toilets
- Café

Real Alcázar, the Courtyard of the Maidens

© Barone Firenze/Shutterstock.com

and the **Salón de Embajadores (3)** (Ambassadors' Hall), the most sumptuous room in the Alcázar, with a remarkable 15C half-orange cedarwood **cupola**★★★ with stucco decoration and exceptional azulejo paneling, as well as pendentives with decorative Moorish motifs (*mocárabes*). This room connects with the **Salón del techo de Felipe II (4)**, which boasts a magnificent Renaissance cedarwood ceiling. The Salón de Embajadores leads to the smaller **Patio de las Muñecas (5)**, in the family area. The upper floors are from a 19C restoration. This patio opens to the Cuarto del Príncipe (Prince's Room).

▶ *Starting from the Patio de la Montería, continue through the Corredor de Carlos V, a low-vaulted gallery.*

Palacio Gótico★★ (Salones de Carlos V)

The Baroque doorway to the Gothic Palace is to the rear of the **Patio del Crucero**. Built by Alfonso X, it was restored in the 18C after the Lisbon earthquake. In the Sala Grande you'll find part of a collection of 17C **tapestries**★★ from the Real Fábrica de Tapices in Madrid relating the Conquest of Tunis in 1535. The 13C **Sala de las Fiestas**, or **Sala de las Bóvedas**, the oldest section, retains its original structure and groin vaults

SEVILLA

The Cuarto Real Alto

An optional 30min guided tour (*booking recommended; www.alcaza rsevilla.org*) takes visitors through the King and Queen of Spain's official residence in Sevilla. The various rooms contain an impressive display of 19C furniture and clocks, as well as 18C tapestries and French lamps. Of particular note are the **Capilla de los Reyes Católicos** (Chapel of the Catholic Monarchs) – an exquisite oratory with a ceramic font, by Nicola Pisano – and the Mudéjar Sala de Audiencias.

(*bovédas*). It was here that Carlos V married Isabel of Portugal. The walls, with 16C *azulejo* paneling, are hung with the remainder of the tapestry collection. Take a moment to appreciate views of the enchanting gardens visible through the room's large windows.

Gardens★

Like the palace, these gardens were created over different periods, reflecting Moorish, Renaissance and Baroque styles. Their terraces and ornamental basins occupy 80% of the Alcázar's total area.
Leave Carlos V's Rooms and pass the Mercurio Pool to reach the 17C **Galería del Grutesco★**, which masks the front of an old wall and affords the best views.
Lower down is the Jardín de las Danzas (Dancing Garden). From here, head to the baths (*baños*) of Doña María de Padilla, a large vaulted pool.
Beyond the 15C **Pabellón de Carlos V** (pavilion) is a clipped-hedge labyrinth, with a modern, English-style garden on the right. Take a moment to wander around these gardens, where you'll be accompanied by nothing more than the gentle bubbling of water in the background.
The Baroque *apeadero* (to alight from horses) leads to the Patio de Banderas.

Patio de Banderas

Filled with orange trees, the Flag Court was the parade ground of the original Alcázar.

Real Alcázar decorations

© Massimiliano Pieraccini/Shutterstock.com

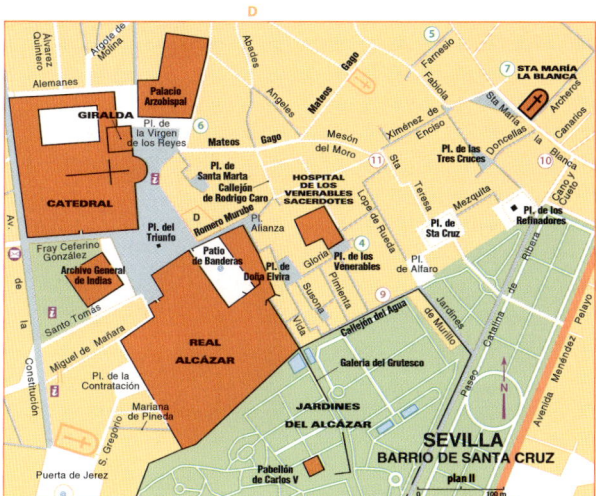

SEVILLA
BARRIO DE SANTA CRUZ
plan II
0   100 m

WHERE TO STAY	
Hostería del Laurel	④
Hotel Amadeus Sevilla/La Música ..	⑤
Hotel Doña María	⑥
Hotel Las Casas de la Judería	⑦

WHERE TO EAT	
Corral del Agua	⑨
La Cava del Europa.................	⑩
Las Teresas...........................	⑪

BARRIO DE SANTA CRUZ★★★

Map above.

Welcome to Sevilla's quintessential *barrio*, a delightful mix of twisting streets, whitewashed houses, flower-filled patios and shady squares. During the Middle Ages this was the Jewish quarter (*Judería*), and remained under royal protection until the end of the 14C, when the barrio was seized by Christians, who converted the synagogues into churches. Today, it is a haven of peace and quiet in the heart of Sevilla. You will want to meander through its alleyways – resplendent in the bright sunshine, and equally delightful at night – to discover its many facets and appreciate its hospitality, particularly during the *paseo*. Many of the barrio's street names are evocative of past times: Mesón del Moro (Moor's Inn), Pimienta (Pepper) and Susona, a name inspired by a legendary love affair between a Jewess and Christian man. One of the best entrances to the quarter is through the **Arco de la Judería**, a covered alleyway leading centuries back in time to the Patio de Banderas. Continue to the **callejón del Agua**, which runs alongside the district's outer wall. You'll find a less theatrical, yet equally interesting route upon leaving the Patio de Banderas, passing through the **calle Romero**

The Barber of Seville

The city provided the inspiration for this comic opera, created in 1816 by Italian composer Gioacchino Rossini (1792–1868). Written in two acts, this masterpiece details the attempts of Bartolo, an elderly doctor, to marry his pretty ward, Rosina. His plans are foiled by another admirer, Count Almaviva, through the help of his acquaintance, Figaro, who also happens to be Bartolo's barber.

Typical calle in the Barrio de Santa Cruz

Murube, continuing along the wall of the Alcázar to the plaza de la Alianza. Cross the square and follow the street, which becomes the twisting yet delightful **callejón de Rodrigo Caro**, ending up at the **plaza de Doña Elvira**, one of Santa Cruz's most typical squares, characterized by *azulejo*-adorned benches shaded by orange trees and a small stone fountain. The calle Gloria leads to the lively **plaza de los Venerables**.

Hospital de los Venerables★

Open daily year-round 10am–2pm and 4–8pm. Closed 1 Jan, Good Fri and 25 Dec. €5.50. 902 09 11 37. focus.abengoa.es.
Founded in 1675, this priests' hospital (now the seat of the Focus-Abengoa cultural foundation) is one of the finest examples of 17C Sevillian Baroque. Its attractive patio is decorated with 19C *azulejos*. The **church★** is covered with **frescoes★★** painted by Valdés Leal and his son Lucas Valdés. *The Last Supper* by Valdés the Younger

and, above it, *The Apotheosis of San Fernando*, by Valdés the Elder, are at the apsidal end. The nave contains four Flemish works on copper and two smaller works painted on marble. Two fine statues by Pedro Roldán, *San Fernando* and *San Pedro*, can be found at the foot of the church. Organ concerts are frequently held here.
The **sacristy** boasts a fresco by Valdés Leal on the theme of the triumph of the Cross. Keep your eye on the balustrade as you move around the room and note how it appears to change position. You can also admire anonymous 18C

Carmen

Fierce, fiery and gorgeous, Carmen was created by French writer Prosper Merimée in 1845 and subsequently used by Bizet as the subject of his famous opera (1874), which describes a triangle of love and jealousy involving Carmen the gypsy, a soldier and a bullfighter.

©Vlas2000/Shutterstock.com

figures of Christ in ivory. Above the attractive **main staircase**★ you'll find an elliptical Baroque dome adorned with stuccoes. *The Presentation of the Infant Jesus*, by Lucas Valdés, hangs on the wall.

Streets and squares

Follow calle Santa Teresa – the artist Murillo, one of the city's favorite sons, lived at no. 7 (now an exhibition room) – or exit plaza de Alfaro to **plaza de Santa Cruz**. Amid the orange trees of the square stands an impressive iron cross, the 17C Cruz de la Cerrajería, where Murillo is buried. Gardens nearby are named in his honor. Calle Mezquita leads to the majestic **plaza de los Refinadores**. Continue via a narrow alleyway to the **plaza de las Tres Cruces**, a triangle with three columns upon which stand three wrought-iron crosses. **Calle Mateos Gago**, which runs into plaza de la Virgen de los Reyes, has a number of popular **tapas bars**.

Iglesia de Santa María la Blanca★

This former synagogue was transformed into a church in the 14C; the simple Gothic portal is from this period, but the façade and the **interior**★ are 17C reconstructions. The barrel vaults adorned with lunettes and the dome over the transept are completely covered with delightful plasterwork decoration. The Evangelist nave contains a *Last Supper*, attributed to Murillo, which is surprising in its dramatic use of light, in keeping with the pure tenebrist style.

THE RIVER BANK★
Map pp28–29 (A-B 4-5).

The **paseo de Cristóbal Colón** runs parallel to the river between the San Telmo and Triana bridges. Along it are the Torre del Oro and the Real Maestranza bullring and other impressive sights. From the paseo you can enjoy fine views across to the Triana district.

Torre del Oro

The splendid Gold Tower was built by the Almohads in the 13C, along with the Torre de la Plata or Silver Tower, as part of the city's defenses. The main part of the tower is a dodecagonal stone structure crowned with merlons, topped by two levels

Don Juan

This legendary seducer, a man who shows no respect for anyone or anything, appears for the first time in Tirso de Molina's *The Trickster of Seville and His Guest of Stone* (1630). According to legend, de Molina's real-life inspiration for the character was Don Miguel de Mañara, the founder of the Hospital de la Caridad (*see p 42*).

Although Don Juan is known to the opera world as Mozart's *Don Giovanni* and has been re-created time and time again over the centuries by writers like Molière, Dumas and Byron, in Spain the best-known version is José Zorrilla's *Don Juan Tenorio* (1844). The statue you can see in the plaza de los Refinadores was erected in the writer's honor.

in brick, the second added in the 18C. The tower houses the **Museo Marítimo** (*open Tue–Fri 9:30am–5:30pm, Sat–Sun 10:30am–1:30pm; closed Mon and public holidays; €1; 954 22 24 19*), which displays documents, engravings, boat models and other elements of maritime life.

Cruises along the Guadalquivir depart from just below the tower. Opposite the Torre del Oro is the **Teatro de la Maestranza**, with an unusual false façade.

Hospital de la Caridad★

Calle Temprado 3. Open year-round Mon–Sat 9am–1:30pm and 3:30–7:30pm, Sun 9am–1:30pm. Closed major holidays. €5. 954 22 32 32. www.santa-caridad.es.

The Hospital of Charity was founded in 1667 by Don Miguel de Mañara (1627–79). The church's façade displays five murals of blue and white ceramics apparently based on drawings by Murillo: theological virtues predominate (Faith, Hope, Charity); the two below show St George slaying the dragon and St James (Santiago), the Moorslayer. Enter the church via the hospital, with its harmonious double patio adorned with panels of *azulejos*

representing scenes from the Old and New Testaments.

Church★★

The single-nave Baroque church contains artistic gems commissioned by Mañara from Sevilla's leading artists of the period. The pictorial representations of Death and Charity were created as reminders of the path the brothers of Charity were expected to follow.

Two **paintings★★** by **Valdés Leal** beneath the chancel tribune are staggeringly severe. In *Finis Gloriae Mundi*, Valdés Leal depicts a dead and half decomposed bishop and knight with macabre realism; the scales held in the hand of Christ refer to the moment of judgement. *In Ictu Oculi* (In the Blink of an Eye) is an allegory of death in which the skeleton has earthly symbols at its feet (a globe, a crown, books, etc). An *Exaltation of the Cross* by the same artist can be seen above the choir.

In the nave, **Murillo** has illustrated the theme of Charity through several **works★**. The sense of submission to one's fellow man is exalted in *St Isabel of Hungary Curing the Lepers*, and in *St John of God Carrying a Sick Man On*

Triana bridge over the Guadalquivir

© Matej Kastelic/Shutterstock.com

🏛 Muelle de Nueva York

Created alongside the Guadalquivir River and named in honor of the location's historic role as the departure point for ships headed across the Atlantic to America, the Muelle de Nueva York (New York Dock) provides visitors with a new and novel way to experience the city. Floating docks, free pontoon boats, a stage, outdoor stands, green zones and kiosk-bars blend together to form an urban riverside park, allowing tourists and townies alike to appreciate Sevilla from the water. Bicycle paths and pedestrian routes crisscross the area, benches line its paths and a relaxing atmosphere pervades this waterway wonderland, creating a user-friendly riverside attraction for anyone who comes to this part of Spain.

His Shoulder, in which the artist demonstrates his mastery of *chiaroscuro*. Two paintings of children on the side altars are also by Murillo. Another side altar has a 17C bleeding Christ casting a distressed gaze toward the sky, by Pedro Roldán. The two horizontal paintings facing each other in the transept are *The Miracle of the Loaves and Fishes* (representing the gift of food) and *Moses Smiting Water from the Rock* (representing the gift of water). The canvases in the dome of the transept are by Valdés Leal: in each echinus is an angel bearing the instruments of the Passion; the Evangelists are depicted in the pendentives. Note also the fine lamp-bearing angels.

At the main altar, a splendid Baroque altarpiece by Pedro Roldán has a sculptural group representing the **Holy Burial of Christ★★**. As you leave, the founder's statue is opposite; to the left is the **Torre de la Plata**.

La Maestranza

Paseo de Colón 12. Visit by guided tours, May–Oct daily 9:30am–8pm, Nov–Apr daily 9:30am–7pm. €7. 954 22 45 77. www.realmaestranza.com.
Sevilla's famed *plaza de toros*, with an attractive red and white façade, was built between 1758 and 1881. Unusually, the bullring itself is not quite circular. Fans carry triumphant bullfighters

on their shoulders through the Puerta del Príncipe (Prince's Gate). The **museum** has an interesting assortment of posters, paintings and costumes.

In front of La Maestranza, where the tragic finale of the opera played out, you'll see a bronze statue to Carmen, the personification of passionate female love. Before the Puente de Triana you'll find the **Monumento a la Tolerancia**, a large sculpture with the stamp of the acclaimed contemporary Spanish sculptor, Eduardo Chillida, who spent time here in April 1992.

Triana★

Triana, one of the city's most colorful areas, is across the Puente de Triana (or Puente de Isabel II), a bridge built in 1845. The bridge offers fine **views** of the Guadalquivir and the east bank. Triana is a fishermen's and merchants' quarter that has produced famous singers and bullfighters. To the left of the bridge, the **plaza del Altozano** has a monument to bullfighter Juan Belmonte (1892–1962), considered a *trianero* even though he was born across the river.

Enter the district by the **calle Pureza**. At no. 55, between simple, well-maintained houses, stands the **Capilla de los Marineros**, a chapel dedicated to sailors, with a statue of the **Esperanza de Triana** (Hope of Triana), one of the most venerated statues of the Virgin Mary, whose procession rivals that of La Macarena.

Parroquia de Santa Ana

Calle Pureza. A little farther on, the Iglesia de Santa Ana in the parish (*parroquia*) of the same name is

"El Cachorro"

The **Capilla del Patrocinio**, a chapel situated at the end of the calle Castilla in the most northerly section of the Triana district, is where the Christ of the Expiration, commonly known as "El Cachorro," is venerated. It is said that the artist, Francisco Antonio Gijón, used a sketch of a murdered gypsy known as "El Cachorro" for the face of Christ in this late-17C masterpiece. Once he had finished carving Christ, the sculpture was so realistic that when people saw it they immediately recognized the dead gypsy, hence its name.

the oldest in Sevilla. The original church, founded by Alfonso X the Wise in the 13C, was restored in the 18C. The most striking feature is the tower, with multifoiled arches in the lower sections showing clear Mudéjar influence, and *azulejo* decoration in the upper part.

A **Renaissance altarpiece** in the chancel comprises a fine ensemble of sculptures and paintings dedicated to the Virgin Mary, with several canvases by Pedro de Campaña. The retro-choir contains a delicate early 16C **Virgin of the Rose**, by Alejo Fernández.

Calle Betis

Stroll this riverside street and enjoy a completely different perspective of Sevilla: the Torre del Oro and La Maestranza in the foreground, dominated by the majestic Giralda. Calle Betis is famous for its **traditional houses**, **bars** and **open-air kiosks**. The street is romantic by night, with moonlight reflected on the river.

SOUTH OF THE CATHEDRAL★
Map pp28–29 (B-C 5-6)

Palacio de San Telmo
This impressively wide late 17C palace is the seat of the Presidencia de la Junta de Andalucía (Regional Council). Originally a naval academy, it became the residence of the Dukes of Montpensier, and later a seminary. Its **main portal★**, one of the finest works of Sevillian Baroque, is by Leonardo de Figueroa. Above, a statue of San Telmo is silhouetted against the sky.

Hotel Alfonso XIII
Calle San Fernando 2.
This is the most famous hotel in Sevilla, built for the 1929 Ibero-American Exhibition in regionalist style with neo-Mudéjar features.

University
The city's university is a fine building with classical, harmonious lines and impressive dimensions, built in the 18C as a tobacco factory (and entrenched in Sevillian legend thanks to Bizet's *Carmen*). The **portal** fronting calle San Fernando has paired columns; in the doorway arch are medallions of Columbus and Hernán Cortés.

Parque de María Luisa★★
This popular park was a gift from the Infanta María Luisa Fernanda, Duchess of Montpensier. Once part of the Palacio de San Telmo gardens, it was landscaped for the 1929 Ibero-American Exhibition by Jean-Claude Nicolas Forestier, and enhanced with gazebos, pools and exhibition buildings, some of which can still be seen today.

But the Parque de María Luisa is much more than just a collection of attractive buildings and long, tree-lined avenues. Its murmuring fountains, gazebos and statues of famous characters give the park an intimate, romantic air. The memorials to Gustavo Adolfo Bécquer and Cervantes, with its *azulejos* illustrating scenes from *Don Quixote* (*at one end of plaza de América*), are just two examples of the surprises awaiting visitors as they stroll around the gardens.

Plaza de España★
Created by Sevillian architect Aníbal González, this magnificent plaza is fronted by a canal where you can rent **rowboats**. The enormity of the plaza is striking, and the ceramics exquisite. Before the brick building with towers at either end are *azulejo* scenes illustrating an episode from the history of each province of Spain.

Plaza de América
Here are three buildings from the 1929 Exhibition: the Isabelline Pabellón Real (Royal Pavilion); the Renaissance pavilion, now the **archaeological museum★** (*see Museo Arqueológico de Sevilla, p 51*), and the Mudéjar pavilion, now a museum of popular arts (*see Museo de las Artes y Costumbres Populares, p 51*).

NORTH OF THE CATHEDRAL★
Map pp28–29 (A-B-C 3-4)

Iglesia de la Magdalena
This church, with an elegant dome ornamented with *azulejos,* was built in the late 17C and early 18C

according to designs by Leonardo de Figueroa. The **interior**★ contains a number of treasures. The ceiling paintings are the work of Lucas Valdés. A lanterned cupola rises majestically above the transept, while the exuberant Baroque altarpiece in the chancel dates from the early 18C; the paintings on the vaults illustrate allegories of saints. The **Capilla del Cristo del Calvario** (*to the right of the presbytery*) takes its name from *The Exposed Christ*, an 18C work by Francisco Ocampo. In the Epistle nave are the fine **high-relief of the Assumption** supported by four small angels, by Juan de Mesa (1619), and the Sacramental and Quinta Angustia chapels. The former contains two canvases by **Zurbarán**: *St Dominic in Soria* and *The Miraculous Healing of the Beatified Reginald of Orleans*.

The **Capilla de la Quinta Angustia**★ is situated in the vestibule of the main entrance doorway. The magnificent sculpture at the altar, depicting a highly moving Deposition, is attributed to the followers of Pedro Roldán. Look up to admire the three Moorish-influenced cupolas. Ten canvases of saints by Valdés Leal hang on the chapel walls. In the left transept, next to the door, stands a 16C sculpture of the **Virgin of the Fever**, an elegant and maternal Virgin holding the Infant Christ in her arms.

Plaza Nueva

This spacious square is on land previously occupied by the Convento de San Francisco. The equestrian statue is of Fernando III the Saint, the city's Christian conqueror.

Ayuntamiento

The west front of the neo-Classical 19C town hall faces the square. The more interesting east side, on plaza de San Francisco, has an attractive Plateresque 16C **façade**★, the work of Diego de Riaño, adorned everywhere with delicate classical motifs (fantastical and grotesque animals, medallions with faces, escutcheons, etc).

The palace opposite the town hall in plaza de San Francisco is the Caja de Ahorros San Fernando (savings bank). It was formerly the seat of the Royal Court of Justice (Audiencia). Its classical late-16C façade is attributed to Alonso de Vandelvira.

Calle Sierpes

This is Sevilla's most famous street, lined with traditional and modern shops, and liveliest in the late afternoon and early evening when locals window-shop or enjoy pastries in its renowned *pastelerías*. The famous **La Campana** coffee and pastry shop, founded in 1885, is at the very end of Sierpes on the corner with Martín Villa.

Capilla de San José★
Calle Jovellanos 10.

This chapel, a masterpiece of Sevillian Baroque, dates from the end of the 17C. Its 18C façade and belfry with bright blue azulejos can be seen from the corner of calle Sierpes and calle Jovellanos. The exuberance of Baroque decoration in the small interior is a surprise, particularly at the apsidal end. Note the large wooden **altarpiece** in the presbytery depicting angels, saints and God the Father, with an image of St Joseph in the center.

Palacio de la Condesa de Lebrija★

Open year-round Mon–Fri 10:30am–7:30pm, Sat 10am–2pm and 4–6pm, Sun 10am–2pm (Jul–Aug only Mon–Fri 9am–3pm, Sat 10am–2pm). €5 (€8 for both floors). 954 22 78 02. www.palaciodelebrija.com.

This private residence provides an opportunity to visit a palace with a typically Sevillian layout, comprising a hallway, central patio and interior garden. Inside you'll discover a floor that appears to be completely covered with Roman **mosaics★** from nearby **Itálica** (*see Excursions*), including mythological scenes; as well as a striking octagonal room with volutes and large vases. The attractive patio also has elegant foiled arches, Moorish-influenced paneling, *alfiz* rectangular moulding and a colorful plinth of Sevillian *azulejos*. The **staircase★**, rich in ceramic tiles, has a mahogany bannister, marble steps and an outstanding Mudéjar marquetry ceiling, which originally graced a palace in Marchena.

Plaza del Salvador

The huge parish church of El Salvador looks over this large square, one of the most popular places for an afternoon drink and lively socializing, especially on Sundays.

Iglesia del Salvador★

This church, rising majestically on one side of the square, replaced the former main mosque, demolished in 1671. Construction lasted until 1712, following plans by José Granados; the cupolas were designed by Leonardo de Figueroa. The elegant pink brick and stone façade is a fine example of ornamental Baroque style. Note the high lanterned cupola above the transept.

Some of the city's most interesting **Baroque retables★★** (all from the 18C) are inside. The one in the chancel, dedicated to the Transfiguration of the Lord, covers the entire wall and is the work of Cayetano Acosta. The frontispiece of the **Capilla del Sagrario**, the sacrarium chapel which opens onto the left transept, is also by Cayetano Acosta and is dedicated to the exaltation of the Sacred Host. Inside, the most interesting object is the 17C **Christ of the Passion**, by Martínez Montañés. Part of an opulent silver altarpiece, it conveys an image of serene suffering on the face of Christ. The chapel to the right displays the 17C **Crucificado del Amor**, by Juan de Mesa, a moving interpretation of the suffering and solitude of Jesus on the Cross.

Casa de Pilatos★★

Open year-round daily 9am–7pm (Nov–Mar 6pm). €8 (ground floor and gardens only €6). 954 22 52 98. www.fundacionmedinaceli.org.

This palace is one of Sevilla's most famous and beautiful monuments, facing out onto the pleasant plaza de Pilatos with a statue of Zurbarán at the center. Although construction on the palace began at the end of the 15C, most of what we can appreciate today was created by Don Fadrique, the first Marquess of Tarifa. According to legend, he took his inspiration from Pontius Pilate's house in Jerusalem, hence the name of

the palace. The building is a mixture of Mudéjar, Renaissance and Flamboyant Gothic styles, although the Mudéjar style predominates.

The delightful **patio** recalls an elegant Moorish palace with its finely moulded stuccowork and magnificent 16C lustre **azulejos★★**. Note the unequal arches and different motifs visible on the various *azulejo* panels. The fountain was carved in Genoa in the 16C. Statues in the palace include **Athena**, a 5C BC Greek original (the others are of Roman origin). Rounded niches in the walls hold superb busts of Roman emperors. The rooms around the patio have fine *artesonado* ceilings, panels of *azulejos*, sculpted plasterwork, groined vaulting and the palaeo-Christian sculpture of the Good Shepherd in the chapel, the oldest part of the house. You can also visit the **gardens**.

The sumptuous *azulejo*-adorned **staircase★★** leading up from a corner of the patio has a remarkable half-orange **wooden dome★**.

On the upper floor, frescoes from the 16C display representations featuring various characters from Antiquity. Several rooms have interesting ceilings. Of particular interest is the ceiling painted in 1603 by Francisco Pacheco, illustrating the Apotheosis of Hercules.

A visit to the nearby **Convento de San Leandro** is particularly recommended. Although access to the church is difficult, it is still worth a visit to buy the convent's famous *yemas*, delicious sweets made with egg yolk and sugar.

Convento de Santa Paula★

Calle Santa Paula 11. 954 53 63 30. www.santapaula.es.

This historic convent of an order of enclosed (Hieronymite) nuns was founded at the end of the 15C. Its elegant and lofty 17C belfry is one of the finest in Sevilla. The nuns prepare and sell tasty cakes and jams to visitors.

Church★

Note the interesting atrium and the fine **portal★**, worked on by Nicola Pisano and completed in 1504. In spite of the evident mixture of styles – Mudéjar in the use of brick, Gothic in the arches, and Renaissance in the medallions and cresting – the overall effect is perfectly cohesive and harmonious. A Catholic monarch escutcheon can be seen on the tympanum, while the central medallion, attributed to Luca della Robbia, represents the Birth of Jesus.

The **interior★**, a single nave topped by a 17C *artesonado* ceiling, comprises a presbytery with Gothic vaults, totally covered with delightful polychrome frescoes. The main altarpiece dates from the beginning of the 18C, though it retains the image of St Paula, in the center, from an earlier retable. Note the movement of the two lamp-bearing angels.

Museum★

Open Tue–Sun 10am–1pm.

The museum is spread out over several tall outbuildings, two of which boast fine *artesonado* ceilings. The museum contains objects of great value, including canvases by **Ribera** (*St Jerome* and *The Adoration of the Shepherds*), two works by Pedro de Mena (*Our Lady of Sorrows* and *Ecce Homo*), an Immaculate Conception by Alonso Cano, and a charming 17C crib.

Iglesia de San Marcos

The impressive 14C façade blends Gothic and Mudéjar features. The attractive **Mudéjar tower★** stands out, clearly Giralda-influenced (multifoiled arches and *sebka* work on the upper frieze). The tower is brick, with the exception of the Gothic stone portal which has three 18C sculptures (God the Father, the Virgin Mary and an angel) and an elegant and unusual *sebka*-style frieze.

The whitewashed interior contains a handsome 17C sculpture of **St Mark** (*Evangelist nave*) and an 18C **Recumbent Christ** (*Epistle nave*).

In the **plaza de Santa Isabel** behind the church, admire the doorway of the **church of the convent of Santa Isabel** (*open only for morning Mass*). An early 17C relief by Andrés Ocampo depicts the Visitation of the Virgin to her cousin Elizabeth.

Basílica de la Macarena

Open year-round daily 9am–2pm and 5–9pm. Museum €3. 954 90 18 00. www.hermandaddela macarena.es.

Built mid 20C, the Iglesia de Nuestra Señora de la Esperanza (Church of Our Lady of Hope) contains one of Sevilla's most famous statues: **La Macarena★**. This carving of the Virgin Mary, the work of an anonymous 17C artist, looks down from the high altar. Sevillians say that only angels could have created such a work. The beauty of her tearful face

La Macarena

© Roberaten/Shutterstock.com

unleashes devout fervor during her procession, held in the early morning of Good Friday. A Christ under Sentence in a chapel on the Evangelist side of the church is also venerated, and carried alongside the Virgin.

The **museum** displays cloaks and skirts, as well as the impressive floats that bear La Macarena and Christ, conveying the splendor of these occasions.

Iglesia de San Luis de los Franceses★

Calle San Luis.

Designed by Leonardo de Figueroa, this church is an excellent example of Sevillian Baroque architecture. The **façade** is clearly compartmentalized: two storeys, with octagonal towers on each side, and a central cupola with ceramic decoration.

The **interior★★** is surprisingly exuberant, with murals on the magnificent cupola by Lucas Valdés and retables by Pedro Duque Cornejo.

MUSEUMS

Museo de Bellas Artes★★★

Map pp28–29 (A3). Plaza del Museo 9. Open year-round Tue–Sat 9am–8:30pm, Sun 9am–2:30pm. Closed 1, 6 Jan, 28 Apr, 1 May, 24, 25, 31 Dec. €1.50 (free for EU citizens). 954 78 65 00. www.museosdeandalucia.es.

This remarkable museum contains one of the world's largest collections of Spanish paintings from the Golden Age. It is housed in the former Convento de la Merced (17C), designed by Juan de Oviedo; the Baroque doorway was added in the 18C. The museum is built around three delightful patios and a magnificent staircase, covered by a cupola decorated with Mannerist stucco designs. The gallery displays significant works from the Middle Ages through the 20C.

Room V★★★
Ground floor.

This is undoubtedly the museum's main attraction. The church, its walls decorated with paintings by the 18C artist Domingo Martínez, provides the perfect backdrop to an outstanding collection of work by Murillo and one of Zurbarán's masterpieces, *The Apotheosis of St Thomas Aquinas* (in the nave).

Murillo (1617–82), a master of both the pictorial technique and the use of light in his canvases, concentrated on religious subjects and children. His characters are always very human, exuding tenderness and gentleness in a world that avoids drama and excess. His canvases can be found in the transept and in the apse, where you can appreciate

his monumental *Immaculate Conception*. Around it are notable paintings of saints: *Santa Rufina* and *Santa Justa*, who are clutching the Giralda, and *San Leandro* and *San Buenaventura*. In the right transept there is a particularly interesting *Virgin of the Cloth* (note the way the child seems to move toward you). Note also *St Francis Embracing Christ on the Cross* and another Immaculate Conception, known as *La Niña* (*The Child*). On the left-hand side you'll find *St Anthony and Child*, *Dolorosa* and *St Felix of Cantalicio and Child*.

Room X★★
Upper floor.

This room features works by **Francisco de Zurbarán** (1598–1664), who had a particular skill for painting the shades of white of monks' habits and the pure cloth of Christ, visible in his *Christ on the Cross*, in which the body of Christ, painted against a dark background, appears as if sculpted in relief. A lack of correct perspective can be seen in the otherwise quite outstanding *St Hugh and Carthusian Monks at Table*. Zurbarán's preoccupation with the treatment of cloth, seen in his depiction of the Fathers of the Church in *The Apotheosis of St Thomas Aquinas*, is also evident in the splendid velvet brocade in *San Ambrosio*. His saints, *Virgin of the Caves* and *San Bruno's Visit to Urbano II* are all interesting. Sculptures in the same room include *St Dominic* by Martínez Montañés (1568–1649). Note the splendid *artesonado* ceiling in the inner room.

Other rooms

Room I displays medieval works. **Room II**, once the refectory, is dedicated to Renaissance art, in particular a fine sculpture of *St Jerome* by Pietro Torrigiani, a contemporary of Michelangelo. Other works of note include Alejo Fernández's *Annunciation*, a painting by El Greco of his son *Jorge Manuel*, and a diptych of *The Annunciation and Visitation* by Coffermans. Two magnificent portraits of *A Lady and a Gentleman* by Pedro Pacheco are the highlights in **Room III**.

On the upper floor, **Room VI** displays a fine collection of richly decorated female saints (anonymous, some by followers of Zurbarán) and two male saints. **Room VII** contains more works by Murillo and his disciples while **Room VIII** is devoted to the other great Baroque artist, Valdés Leal. European Baroque is represented in **Room IX** by Ribera's powerful *St James the Apostle*, canvases by Brueghel and the supreme *Portrait of a Lady* by Cornelis de Vos, among others. **Room XI**, devoted to 18C art, is enlivened by Goya's *Portrait of Canon José Duato*, and several works by Lucas Valdés. The following two rooms (**XII** and **XIII**) display 19C art, in particular superb portraits by Esquivel, while the final room (**XIV**) shows 20C canvases by Vázquez Díaz and Zuloaga, among others.

Museo Arqueológico de Sevilla★

Off map, south of the Cathedral. Open year-round Tue–Sat 9am–8:30pm, Sun and public hols 9am–2:30pm. Closed major holidays. 955 12 06 32.

www.museosdeandalucia.es. Housed in a Renaissance pavilion in the Parque María Luisa, Sevilla's archaeological museum contains an interesting collection of prehistoric and Roman objects. The prehistoric collection (ground floor) includes items discovered at archaeological excavations in the region. The exhibits in **Room VI** are particularly interesting, comprising the 7C–6C BC **El Carambolo treasure★**, a superb collection of gold jewelery of Phoenician inspiration, and the Goddess Astarte (8C BC), a small bronze statue bearing an inscription said to be the oldest script found on the Iberian peninsula.

The first floor is dedicated exclusively to the **Roman collection★** (Rooms XII to XXV), largely discovered at Itálica (*see Excursions*). Exhibits include magnificent sculptures and mosaics that provide an insight into Roman artistic development in the region.

Museo de las Artes y Costumbres Populares

Off map, Parque de María Luisa, plaza de América 3. Open year-round Tue 3pm–8pm, Wed–Sat 9am–8pm, Sun and public holidays 9am–2pm. Closed major holidays. €1.50 (free for EU citizens). 955 54 29 51. www.museosdeandalucia.es.

The Museum of Popular Art and Traditions, in the Mudéjar pavilion of María Luisa park, displays costumes worn for *romerías* and *fiestas*, models of workshops, musical instruments, farming tools and more.

EXCURSIONS

ITÁLICA★

9km/5.5mi northwest of Sevilla along the A 66–E 803. Bear left after Santiponce. Open Apr–Sept Tue–Sat 8:30am–9pm, Sun and public holidays 9am–3pm; Oct–Mar Tue–Sat 9am–6:30pm, Sun and public hols 10am–4pm. Closed 1, 6 Jan, 1 May, 24, 25, 31 Dec. 600 141 767. www.museosdeandalucia.es.

The remains of Roman Itálica, founded by Scipio Africanus in 206 BC, stand on a cypress-shaded hill above the Guadalquivir Plain. Itálica's golden age was in the 2C AD. Emperors **Trajan** (AD 53–117) and **Hadrian** (AD 76–138) were born here. Hadrian granted Itálica the title of Colony, transforming it into a monumental city. Its decline began in the Late Empire period. The excavated area is a district created under Hadrian, with streets laid out according to an orthogonal plan and lined by public buildings and luxurious private houses. You can appreciate original **mosaics** of Neptune, birds and various divinities.

Amphitheater

Capable of seating as many as 25,000 people, this elliptical amphitheater was one of the largest in the Roman Empire. Sections of tiered seating and the pits beneath the arena remain. The town of **Santiponce** stands on the oldest part of Itálica. The former Roman theater can be seen at its center.

CARMONA★★

39km/24.2mi northeast of Sevilla. Set on a plateau overlooking a fertile plain irrigated by the River Corbones, Carmona is one of Andalucía's oldest towns. It was founded by the Carthaginians, and played an active political role during Roman occupation and under both Moors and Christians.

Walls

The Moorish-arched **Puerta de Sevilla★** in the lower fortress (*alcázar de abajo*), served as an entrance to the old quarter, where sections of Carthaginian walls remain. The **Puerta de Córdoba★** has two superb octagonal Roman towers.

Iglesia de San Pedro★
Calle San Pedro.
The 15C Church of St Peter, on the paseo del Estatuto, has a fine **bell tower★**, similar to the Giralda in Sevilla (hence the nickname "Giraldilla"). The **Capilla del Sagrario** (sacrarium) is richly decorated, and there is an extraordinary 16C green ceramic **baptismal font**. The church was heavily restored during the Baroque period.

Iglesia de San Felipe★

A fine 14C Mudéjar church with a handsome tower, *artesonado* work bearing the coat of arms of the Hurtado de Mendoza family, and chancel with 16C *azulejos*.

Plaza Mayor

Mudéjar and Renaissance mansions line this attractive square.

Ayuntamiento
Calle El Salvador 2. 954 14 00 11. www.carmona.org.

Countryside around Carmona

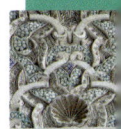

© Jmarijs/Shutterstock.com

The interesting Baroque town hall has an attractive Roman **mosaic** in its courtyard.

Iglesia de Santa María la Mayor★

Calle San Ildefonso.
This large 15C Gothic church replaced a mosque. Note the Patio de los Naranjos (Orange Tree Patio) and beautiful horseshoe arches that were once part of the original Moorish building. You can see a 6C **Visigothic calendar** on one column. A monumental **Plateresque altarpiece★** depicts sculpted scenes of the Passion. Side chapels hold magnificent retables such as the Christ of the Martyrs behind 16C **Plateresque grilles**.

Convento de las Descalzas★

This magnificent example of 18C Sevillian Baroque has a Latin-cross ground plan, a tower with a double campanile and *azulejo* decorations.

Alcázar de Arriba

Providing superb **views★** of the surrounding countryside, this old Roman fortress was extended by the Almoravids and later converted into the palace of Pedro I. Only fragments of the original structures remain, but the magnificent **parador**, former residence of the Catholic Monarchs, now stands in the parade ground and is open to the public for the price of a coffee.

Roman necropolis★

At the end of calle Jorge Bonsor, on the road from Sevilla. Open year-round Tue–Fri 9am–6pm, Sat–Sun 9:30am–2:30pm. 954 14 08 11. www.museosdeandalucia.es.
This impressive site, in use around 1 and 2BC, holds over 300 tombs, mausoleums and cremation kilns. The **Tumba del Elefante** (named for an elephant statue) holds three dining rooms, while the **Tumba de Servilia** is the size of a villa.

PARQUE NATURAL DE LA SIERRA NORTE DE SEVILLA

Map of Andalucía.

Drive to Lora del Río (58km/36mi northeast of Sevilla, via A 4 and A 457).

This park extends for 164,840ha/407,320 acres of outstanding natural beauty into the **Sierra Morena** north of Sevilla. Along its rivers – the Viar, Huéznar and Retortillo – lush vegetation

Touring Tip

The **Centro de Información del Parque** in El Robledo, 2.5km/1.5mi southwest of Constantina, provides maps and brochures detailing activities in the park. *955 88 15 97.*

includes cork oak, horse chestnut, elm, holm oak and hazel.

Fauna include wild boar, harrier eagles and tawny vultures. The park is particularly attractive in the springtime, when its mountainsides are covered with blooming flowers of all shapes, sizes and colors.

Lora del Río

Peaceful and steeped in tradition, Lora is located on the Guadalquivir, at the base of the Sierra Morena foothills (just outside the park's borders). Local delicacies include snails (*caracoles*), *sopeaos* (a variant of gazpacho), and *gachas con coscurros*, a flour-based pureé sprinkled with fried breadcrumbs.

Constantina

29km/18mi north of Lora del Río.
Surrounded by delightful forests and streams of crystal-clear water, this town is named for Roman emperor Constantine. Its center is

Cep Mushrooms

The area around Constantina is a mushroom-lover's paradise. In autumn, the town is inundated by visitors who come here to pick them or simply to enjoy them in one of Constantina's many bars and restaurants.

a mix of Moorish and distinctive 15C–17C noble edifices. The Moorish quarter (**barrio de la Morería★**) sits at the foot of the old fortress above Constantina. Steep, winding alleyways lined with whitewashed houses and connected by flights of steps preserve the flavor and feel of an Arab district.

El Pedroso

18km/11mi west of Constantina.
Set in a landscape of outstanding beauty, El Pedroso has two impressive religious buildings: the church of Nuestra Señora de la Consolación and the Ermita de La Virgen del Espino. The nearby hills of Monteagudo and La Lima offer **views** of the sierra.

Cazalla de la Sierra

17km/10.5mi north of El Pedroso.
This delightful town is hidden in the heart of the Sierra Morena amid holm and cork oak forests. The center is characterized by picturesque streets, attractive houses and elegant stone façades. **Plaza Mayor**, the hub of Cazalla, is bordered by a singular array of 16C popular Andalusian architecture. The town is renowned for its brandies.

Alanís

17km/10.5mi north of Cazalla.
Alanís stands in a near-impregnable mountain area, at the foot of a medieval castle. The **Iglesia de Nuestra Señora de las Nieves**, originally a Gothic church, was rebuilt in neo-Classical style. If you have time, be sure to view the marvelous Mudéjar **azulejos** on display in the 16C Capilla de los Melgarejo.

Guadalcanal

11km/7mi northwest of Alanís.
This old fortified settlement retains interesting vestiges of its medieval walls.

PARQUE NATURAL DE LA SIERRA DE ARACENA Y PICOS DE AROCHE★★

Map of Andalucía.

Accessible from Huelva on the N 435 and Sevilla via the N 433 and A 66, the park borders Portugal to the west and Extremadura to the north.

This superb nature park boasts mountain landscapes and picturesque villages. Vast forests punctuated by slender peaks offer delightful views of the sierra, while the rush of flowing water blends with the sound of wind whistling through the treetops.

Aracena★

93km/58mi northwest of Sevilla.
The whitewashed houses of Aracena rise in tiers on a hillside, overlooked by remains of a Templar castle. Its splendid **caves** attract a steady stream of day visitors, while the **Museo al Aire Libre de Escultura Contemporánea**, an open-air exhibition of modern art, adds a touch of modernity and culture.

Gruta de las Maravillas★★★

Open year-round daily by guided tours (45min) only 10am–1:30pm and 3pm–6pm. Closed 24, 25, 31 Dec. €8.50. 663 93 78 76. www.cuevasturisticas.com.
The aptly named **Cave of Marvels** descends over 100m/330ft deep, boasting underground lakes that

Serrano and Pata Negra hams

Many bars (*mesones*) around Aracena offer ample opportunity to try local cuisine, and the region's renowned **jamón serrano** in particular.
Pata negra from Jabugo is considered the king of Spanish cured hams, boasting a silky texture, sublime aroma and strong flavor. Beware: it comes with a hefty price tag!

mirror the limestone ceilings to superb effect. Points of interest include the organ chamber (*salón de los órganos*); the cathedral chamber (*sala de la catedral*) with a Virgin and Child formation; Sultana's bath (*baño de la sultana*); and the stunning **God's Crystal Chamber★★** (*salón de la Cristalería de Dios*). The 70m/231ft high **salón del gran lago** (hall of the great lake) hosts performances of the *Sinfonía del Agua* by local musician Luis de Pablo and the Suite *Gruta de las Maravillas* by Don Primitivo Lázaro.
The **Museo Geológico Minero** (*open 10am–6:30pm*) geological and mining museum is part of the complex.

Touring Tip

The **Centro de Información del Parque Natural Sierra de Aracena y Picos de Aroche** in Aracena provides information on the park and surrounding area. *Open Tue–Sun 10am–2pm and 4–6pm (Jul–Aug, 6–8pm). 959 12 95 53/4. www.aracena.es.*

Castle

Open daily 10am–7pm (winter, 5:30pm). 663 93 78 77 (Oficina de Turismo. www.aracena.es.
Built over a 9C Almohad fortress, this castle dominates Aracena and the surrounding countryside. The compound includes a Gothic church and a **Mudéjar-style tower** – once a minaret – with *sebka* paneling similar to that on the Giralda in Sevilla.

Iglesia de Nuestra Señora del Mayor Dolor

The Church of Our Lady of Great Suffering was built between the 13C and 14C on a site affording superb **views★★**. It contains a sculpture of the Virgin Mary, the town's patron saint, as well as a recumbent statue by Pedro Vázquez.

Plaza Alta

This tranquil square, the hub of local life, borders several notable buildings, including the solemn Renaissance-style 16-17C **Iglesia de Nuestra Señora de la Asunción** and the 15C former municipal storehouse and town hall, **Cabildo Viejo**, which today hosts the **Centro de Información del Parque Natural Sierra de Aracena y Picos de Aroche**.

Alájar★

18km/11.3mi southwest of Aracena.
This whitewashed village, nestled at the foot of a church with a pointed belfry, is popular with walkers. The area around Alájar is a microcosm of the park: dark cork and holm oak forests, steep rugged rocks and stunning views.

Peña Arias Montano

This impressive rock (*peña*) several kilometers north of Alájar provides superb **views★★** of this extraordinary landscape. Its name recalls the learned **Benito Arias Montano**, tutor to Felipe II, diplomat and royal librarian, who retired to a contemplative existence in Alájar. The **Ermita de Nuestra Señora de los Ángeles** chapel can be seen perched atop a rocky outcrop.

Jabugo

20.4km/12.6mi northwest of Alájar.
This isolated mountain village is world-famous for its prized **cured hams** (*jamones*) and **sausages** (*embutidos*).

Castaño del Robledo

6.2km/3.8mi southeast of Jabugo.
Hikers come to this village to walk trails through groves of chestnut trees, scale peaks and admire birds of prey gliding through the air.

Almonaster La Real★

15.5km/9.5mi west of Castaño.
Almonaster is a pleasant surprise. Located amid dense stands of chestnut, eucalyptus, cork and holm oak, this little town is a labyrinth of quiet streets and mansions where it feels as if time has stood still. Local cuisine is based on pork products. A major attraction is the *Cruces de Mayo* festival in May. A **park information point** can be found in the **town hall** (*959 14 32 06*).

Mezquita★

This 10C mosque is one of the few Caliphal structures left in the area. A stroll atop its reddish walls provides superb mountain views.

You can see an unusual bullring to one side, while the castle-fortress in the mosque enclosure offers **views** of the town below.

Cortegana

9km/5.5mi northwest of Almonaster La Real.
This pleasant town specializes in local meats, cork, and making scales and pottery. Historic buildings of note include the elegant 16C Gothic-Mudéjar **Iglesia del Salvador**, the Gothic-Renaissance **Iglesia de San Sebastián** and the medieval **castle**.

 **Medieval festivities**
On 9–12 August every year, the streets of **Cortegana** become a backdrop for theater performances, processions, medieval banquets, re-enactments of scenes of daily life in the Middle Ages and concerts of sacred Andalusian music, attracting thousands of visitors of all ages.

Aroche

27.5 km/16.9 mi west of Cortegana.
Aroche is one of the oldest towns in the area, as evidenced by the **Piedras del Diablo** (Devil's Stones), dolmens in a delightful setting 3km/2mi to the southeast along the H 9002 (near the **Ermita San Mamés**). You can explore a maze of narrow, twisting alleyways, mansions, old buildings and small workshops specializing in saddles and leatherwork on your way up to the **castle★**, a sober 12C construction that King Sancho IV ("the Brave") once used as a refuge. It houses a bullring,

as well as a **park information point** dedicated to the black vulture, a local species in danger of extinction. The park has one of the biggest black vulture breeding colonies in Spain.

MINAS DE RIOTINTO★★
Map of Andalucía.

Minas de Riotinto is in the Sierra de Aracena, near Parque Natural Sierra de Aracena y Picos de Aroche, 73km/45mi northeast of Huelva by the N 435, and 85km/53mi northwest of Sevilla.

This small community is set in a breathtaking landscape of oak forests, reservoirs and lakes like the Cobre-Gossan, Campofrío and Agua. Deep red scars of excavated mountain slopes attest to a mining tradition dating back some 5,000 years.

Parque Minero de Riotinto★
Hours and prices vary, check via Internet. Closed 1, 6 Jan, 25 Dec. 959 59 00 25. www.parqueminero deriotinto.com.
This mining-themed park lies within the town and in the surrounding area.

Museo Minero y Ferroviario★
The mining and railway museum is set in a former British hospital. Exhibits include early-20C locomotives and the popular **Maharajah's carriage★★★**, built in England for a planned journey to India by Queen Victoria. The museum also displays mining artefacts dating as far back as the Bronze Age, and a reconstruction of a **Roman mine**. **Casa 21** is a restored grand dwelling that

depicts how English mine owners and their families lived around the turn of the 20C. Inquire at the mine about the following excursions:

Corta Atalaya★★★
2km/1.2mi northwest.
This huge open-cast mine is over 1,000m/3,280ft in length, 900m/2,950ft wide and 350m/1,150ft deep. Enjoy exceptional **views**★★★ of the striated crater from the lookout point. Nearby facilities show visitors how gossan (mineralized iron) is extracted and transported in enormous vehicles capable of carrying up to 200 tons each.

Cerro Colorado★★
2.5km/1.5mi northwest.
The pit of the second largest mine in Riotinto is an unusual red color. If you visit in the late afternoon you can enjoy the surprising way its walls and terrain appear to sparkle in the sunlight.

The British in Riotinto
It is odd to discover the vestiges of Anglo-Saxon culture, so out of keeping with the character of the local population and landscape, in an isolated backwater such as Riotinto. It should be remembered, however, that at the beginning of the 20C, Britain had developed into a huge economic power, partly due to its colonial possessions and to the role it played in global economic development through mining operations in outposts such as Riotinto.

Local Specialties
Typical products from Minas de Riotinto area include **migas** (breadcrumbs fried in olive oil and garlic, traditionally served with grilled sardines); **gurumelos** (a local cep mushroom); **pestiños** (honeyed doughnuts); and a wide variety of pork-based products.

Tourist train★★
The train runs from an old station to Cerro Colorado. Trips (10km/6mi or 23km/14.5mi) extend along the river on a line built at the end of the 19C to carry ore to Huelva for export to Great Britain. This journey in old-fashioned carriages offers surprises at every turn, including stunning glimpses of the reddish-colored River Tinto as it winds through dense woods; views of the very first stations; and an impressive bridge, the Puente de Salomé, which provides spectacular views of the river and surrounding landscape.

Bellavista district
The Victorian-style houses in this district were built at the beginning of the 20C to accommodate huge numbers of British workers. Though now uninhabited, a Presbyterian church, social club and British cemetery remain.

Zalamea la Real
7km/4.4mi west of Minas de Riotinto.
A panoramic **road**★★ winds across mountain spurs past the Cobre-Gossan Reservoir (*embalse*) to the village of Zalamea, renowned for its **anise-flavored liqueurs**.

FOR FUN

TAPAS & CAFÉS
See map pp28–29.

Bar Santa Ana
Calle Pureza 82 (A5). 954 27 21 02.
www.kioscodelasflores.com.
A cheerful tapas bar open early into the morning where you can enjoy classic Sevilla treats. If the weather's nice, make sure you grab a table outside, to the lee of the church.

Bodeguita Romero
Calle Harinas 10 (B4). 954 22 95 56.
bodeguita-romero.com.
Next to the Maestranza bullring. Famous for its exquisite *pringá* (roast or stewed meat eaten with bread). Regional decor.

El Rinconcillo
Calle Gerona 40 (C3). 954 22 31 83.
www.elrinconcillo1670.com.
Charming old-world taverna dating to 1670, with 18C and 19C *azulejo* paneling and fine wooden ceiling.

Horno San Buenaventura
Avenida de la Constitución 16 (B4).
954 45 87 11.
Near the cathedral with a spacious and popular ground floor tearoom. Its cakes, baked in its own *horno* (oven) are justifiably famous.

Kiosco de Las Flores
Calle Betis (A5). 954 27 45 76.
www.kioscodelasflores.com.
Founded in 1930, this family-run riverside tapas bar specializes in fried fish and seafood.

La Campana
Calle Sierpes 1 (B3). 954 22 35 70.
www.confiterialacampana.com.
One of Sevilla's classic coffee houses, dating from 1865. Everyone from local seniors to tourists enjoys pastries served in a pleasant Rococo atmosphere.

La Cava del Europa
Calle Santa María La Blanca 40 (C4). 954 53 16 52.
Here tapas amount to a gourmet experience, all prepared with top quality ingredients and creative flair, from shrimp ala *salmorejo* (tomato purée) to Argentine beef specials. A vast wine selection.

See map p39 – Barrio de Santa Cruz.

Calle Mateos Gago
This street by the Giralda is full of bars and restaurants. **Bodega de Santa Cruz** attracts a young crowd that spills onto the street. The **La Giralda** *cervecería* (*no 1*) is a very traditional bar with tasty raciones. **Bodega Belmonte** (*no 24*) is known for its *lomo a la pimienta* (spicy pork loin).

Las Teresas
Calle Santa Teresa 2. 954 21 30 69.
A small, typically Sevillian tavern – one of the oldest in the Barrio Santa Cruz – with attractive early-19C decor, set on a picturesque alley. **Casa Plácido**, opposite, is also recommended.

NIGHTLIFE
See map pp28–29.

In the evenings, to *tomar una copa* (have a drink) amid an atmosphere rich in history, you can explore the area around the cathedral, head for the more

touristy Santa Cruz neighborhood, or visit El Arenal, near the arena. Other areas worth investigating include the Triana neighborhood (especially calle Betis, along the river), and piazza Alfalfa, in particular calle Pérez-Galdós. At night the alternative crowd heads for Alameda de Hércules, where interesting haunts include **Fun Club**, a popular concert venue, and the **La Habanilla** café/bar with its large and unusual collection of old coffee pots. In summer, the action moves down to the river, where several kilometers of bars and outdoor terraces are popular with people of all ages and tastes.

Café Habanilla

Plaza de la Alameda de Hércules 63 (off map, A3). 954 90 27 18.
A cheerful café/bar with live music and a large and unusual collection of old coffee pots.

Casa de la Memoria

Calle Cuna 6 (B3). Information on performances (7:30pm or 9pm) available online. Reservations are recommended. 954 56 06 70. casadelamemoria.es.
Set on the patio of an 18th-century palace, this is the perfect spot for enjoying an authentic flamenco dance show. Singing, dancing and guitar playing by the best artists in Sevilla are held here every night.

El Patio Sevillano

Paseo de Cristóbal Colón 11 A (A4). Shows at 7pm and 9pm. 954 21 41 20. www.elpatiosevillano.com.
An institution since 1952, offering a flamenco retrospective. Near the bullring.

Fun Club

Alameda de Hércules 86 (off map, A3). Open Thu–Sat 9:30pm–6/7am (if no concerts are scheduled, the club opens at midnight). funclubsevilla.com.
This lively disco-bar is a must for anyone who wants to enjoy live music of all kinds. DJ set and dance floor.

La Carbonería

Calle Levies 18 (C4). Open 8pm–4am. 954 21 44 60. www.levies18.com.
Until recently the watering hole for Sevilla's bohemians, this locale has lost a little of its authenticity, but remains a must. In various parts of this former coal warehouse in the Jewish Quarter, you can listen to an intimate recital around a fireplace, watch live flamenco, or view an art or photography exhibition.

Tablao El Arenal

Calle Rodó 7 (A4). Performances at 8pm and 10pm. Reservations required. 954 21 64 92. www.tablaoelarenal.com.
One of Sevilla's most important *tablaos*, said by those in the know to feature flamenco at its purest. Stop here to experience dance and music as pure emotion, with fine Andalusian cuisine served to you just a pirouhette away from the dancers on stage.

Teatro de la Maestranza

Paseo de Cristóbal Colón 22 (A5). 954 22 33 44. www.teatrodela maestranza.es.
Full season of theater, dance opera and flamenco with performances by international stars.

Teatro Lope de Vega

Avenida María Luisa (B6). 954 59 08 53. www.teatrolopedevega.org.
This theater overlooking the Parque de Maria Luisa concentrates on drama and  flamenco, but also offers jazz, Andalusian copla or new age. Built in 1929 for the Exposición Iberoamericana, the interior is elegant and rich in typical Spanish reds.

SPAS

See map pp28–29.

Aire de Sevilla – Arab Baths and Tea House

Calle Aire 15 (B4). 995 01 00 24/25/26. www.airedesevilla.com.
This late 16th-century building houses magnificent thermal baths with Arabic and Andalusian themes. Inside you can enjoy aromatherapy, relaxing massages and other wellbeing treatments. An entire floor is dedicated to the tearoom, perfect for relaxing and enjoying the ambiance!

SHOPPING

Among all the shopping districts in Sevilla, the most traditional is centered in the historic center, in calle Tetuán, plaza del Duque de la Victoria, calle San Eloy and other pedestrian streets in the neighborhood, including **calle Sierpes** (B3-4). You'll also find good shopping on the streets perpendicular to calle Sierpes, and those around the Iglesia del Salvador. Plaza Pan and calle Alcacería are rife with jewelry shops. At the former train station in **plaza de Armas** (A3) – an interesting early 20C regional building in neomudéjar style – you'll find a shopping mall complete with supermarket, shops (open daily 10am–10pm), restaurants and a movie theater.

Markets

There are many open-air markets, each with its own specialties. On Thursdays, a picturesque antiques market is held in **calle Feria**, perfect for browsing. A thriving **flea market** is held in **Alameda de Hércules** on Sunday mornings.

The Ceramics Quarter

A number of ceramics workshops and boutiques can still be seen in the area near the **plaza del Altozano** (A4), in calle de Callao, calle Antillano and calle de Alfarería in particular, perpetuating an artistic tradition that has always existed in this quarter. The façades of some of these shops and workshops are decorated with *azulejos* advertising the wares inside.

FIESTAS & EVENTS

In spring, Sevilla gears up for two fiestas that have brought it international fame: Holy Week (Semana Santa) and the April Fair (Feria de Abril). For those yet to experience either, it is difficult to imagine their splendor or how *Sevillanos* embrace these two authentic, yet totally distinct expressions of the Sevillian soul.

Semana Santa

Holy Week is celebrated between Palm Sunday and Easter Sunday, in March or April, depending on the dates. The origins of Sevilla's Semana Santa date back to the 16C, when the first brotherhoods or fraternities were formed to assist guild associations. Over 50 brotherhoods participate in the Holy Week processions, each carrying its own statue of Christ or the Virgin Mary.

The spectacle is impressive, with the streets and street corners of the city providing a magnificent backdrop to processions. In an extravagant religious ritual, breathtakingly beautiful statues are borne aloft on floats, each exquisitely adorned with gold and silver, as popular religious fervor erupts in an atmosphere bordering on ecstasy.

The processions

These take place throughout the week. Every brotherhood departs from its own church or chapel and usually carries two floats (*pasos*): one bearing Christ, the other the Virgin Mary. They make one journey to the cathedral and then return to their headquarters, always by way of calle Sierpes and the town hall. More than 100 floats wind through the city's streets; each carried by *costaleros* – young men who take immense pride in transporting these holy figures. They are accompanied by a band of musicians. A number of these famous processions take place on the **madrugá**, the early morning of Good Friday, including those of El Silencio (the oldest brotherhood, who, as their name suggests, march in complete silence), La Macarena, La Esperanza de Triana, Los Gitanos and, on Friday afternoon, El Cachorro.

Pick up an **official program** or look in the local paper for the full schedule.

Feria de Abril

This started from humble beginnings in the mid-19C as a purely commercial animal exchange, but soon developed

The annual Feria de Abril

into a very colorful and boisterous celebration. It is now the major annual fiesta held in Sevilla, which for a city with a huge reputation for partying, says something! The April Fair takes place two or three weeks after Holy Week in the Los Remedios district, where a veritable city of light is created by thousands of electric bulbs and decorative lights. The streets are also full of traditional *casetas* – stands or marquees, which hold their own little parties. Festivities commence late Monday evening and in the early hours of Tuesday, and continue until the closing fireworks display the following Sunday. During the *feria* a high-spirited, good-humored crowd throngs the streets. Sherry from Jerez and *manzanilla* from Sanlúcar flow in the *casetas*, tapas are munched, and *sevillanas* are danced with great passion until the early hours. During the day, the women of Sevilla do their best to upstage each other with the beauty and grace of their flamenco costumes as they dance, stroll the streets with friends and family, or wander around the *feria* area itself. In the Feria parade, horsemen dress in tight-fitting costumes and wide-brimmed *sombreros cordobeses*. Carriages are drawn by horses with colorful harnesses. The calle del Infierno funfair has attractions to delight young and old alike.

El Rocío

Any mention of local fiestas would not be complete without El Rocío (*80 km/50mi southwest of Sevilla*). This religious **pilgrimage**, a combination of devotion to the Virgin and devotion to the festive spirit, converges at a chapel in the village of El Rocío, south of Almonte in the province of Huelva, at the edge of the **Parque Nacional de Doñana** (*see COSTA DE HUELVA*).

FOR KIDS

🚠 Isla Mágica★

5km/3mi northwest of the city center (off map, A4). Rotonda Isla Mágica (Isla de la Cartuja). Buses C1 and C2. Open daily Apr through Sept, certain days Oct–Dec and Jan following Christmas holidays. Consult the website for opening times. Prices vary according to season (half-day tickets available). Full day ticket prices: Adults €29; child €21. 902 16 17 16. www.islamagica.es.
The Isla Mágica (Magic Isle) amusement park, spread over 40ha/99 acres on the island of La Cartuja, is themed to take visitors on a journey back to the century of discovery. The park's eight areas are: Sevilla, the Gateway to the Indies; Quetzal, the Fury of the Gods; The Balcony of Andalucía; The Gateway to America; Amazonia; The Pirates' Den; The Fountain of Youth; and El Dorado. Facilities and attractions include all manner of rides (from terrifying white-knuckle rides for teens to gentle traditional funfair rides for little ones), live shows, spectacular audio-visual shows, street entertainers, souvenir shops, and a good selection of bars and restaurants.

COSTA DE HUELVA ★

Threading your way southeast from Portugal along the Huelva coast, you'll pass a succession of sparkling beaches and river deltas where the Guadiana, Guadalquivir and Tinto enter the Atlantic. Relatively undeveloped, the Huelva forms part of the Costa de la Luz (Coast of Light), a brilliant, sun-kissed corner of Spain.

COSTA DE HUELVA

FROM HUELVA TO AYAMONTE
Map of Andalucía.

Huelva ★
82km/51mi west of Sevilla.
Huelva, the capital of the westernmost province of Andalucía, lies inland amid marshland and channels, and is associated with Columbus, who departed from the Costa de Huelva for America. The clime and nearby beaches make it a popular summer vacation destination for Spaniards.

Cathedral
Plaza de la Merced. Open for services only. 959 24 30 36.
Built in 1605, the cathedral boasts a Renaissance façade, a sculpture of Christ of Jerusalem and a carving of the Virgen de la Cinta, the city's patron saint, by Martínez Montañés.

Barrio Reina Victoria ★
The English-style houses in this district were built for the families of employees of the Río Tinto Company.

Monumento a la Fe Descubridora
This large sculpture dedicated to the spirit of discovery is by American artist **Gertrude Vanderbilt Whitney**. It was erected in 1929 on **Punta del Sebo**, directly opposite the city.

🛶 Paraje Natural de las Marismas del Odiel ★★
2km/1.2mi southeast of Huelva. Visitor Center in Carretera del Dique Juan Carlos I. 959 52 43 33/34.
This marsh *(marisma)* is a World Biosphere Reserve, home to over 200 bird species, despite nearby chemical factories. The marsh is particularly beautiful in February and March, when the area fills with various species of migrating waterfowl. One third of Europe's spoonbill population lives here. Visit El Burro and Isla de Enmedio sections by 🛶 **canoe**.

The World Biosphere Reserve of Marismas del Odiel

© Ashiga/Shutterstock.com

Practical Information

Location

The Costa de Huelva extends from Ayamonte, at the mouth of the River Guadiana, to the Parque Nacional de Doñana.

Getting There and Around

♦ **By Car** – You can reach Huelva from Sevilla via the A 49-E 1 highway in roughly 1hr 10 mins. The A 49-E 1 runs between Ayamonte and Huelva, while the N 442 and A 494 follow the coast.

♦ **By Train** – Trains run daily between Sevilla and Huelva (roughly 1hr 30 mins).
For information and reservations, 902 32 03 20, www.renfe.com.

♦ **By Bus** – From Sevilla, in plaza de Armes, a number of different Damas buses depart daily for Huelva (902 45 05 50; www.damas-sa.es; siu.cthu.es). In Huelva, at the bus station in calle Dr. Rubio, Damas provides connections with various towns in the Huelva province, including Ayamonte and Palos de la Frontera. Eva Transportes connects Huelva and Ayamonte with several cities in southern Portugal (www.eva-bus.com). Socibus connects Huelva with Ayamonte, Cádiz, Córdoba and Jerez de la Frontera (902 22 92 92, www.socibus.es).

Visitor Information

Tourist offices can be found in: **Ayamonte** (calle Huelva 27, 959 32 07 37), **Huelva** (Plaza Alcalde Coto Mora 2, 959 65 02 00; www.turismohuelva.org), **Palos de la Frontera** (calle Rábida 3, 959 35 01 00).

Punta Umbría

21.5km/13.5mi south of Huelva. In summer, Punta Umbría can be reached by ferry from Huelva.
This popular resort is located in the salt marshes of the **Paraje Natural de Enebrales de Punta Umbría** nature reserve, and has a small marina and attractive beaches. The daily early-morning fish auction is worth seeing, as is the fishermen's procession to honor the Virgin Mary, held on 15 August every year. The nature reserve is a protected area of **sand dunes** in a landscape dominated by savin, juniper, mastic and hawthorn.

El Rompido

14.5km/9mi west of Punta Umbría.
This small fishing port has a pleasant dune-lined beach popular with summer visitors. The **Paraje Natural Marismas del Río Piedras y Flecha de El Rompido★** is a protected salt marsh (*marisma*) off the road toward La Antilla, home to black-headed gulls, pintails, oystercatchers and common egrets.

Cartaya

8km/5mi north of El Rompido.
The **plaza Redonda** is a tranquil square adorned with orange trees and elegant wrought-iron street lamps. Around the square are the 16C Iglesia de San Pedro, with its *azulejo*-decorated bell towers, the town hall and the Casa de Cultura.

La Antilla

14.5km/9mi southwest of Cartaya.
Crowds flock to La Antilla's

Costa de la Luz

delightful **beaches**, yet the quiet town of older houses remains sedate, in contrast to nearby Islantilla, a modern complex of apartment blocks and a luxurious golf course. At the mouth of the River Piedras is **El Terrón**, worth a visit to watch fishermen and enjoy local seafood.

Isla Cristina
10.5km/6.5mi west of La Antilla.
Many houses in Isla Cristina's old quarter boast tiled *azulejo* decoration. You will find a marina, protected marshes and beaches.

Ayamonte★
16km/10mi northwest of Isla Cristina.
Located on the border with Portugal, in Ayamonte the sounds of fishing fleets unloading the day's catch and the hubbub of fish auctions blend in with lively conversation in waterside cafés. Colonial-style houses were built by Spanish emigrants who returned from the Americas at the end of the 19C.

Iglesia de las Angustias
Nestled between old houses, this 16C church with a colonial air has a spacious triple-nave interior,

crowned by a tower dominating Ayamonte.

FROM PALOS DE LA FRONTERA TO MATALASCAÑAS
Map of Andalucía.

Palos de la Frontera★
14.5km/9mi southeast of Huelva.
In 1492 **Columbus** sailed forth from this picturesque small town on his voyage of discovery. It is also the birthplace of the Pinzón brothers, who accompanied Columbus. The charm of Palos lies in its whitewashed houses, narrow alleyways and lively atmosphere, best enjoyed in its charming squares.

Casa-Museo de Martín Alonso Pinzón
Calle Colón 48. Free. 959 35 01 99.
The home of the local navigator who accompanied Columbus to the New World, where numerous personal mementoes (signed letters, navigational equipment etc.) are on display.

Iglesia de San Jorge
This fine 15C Gothic-Mudéjar church faces a small, attractive square. Columbus prayed here on the

© Algecireño/Shutterstock.com

morning of his departure (3 August) in 1492. Behind the church, **La Fontanilla**, a fountain crowned by a small Mudéjar shrine, supplied the water for the three caravels.

Mazagón

15km/9.3mi southeast of Palos de la Frontera.

The fine sands of **Playa de Mazagón** extend 10km/6mi from the mouth of the River Tinto to the Torre del Loro. Flanked by steep cliffs, this quiet beach has nice campsites, chalet complexes and a marina. The **Parador de Mazagón** (*see Must Stay*) commands delightful **views** of this part of the Atlantic coastline.

Matalascañas

29km/18.3mi southeast of Mazagón.

Bordering the Parque Nacional de Doñana, Matalascañas is one of the busiest resorts in this part of the coast, with numerous outdoor bars, nightclubs and a wide range of leisure facilities.

❍ *8km/5mi northwest of Matalascañas you'll find the El Acebuche Visitor Center of Parque Nacional de Doñana.*

PARQUE NACIONAL DE DOÑANA★★★

Map of Andalucía.
This famous wetland is one of Europe's great wilderness sites. Comprising 54 500ha/134,700 acres, it is said to be the largest road-free area in Europe. The park encompasses the right bank of the River Guadalquivir. See Visitor Centers below. 959 44 87 39 or 956 38 16 35. reddeparquesnacionales. mma.es/parques/donana.

Touring Tip

On foot
Marked trails run from each information center. Wardens can provide information on difficulty and duration for each walk.

By four-wheel drive
Book in advance. Official park guides provide two visits per day, one in the morning and another mid-afternoon.

By horse
Horseback tours and horse-drawn carriages are available by arrangement, with an optional picnic for groups.

By boat
From Sanlúcar de Barrameda (*see p 75*).

Salt marshes, coastal dunes and dry, undulating scrublands (cotos) combine to form this exceptional park. Its vast wetland, best viewed in spring and autumn, is a winter paradise for over 150 African and European birds. In addition to bird-watchers, Doñana attracts thousands of visitors every year who come to admire the contrasting landscapes of subtly moving sand dunes, marsh, and forests inhabited by lynx, deer, horses and wild boar. The national park is named for Doña Ana Gómez de Mendoza y Silva, wife of the seventh Duke of Medina Sidonia and daughter of the famous Princess of Éboli, who established a hunting reserve here in the 6C.

Visitor Centers

Entry to the park is rigorously monitored. Excursions into the park depart from four visitor centers in the nothern sector (for people arriving from the Costa de Huelva) or from the Sanlúcar de Barrameda visitor center in the south. Excursions last approximately 3hr 30min, and are best booked in advance.

El Acebuche

8km/5mi northwest of Matalascañas (follow the A 483, then turn left onto Carril del Abalari/H-9015). Open summer daily 8am–9pm, winter 8am–7pm. 959 43 96 29.

This visitor center handles all reservations, and offers an **exhibition** focusing on the park's wetlands. Walks from this center provide a closer look at the aquatic birds found in the lagoon.

La Rocina

12km/7.5mi northeast of El Acebuche. Open summer daily 10am–3pm, 4pm–8pm; winter 9am–7pm. 959 43 95 69.

La Rocina is just a few kilometers from **El Rocío**, along the Almonte-Matalascañas road, and marks the starting point of the popular **Charca de la Boca trail** (*14km/9mi*), which provides a number of **bird-watching** spots.

Ecosystems

Doñana National Park encompasses three primary ecosystems. 27,000ha/66,700 acres of **salt marshes** provide an ideal habitat for wintering birds and include unusual features such as *caños* (depressions formed by water), *lucios* (permanent lagoons), *paciles* and *vetas* (mounds of land rising above water, favored areas for saltwort). The **sand dunes**, parallel to the Atlantic, are advancing at an alarming 6m/20ft per year. The land between the dunes is known as a *corral*, while sand-leveled trees are *cruces* (crosses). Originally hunting reserves, *cotos* are dry, undulating areas covered with aromatic shrubs such as heather, rockrose, rosemary and thyme. Alongside these ecosystems are *vera*, strips of land between woodlands and marshes. **Lagoons** include Santa Olalla, a nesting place for ducks, geese and swans; and La Dulce, filled with crustaceans – tasty treats for the park's pink flamingoes.

Parque Nacional de Doñana

© Giraudou/Hemis.fr

🐾 Fauna

Most visitors come to Doñana to birdwatch, since its numerous winged inhabitants are augmented by birds from north and central Europe in the winter and others from Africa in the summer, the most colorful of which are **pink flamingoes**. Many visitors have caught glimpses of the majestic **imperial eagle** here, while only a very lucky few are given the chance to spot an **Iberian lynx** (*Lynx pardina*), endemic to the Iberian Peninsula and the park's critically endangered emblem.

Palacio del Acebrón

5.5km/3.5mi west of La Rocina. Open summer daily 10am–3pm, 4pm–8pm; winter 9am–7pm. 959 50 61 62.

This center exhibits the "Man and Doñana" presentation, detailing the park's evolution and man's presence in it. The upper floor affords fine views. El Acebrón is the starting point of a 12km/8mi **forest walk**.

José Antonio Valverde

18.5km/11.5mi southeast of El Acebrón. Open summer 10am–8pm; winter 10am–6pm. 671 56 41 45.

This modern structure boasts large windows for bird observation.

🐾 Fábrica de Hielo

In Sanlúcar de Barrameda (see p75), 18.5km/16.5mi northwest of Jerez de la Frontera. Open summer 9am–8/9pm; winter 9am–7pm. 956 38 65 77.

The Fábrica de Hielo (ice factory) provides an overview of this attractive nature area, giving visitors a chance to touch, feel and explore some of the natural resources that can be found in this part of the world. Buy tickets here for a half-day trip on the *Real Fernando* **boat** that includes full commentary on the wildlife and habitat of the park and two short guided walks. You can also book a guided tour by Landrover here.

JEREZ DE LA FRONTERA★★

Visiting Jerez, think horses and sherry. The aroma of this sweet dessert wine wafts through streets and alleyways in the city, while elegant horses dominate local festivals. Some of the finest architecture in the region can be found here, and flamenco and the *bulería*, a traditional Andalusian dance, developed in this region.

A Bit of History

After Fernando III (the Saint) captured Sevilla in 1248, the Lower Guadalquivir Valley opened up to Christian troops, who subsequently occupied cities such as Arcos, Medina and Jerez de la Frontera. Jerez finally came under Castilian control on 9 October 1264, the feast day of St Dionysius. During this period, the city was surrounded by a rectangular wall stretching over 4km/2.5mi, built by the Almohads, remains of which can still be seen in calle Porvera and calle Ancha. Three gates led into the city, which was divided into six parishes or *collaciones*, named after the four Evangelists, St Dionysius (the city's patron saint) and the Savior. Neighborhoods like San Miguel and Santiago, as well as Dominican and Franciscan monasteries, stood outside its walls. From the 13C onwards, the city played a key role in the defensive border system established between the Christian and Nasrid kingdoms.

HISTORIC JEREZ★★
Map p72 (A-B 1-2)

Take some time to explore the town's medieval quarter, where you'll find several "churches of the Reconquest" (*most open during services only, from 7pm*). The medieval districts of San Miguel and Santiago are filled with eye-catching architecture, and today their streets are lined with lively outdoor cafés and shops.

Plaza del Mercado

The Moorish market once stood on this square in working-class San Mateo. The surviving façade of the Renaissance **Palacio de Riquelme** stands out like a stage set. You'll also find the **Museo Arqueológico** (*see p 74*) here.

Iglesia de San Mateo

One of the first churches built by Alfonso X in the 13C, erected where a mosque once stood. The present buttressed building dates from the 15C.

Iglesia de San Juan de los Caballeros★

This 15C church has a façade added in the 17C. Its magnificent nine-sided 14C **polygonal apse★** is topped by a ten-rib cupola with

Real Escuela Andaluza del Arte Ecuestre

R.Mattes/Hemis.fr

Practical Information

Location

Jerez is 90km/56mi south of Sevilla, 35km/22mi northeast of Cádiz, and 30km/19mi west of Arcos de la Frontera.

Population

215,180.

Getting There and Around

♦ **By Air** – La Parra airport (www.aena.es) is located 7km/4.5mi northeast of the city center along the A 4. You can reach downtown Jerez in 30 mins by bus (siu.cmtbc.es) or in 6 mins by train (www.renfe.com) from Cádiz and Sevilla.

♦ **By Car** – From Sevilla, approx 1hr 23 mins on the A 4-E 5 highway. From Jerez you can reach Sanlúcar de Barrameda in 33 mins on the A 480; and Cádiz in 48 mins on the A4.

♦ **By Train** – Jerez has two train stations: one at the airport and another downtown in Plaza de La Estación. Trains arrive in Jerez from Cádiz (approx 36 mins), Sevilla (approx 1hr 6 mins), Córdoba (approx 1hr 57 mins) and other major cities. For information and reservations, 902 32 03 20, www.renfe.com.

♦ **By Bus** – Transportes Generales Comes (956 29 11 68; siu.cmtbc.es) runs lines from Sevilla and Cádiz. Socibus (902 22 92 92; www.socibus.es) runs lines from Córdoba. The bus station is on calle Cartuja.

♦ **By Taxi** – Tele-Taxi: 956 34 48 60 / 35 05 07 / 05 30 53.

Visitor Information

You'll find tourist offices in Plaza del Arenal, Edificio Los Arcos (956 33 88 74 / 34 17 11) and calle Paúl (956 14 98 65). www.turismojerez.com.

---

jagged decoration. Nearby, the **Centro Andaluz de Flamenco** is on plaza San Juan.

Palacio de los Ponce de León

Plaza Ponce de León.
This Plateresque palacio has a lovely **corner window**★★.

Iglesia de San Marcos

Plaza San Marcos.
This 15C church features a beautiful 16C **star vault** and a striking 17C polygonal **retable**★.

Plaza de Rafael Rivero

This small square is bordered by the Palacio de los Pérez Luna, with its beautiful late-18C **doorway**,

and next to it, the **Casa de los Villavicencio**.

Palacio Domecq★

Plaza Aladro.
This is an elegant late-18C Jerez Baroque-style palace with a highly decorative marble **doorway**★. Note the graceful iron balustrade on a curving cornice.

Plaza del Plateros

This was a medieval commercial center. The **Torre Atalaya** is an early 15C watchtower.

Plaza de la Asunción★

The Renaissance **Casa del Cabildo**★★ (town hall, 1575) is adorned with figures.

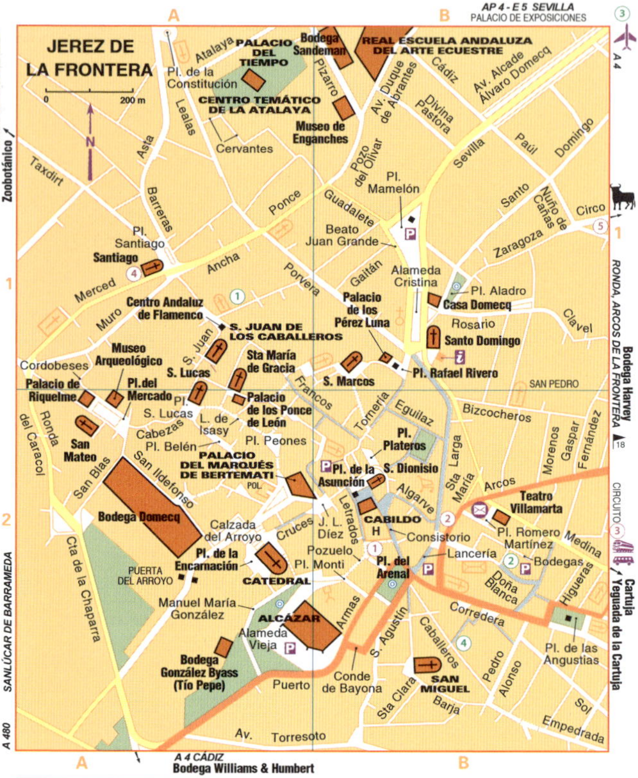

JEREZ DE LA FRONTERA

0 ————— 200 m

A

B

PALACIO DEL TIEMPO
Bodega Sandeman
REAL ESCUELA ANDALUZA DEL ARTE ECUESTRE
Pl. de la Constitución
Atalaya
Pizarro
Cádiz
Av. Alcalde Álvaro Domecq
A 4
CENTRO TEMÁTICO DE LA ATALAYA
Leales
Av. Duque de Abrantes
Divina Pastora
Sevilla
Paul
Domingo
Museo de Enganches
Cervantes
Asta
Taxdirt
Barretas
Ponce
Pozo del Olivar
Guadalete
Pl. Mamelón
Beato Juan Grande
Santo
Nuño de Cañas
Circo
Zaragoza
Pl. Santiago
Santiago
Merced
Muro
Ancha
Porvera
Galtán
Alameda Cristina
Pl. Aladro
Casa Domecq
Clavel
Centro Andaluz de Flamenco
S. JUAN DE LOS CABALLEROS
Palacio de los Pérez Luna
Rosario
Santo Domingo
Museo Arqueológico
Cordobeses
Ronda del Caracol
S. Juan
Sta María de Gracia
S. Lucas
Pl. del Mercado
Palacio de los Ponce de León
S. Marcos
Francos
Pl. Rafael Rivero
SAN PEDRO
Palacio de Riqueme
L. de Isasy
Cabezas
Pl. Belén
Bizcocheros
Torneria
Eguilaz
Gaspar Fernández
San Mateo
San Blas
San Ildefonso
PALACIO DEL MARQUÉS DE BERTEMATI
POL.
Pl. Peones
Pl. Plateros
Sta Larga
Morenos
Arcos
A 18
Bodega Domecq
Calzada del Arroyo
Cruces
Pl. de la Asunción
S. Dionisio
Algarve
Sta María
Teatro Villamarta
CIRCUITO
③
Cta de la Chaparra
PUERTA DEL ARROYO
Pl. de la Encarnación
J. L. Díez
Pozuelo
Pl. Monti
CABILDO
Larados
Consistorio
Lancería
H
Pl. Romero Martínez
Bodegas
Medina
Higuera
Manuel María González
CATEDRAL
Pl. del Arenal
Armas
S. Agustín
Doña Blanca
Corredera
Pl. de las Angustias
A 480
Bodega González Byass (Tío Pepe)
ALCÁZAR
Alameda Vieja
Puerto
Conde de Bayona
SAN MIGUEL
Sta Clara
Barja
Caballeros
Pedro
Alonso
Sol
Empedrada
Av. Torresoto

A 4 CÁDIZ
Bodega Williams & Humbert

Zoobotánico
SANLÚCAR DE BARRAMEDA
Bodega Harvey
RONDA, ARCOS DE LA FRONTERA
Cartuja / Yeguada de la Cartuja

A **B**

WHERE TO STAY		WHERE TO EAT	
Hotel Chancillería . . . . ①		Bar Juanito. . . . . ①	
Hotel Doña Blanca . . . . ②		El Gallo Azul . . . . ②	
Hotel Jerez & Spa . . . . ③		La Carboná . . . . ③	
Nuevo Hotel . . . . ④		La Taberna Flamenca. . . . . ④	
		Tendido 6. . . . . ⑤	

Palacio del Marqués de Bertemati★

Plaza del Arroyo.

This palace, built toward the end of the 18C, boasts one of the most impressive façades in Jerez.
The first section of the **left doorway★** represents the secular world; the second portrays the world of religion.

Cathedral★★

Plaza del Arroyo. Open year-round Mon–Sat 10am–6:30pm. €5. 956 16 90 59.

The Colegial del Salvador was the first church built after the Reconquest. The present building was constructed in the 18C, along with new streets and squares. The tiled **cupola★** above the

MUST SEE · JEREZ DE LA FRONTERA

Jerez de la Frontera

© Vladimir Melnik/Shutterstock.com

transept is visible from much of the city.

Alcázar (Mosque, Arab Baths and Camera Obscura)★

Calle Alameda Vieja. Open Mon–Sat 10am–6pm (May–mid Sept, 8pm), Sun 10am–3pm. €7. 956 32 69 23.
There is an excellent **view★★** of the cathedral from here. The old Moorish fortress was part of the 12C Almohad wall. Enter via the angled **Puerta de la Ciudad** (City Gateway), a typical Almohad structure. Note the 15C **Torre de Ponce de León** along the walls.

Tocino de Cielo

This delicious dessert (literally "heavenly bacon") is thought to have its origins in the Jerez wine-cellars, where local wine-producers once used beaten egg whites to clarify their wine. Not knowing what to do with the leftover yolks, they gave them to the neighboring convents, where the nuns used them to make these delicious custard puddings.

The **mosque★★** is in unadorned early Almohad style, while you'll find 12C Roman-style baths on the other side of the garden.

Camera Obscura

This was only the second camera obscura built in Spain, and is housed high in the tower of the **Palacio de Villavicencio**, providing a unique **view★★** of Jerez. This is an ideal first stop on a tour of the city.

Iglesia de San Miguel★★

Plaza de San Miguel.
The 1480 Hispano-Flemish **San José façade** is the oldest part of the church. St Joseph is flanked by two imposing Flamboyant pillars. The three-tiered Baroque tower is topped with a Jerez-style *azulejo* roof. The highly decorated transept and main chapel are covered by an elaborate star vault. The extraordinary late-Renaissance **retable★** is by Martínez Montañés, with Baroque additions by Juan de Arce. Attached to the church is the Baroque-style **Capilla Sacramental** (Sacramental Chapel).

MUSEUMS

Museo Arqueológico

Open Tue–Fri 10am–2pm and 4–7pm (mid June–mid Sept 9am–2:30pm only), Sat–Sun and public holidays 10am–2pm. Closed Mon €5. 956 14 93 00. www.jerez. es/webs_municipales/museo.
Housed in a restored 18C Mansion, the archaeological museum boasts a number of locally-discovered artifacts, including a **Greek helmet**★ dating from the 7C BC, found in the River Guadalete, and simple marble Copper Age **cylindrical idols**★, discovered in Cerro de las Vacas (Lebrija) and Torrecera.

Palacio del Tiempo★★

Calle Cervantes 3, Museo La Atalaya. Open Mon–Fri 9:30am–1:15pm. €6. 956 18 21 00.
This remarkable **clock museum**, in the 19C neoclassical Palacete de la Atalaya, is surrounded by peacock-filled gardens. The collection includes roughly 300 valuable antique (17C–19C) timepieces, all chiming, memorably, on the hour.

Misterio de Jerez

Atalaya gardens. Opening days and months same as Palacio del Tiempo. €6. 956 18 21 00.

The "Mystery of Jerez," housed in a 19C bodega, uses state-of-the-art technology to explore Jerez **winemaking**.

Real Escuela Andaluza del Arte Ecuestre★

Avenida Duque de Abrantes 50, Palacio Recreo de las Cadenas. See website (Calendar of Events) for days and times. Horse shows €21–27. 956 31 96 35. www.realescuela.org.
This 19C French-style palace houses both the **Museo del Arte Ecuestre** (Museum of Equestrian Art) and the **Royal Andalusian School of Equestrian Art**. Visitors can explore interactive and audio-visual displays detailing the **history of the horse** and its revered role in Andalucía. You can also stroll through beautiful **Botanical gardens**. But the highlight of any visit is the **equestrian show**★★ "How the Andalusian Horses Dance": an equestrian ballet featuring Spanish music and costumes inspired by 18C and 19C fashions.
The adjacent **Museo del Enganche** displays sumptuous coaches.

Manzanilla

This superb sherry is both penetrating and dry on the palate. From May onwards, the triangle between Sanlúcar de Barrameda, El Puerto de Santa María and Jerez is a swathe of leafy **Palomino** vines. The harvest takes place in September, after which the grapes are turned into a dry sherry that is fortified to 15% and then transferred to American oak barrels. The difference between manzanilla and fino sherry is due to Sanlúcar's climate: a layer of yeast (flor) remains in place during ageing.

EXCURSIONS

LA CARTUJA★

6km/3.5mi southeast of Jerez along A 381 on the Medina Sidonia road. Interior open for Mass only (Tue–Sat 8am and 5:30pm, Sun–Mon 5:30pm). Visits to the patio and gardens allowed daily 7am–6pm. Closed holidays. Free entrance. 956 15 64 65.

The Renaissance doorway leads to a paved courtyard featuring a remarkable four-part church **façade★★★**, adorned with the saints of the Order, an Immaculate Conception and, above the rose window, the figure of St Bruno, founder of the Order.

YEGUADA DE LA CARTUJA★

Leave Jerez on the Medina Sidonia road. The Finca Fuente del Suero is at km 6. Guided tours and shows (2hr 30 mins), Sat at 11am. €15.50–21. Reservations advised by phone or online. 956 16 28 09. www.yeguadacartuja.com.

On Saturdays, the public can visit the state-run **Cartujana** stud farm and get a close-up look at how Andalucía's finest horses are trained.

SANLÚCAR DE BARRAMEDA★

26km/16mi northwest of Jerez.

In the 15C, Sanlúcar's location made it a perfect stopping point for galleys returning to Sevilla from the Americas. In 1519 Magellan left to circumnavigate the globe, and his expedition returned here three years later under **Juan Sebastián Elcano**. The soil and climatic conditions around Sanlúcar have produced one of Andalucía's best dry sherries, *manzanilla (see box)*. Sanlúcar's historical neighborhood hosts numerous **sherry** *bodegas*, while the waterfront is lined with superb seafood restaurants. **Plaza del Cabildo**, embellished with orange and palm trees, is the town's epicenter. Note the 18C former **town hall** (*cabildo*) to one side. The **Iglesia de la Trinidad** contains a magnificent 15C Mudéjar **artesonado★★** ceiling.

Covachas★

Recently restored, these five ogee stone arches are decorated with Gothic tracery and winged dragons. They were probably part of the 15C palace of the Dukes of Medina Sidonia.

❯ *Follow avenida del Cabo Nobal to avenida Bajo de Guía where you will find a visitor center (see p 69) devoted to the Parque Nacional de Doñana on the opposite bank of the Guadalquivir.*

🏇 Horseracing

Horse races have been held on the beaches of Sanlúcar for the past 150 years. Today, the Sanlúcar beach race is one of Spain's most picturesque events, combining water, light and superb horsemanship all within a spectacular setting. Its origins date to the 19C, a time when horse races were a novelty. The race is held every August at low tide, around 6pm, on the 2nd and 4th weekends of the month from Thursday to Saturday.

JEREZ DE LA FRONTERA / EXCURSIONS

FOR FUN

TAPAS & CAFÉS

See map p72.

Bar Juanito

Calle Pescadería Vieja 8–10 (B2). 956 34 12 18. www.bar-juanito.com.
On a pedestrian street teeming with outdoor cafés, the venerable Bar Juanito serves award-winning tapas. Quintessentially Andalusian: *azulejos* and bullfighting paintings and posters adorn the walls.

El Gallo Azul

Calle Larga 2 (B2). 956 32 61 48.
This tapas bar is a great place to escape the daily bustle. Enjoy the elegant columned façade.

NIGHTLIFE

Jerez is famous for flamenco clubs (peñas flamencas/tablaos): if you want the real thing, try **Peña Tío José de Paula** (*calle Merced 11, A1; 956 30 32 67/01 96*), or **Peña el Garbanzo** (*calle Santa Clara 9, B2; 956 33 76 67*).

See map p72.

Tablao del Bereber

Calle de las Cabezas 8-10 (A2). 956 34 17 20.
The most famous dinner show and nightspot in Jerez, set in a 13C palace with spaces decorated in Andalusian or Moorish style; includes bars and a large discoteca in adjacent cellars, as well as a flamenco *tablao*.

Shopping

The main shopping district extends around calle Larga. At one end, you'll find a traditional market in plaza Estévez. You can buy sherry everywhere, but for expert advice visit **La Casa del Jerez** (*Divina Pastora 1; 956 33 51 84*).

Kapote Kafé Kopas

Avenida Álvaro Domecq 13 (B1). 902 99 57 73. www.kapote.es.
Modern bar in bullfighting dress, where patrons drink and dance 'til dawn.

Teatro Villamarta

Plaza Romero Martínez (B2). 956 32 73 27. www.villamarta.com.
Opera, classical concerts and occasional flamenco.

SPAS

See map p72.

Baños Árabes Hammam Andalusí (Moorish Baths)

Calle Salvador 6 (A2). Open 10am–10pm. 956 34 90 66. www.hammamandalusi.com.
It's back to the future in these beautiful candle-lit, carefully re-created baths with Moorish decor and a **tea house** with Cathedral views. Enjoy baths, massages and special wellness treatments including full body exfoliation and facial masks.

JEREZ DE LA FRONTERA

MUST DO

SHERRY

Learn about sherry and other bodega tours at www.sherry.org.

"Sherry" is an anglicized version of the name "Jerez." It is produced in the territory between **Jerez**, **Sanlúcar** and **El Puerto de Santa María**, where wines are given official **Denominación de Origen Jerez-Xerez-Sherry** status. Other terms you will probably come across include:

Palomino – 95% of the grapes grown in Jerez are of the Palomino variety, introduced to the region during the time of Alfonso X.

Pedro Ximénez – This grape variety was introduced in 1680 by a Flemish soldier.

Botas – Three types of barrels are used in sherry production: *bocolles*, *toneles* and *botas*. The *botas* (500 liters), made from American oak, are most common.

Solera and **Criaderas** – The *solera* is the row of casks (*barricas*) closest to the floor, which contain the oldest wine. The rows above are *criaderas*. The wine descends from the top level (the first *criadera*) to the *solera*, a process known as "running down the ladder."

Sherry cellar

© Vladimir Melnik/Shutterstock.com

Types of sherry

Fino – A very dry wine with a light, straw-like color. Best with seafood.

Amontillado – An amber sherry, medium dry and aromatic.

Oloroso – A dark sherry with a sharp aroma.

Cream – A sweet, dark sherry, best with desserts.

Pedro Ximénez – A sweet ruby wine made from the Pedro Ximénez grape.

BODEGA TOURS

These bodegas are open by guided tour only. Many require advance booking; inquire at the tourist office.

Pedro Domecq

Calle S.Ildefonso 3. 956 15 15 50.
www.bodegasfundadorpedro domecq.com.
An impressive, 18C El Molino bodega.

González Byass (Tío Pepe)

Calle Manuel María González 12.
www.gonzalezbyass.es.
Founded in 1835, La Concha bodega was designed by Gustave Eiffel in 1892; barrels in La Constancia bear famous signatures (including Margaret Thatcher, Steven Spielberg and King Juan Carlos).

Williams & Humbert

Highway 4 Km 642. 956 35 34 06.
www.williams-humbert.com.
Inquire about the equestrian show.

Sandeman

Calle Pizarro 10. 956 31 29 95.
www.sandeman.com.
Guided tours in English held several times a week.

CÁDIZ★★

Touched by water on three sides, Cádiz is Spain's oldest seafaring city, inhabited for over 3,000 years. It is also one of the most delightful and engaging capitals in Andalucía, with charming parks, squares and 19C streets, as well as a quiet, confident air. Only February's exuberant Carnival, the best on the peninsula, interrupts the city's tranquillity. Visitors will discover a friendly, cosmopolitan metropolis that may be poor in monuments, but remains rich in spirit.

A Bit of History

Cádiz might well be Europe's oldest city. It was colonized in 1100 BC by Phoenicians from Tyre who landed on an islet and founded Gadir ("fortress"). This first settlement extended from the castle of Santa Catalina to the island of Sancti Petri. Initially a dependency of Tyre and later of Carthage, the trading outpost came under Roman rule in 206 BC, as Gades. Trade developed through Gades between Baetica and Rome, but apparently declined under the Visigoths and Moors. The city fell to Fernando III (the Saint) in 1240. His son, Alfonso X (the Wise), transformed Cádiz into a strategic port. The Pópulo district was developed and protected by walls. Three of the four original gateways remain: **Arco de los Blancos**, **Arco del Pópulo** and **Arco de la Rosa**. In the late 15C, Cádiz expanded into the present-day district of Santa María. The Earl of Essex sacked

Cádiz in 1596. The city boomed during the 17C, as testified by numerous examples of Baroque architecture still visible today. Its zenith, however, followed the transfer of the **Casa de Contratación** (Exchange) from Sevilla to Cádiz in 1717, when it became the port of entry for all goods from America.

AROUND THE SANTA MARÍA AND PÓPULO DISTRICTS★★★
Map pp80–81 (C2 and zoom)

The Pópulo district is the early medieval section, while Santa María developed in the 15C beyond the Arco de los Blancos. Restoration projects have been undertaken in recent years on the houses, many of which date to the 17C. A walk here passes through two gypsy quarters where flamenco, guitar music and dancing are part of everyday life.

Cádiz's skyline

© Vladimir Melnik/Shutterstock.com

Practical Information

Location

Cádiz is 138km/86mi northwest of Gibraltar and 35km/22mi southwest of Jerez de la Frontera.

Population

123,948.

Getting There and Around

◆ **By Air** – The airport at Jerez de la Frontera (www.aena.es) is just 35 mins away on the A 4. Connections to Cádiz are available by train (46 mins; www.renfe.com) from the station in the airport, and by bus (1hr; siu.cmtbc.es).

◆ **By Car** – Cádiz can be reached from Sevilla in 1hr 45 mins via the A 4-E 5 highway. The N340 follows the Costa de la Luz southeast all the way to Algeciras (125km/77.5mi), passing through Vejer de la Frontera and Tarifa. The A381 will bring you to Algeciras, crossing through the Parque Natural de los Alcornocales.

◆ **By Train** – The station is in plaza de Sevilla, near the center and port. Trains are available for Jerez de la Frontera (36 mins), Sevilla (1hr 40 mins) and other major cities. For

information and reservations, 902 32 03 20, www.renfe.com.

◆ **By Bus** – Transportes Generales Comes (Plaza de la Hispanidad 1; 956 29 11 68; siu.cmtbc.es) serves Cádiz province (Arcos de la Frontera, Chiclana de la Frontera, Jerez de la Frontera, Algeciras) and Sevilla. Local bus stops are in plaza de España and close to the port. Córdoba can be reached via Socibus (902 22 92 92; www.socibus.es) lines. Five different local bus lines can take you around the city.

◆ **On foot** – This is undoubtedly the best way to discover the delightful squares, gardens and old streets of Cádiz.

◆ **By Taxi** – 956 21 21 21 / 22; 956 26 26 26.

Visitor Information

In Cádiz you can visit the tourist offices in Playa Victoria, Paseo Marítimo (956 25 04 26), avenida José León de Carranza (956 28 56 01), Paseo de Canalejas (956 24 10 01) and Paseo Antonio Burgos; www.turismo.cadiz.es. General information on the Cádiz province is available in Plaza de Madrid, 956 80 70 61 / 72 23; www.cadizturismo.com.

The castle of santa Catalina

CÁDIZ

Plaza de San Juan de Dios

This 16C square is, along with plaza de San Antonio, the oldest in the city. Its strategic position facing the port made it the hub of Cádiz life; for a long time the square was also the site of the city's market. On one side stands the neo-Classical façade of the **town hall** dating from 1799, a work by Torcuato Benjumeda; next to it is the Baroque tower of the **Iglesia de San Juan de Dios**. This square is popular with locals and visitors alike. Enjoy a break from sightseeing at two of the city's most popular cafés: the traditional-style **Novelty Café**, and **La Caleta**, with its boat-shaped counter.

Calle Sopranis

This street contains some of the best examples of Baroque civil architecture in Cádiz. The façades of nos 9–10 (known as the "Houses of the Lilacs" because of the doorway decoration) and the staircase in the patio of nos 17–19 are particularly noteworthy. At the intersection with Calle Plocia, to the left, is the old iron-and-brick **tobacco factory**, a superb example of 19C industrial architecture, now the city's conference center (*Palacio de Congresos*). Opposite stands the **Convento de Santo Domingo**.

Cárcel Real★

Built by local architect Torcuato Benjumeda in 1792, the royal jail was the first neo-Classical building in the city. Four Tuscan-style engaged columns and two lions flank the royal escutcheon. The interior was restored in 1990 to house local courts of law.

A T L Á N T I C O

WHERE TO STAY		WHERE TO EAT	
Hospedería Las Cortes de Cádiz	①	Aurelio	①
Hostal Bahía	②	El Faro	②
Hotel Argantonio	③	La Pepa	③
		Taberna La Manzanilla	④
		Ventorrillo del Chato	⑤

CÁDIZ

Toward Pópulo district

The marble **Casa Lasquetty** in calle Santa María (no 11) is an example of early-18C civil architecture. You can cross calle Félix Soto to the 18C **Arco de los Blancos**, an arch formerly known as the Puerta de Tierra which leads into the working-class Pópulo district.

Casa del Almirante

This fine Baroque palace was built by Admiral (almirante) Don Diego de Barrios at the end of the 17C. The most important feature is the double-section Genoa marble **doorway★★**, with its combination of Tuscan and Solomonic columns on the lower and upper storeys respectively.

Iglesia de Santa Cruz (Catedral Vieja)★

The late-16C Iglesia de Santa Cruz stands on the site of a destroyed mosque and was the city's second cathedral. The sober exterior is broken only by the glazed ceramics covering its umbrella cupolas. The finely proportioned interior consists of three aisles separated by robust Tuscan-style columns.

Teatro Romano

Calle San Juan de Dios. (Closed at the time of publication.) 956 21 22 81. Located immediately behind the Iglesia de Santa Cruz, the Roman theater preserves much of its seating area and several underground galleries.

Cathedral★★

Plaza Fray Félix. Open year-round Mon–Sat 10am–6:30pm, Sun 1:30–6:30pm, holidays 10 am–2 pm. €5 (includes entrance to the museum). Free tour Sun at 11:30. 956 25 98 12.

Construction on Cadíz's main cathedral started in 1722, in pure Baroque style, but was only completed in 1883. Note the brightness and movement in the concave and convex features of its façade. Two towers crowned by pavilions look like astronomical observatories. The large half-orange cupola was completed in 1844 and appears to float high above the city when sea mist envelops Cádiz during winter months.

Casa de la Contaduría (Museo Catedralicio)★

This four-building complex has been superbly restored to house the cathedral museum. The 16C **Mudéjar patio★** is particularly impressive. The museum displays a variety of liturgical objects, vestments and documents, including a letter bearing the signature of St Teresa of Jesus. Other objects of interest are the 16C **Custodia del Cogollo★**, a gold-plated silver monstrance attributed to Enrique Arfe, and the so-called 17C **Custodia del Millón**, named for its numerous precious stones.

NORTH OF THE CATHEDRAL

Map pp80–81 (A-B-C 1-2)

Casa de las Cadenas

Calle Cristóbal Colón. The marble **doorway★** of this late-17C Baroque mansion was made in Genoa. The building is similar to the Casa del Almirante, save for the pair of Solomonic columns framing the main entrance.

Plaza de la Candelaria

Note the late-19C iron-and-glass-fronted building at no 6, and the small Isabelline-style palace at no 15. To one side of the square you can see the birthplace of politician Emilio Castelar, whose bust adorns the square's center.

Oratorio de la Santa Cueva★

Calle Rosario. Open year-round Tue–Fri 11am–2pm and 5:30–8:30pm, Sat–Sun 11am–2pm. Closed Mon and public holidays. €3 (Sun free entrance). 956 22 22 62.
This small neo-Classical jewel is a feast of decoration. The upper, elliptical section consists of a cupola illuminated by lunettes, supported by Ionic columns. Three 1795 **canvases★★** by Goya, recently restored, decorate the chapel.

Plaza de San Francisco

The 16C **Iglesia de San Francisco**, with its simple façade and separate 18C tower, stands to one side of this small square. The interior was restored in the 18C in Baroque style, with stucco and rocaille work. Note the angels below the pendentive-supported false

ceiling, attributed to Pedro Roldán. On the corner of calle Sagasta stands an elegant Baroque edifice with attractive windows, modified in the 19C in Isabelline style.

Callejón del Tinte

There is a fine example of neo-Classical architecture at no 2, and an impressive, thousand-year-old dragon tree opposite.

Plaza de Mina★

In the 19C several squares were created on land expropriated from religious orders. One was the plaza de Mina, created in 1838 on the vegetable garden of the nearby Convento de San Francisco. Today, it is one of the city's most charming squares, boasting fine examples of Isabelline-style

Cádiz cathedral

© Asturianu/Shutterstock.com

CÁDIZ

architecture. In particular, note the houses at nos 11 and 16, as well as the neo-Classical palace housing the **Museo de Cádiz★** (*see Museums*).

Iglesia del Carmen
Plaza San Martín.
This is the most Latin American of the city's churches and provides clear evidence of the reciprocal influences between Spain and her colonies. Built in the mid-18C, note the church's impressive **Baroque façade★**.

Oratorio de San Felipe Neri
Calle Santa Inés. Open Tue–Fri 10am–1:30pm and 5–7:30pm, Sat 10am–1:30pm, Sun 11am–2pm. Closed Mon and public holidays. €3 (Sun free entrance). 956 80 70 18.
Built between 1688 and 1719, this Baroque oratory is one of the few churches in Andalucía with an elliptical ground plan. Inside on the lower level you'll find eight richly decorated chapels and a high altar with an altarpiece dominated by an unusual **Immaculate Conception** in which the Virgin Mary is dark-skinned. Sadly the artist was killed in an accident while creating this work. The Tuscan-ordered upper level, in the form of a bullfighting tribune, supports a lightweight cane-framed cupola.

Parque Genovés★
This is the city's main green area and a delightful place for a quiet stroll. Opposite you'll find the former barracks of Carlos III, which have converted into the main building for the University of Cádiz.

Castillo de Santa Catalina
Avenida Duque de Nájera. Open year-round daily 11am–8:30pm. Free. 956 22 63 33.
The castle is situated at the far end of La Caleta beach. Built by Cristóbal de Rojas in 1598 after

Playa de la Caleta

© Philip Lange/Shutterstock.com

Cádiz was sacked by the Earl of Essex, this fortification has an unusual star shape. The castle often hosts temporary exhibits.

Playa de la Caleta

Once the city's natural harbor, Playa de la Caleta is now the only beach in the old part of Cádiz. At one end, on a small island connected to the city by a small causeway, you can visit the **Castillo de San Sebastián**, built in the 18C and still used by the military today. According to local legend, the temple of Kronos once stood on this site. The handsome white **Balneario de la Palma** spa was built in 1925.

Hospital de Mujeres★

Calle Hospital de Mujeres 26.
Open year-round Mon–Fri
10am–1:30pm and 5:30–8pm,
Sat 10am–1:30pm. Closed Sun.
€1.50. 956 20 31 91.
The Hospital for Women is one of the most significant Baroque buildings in Cádiz. In order to overcome space limitations, the architect designed a narrow façade, behind which the building becomes much broader. It is laid out around two patios linked via an extraordinary Imperial-style **stairway★★** with a cane-framed vault. The 18C *Vía Crucis* created from Triana *azulejos* in the patio is particularly attractive. The church *(inquire at the porter's lodge for access)* contains a painting of **St Francis** by El Greco.

Barrio de la Viña

This working-class district, or barrio, was created in the early 18C. Today it is one of the most colorful quarters of Cádiz, renowned as the

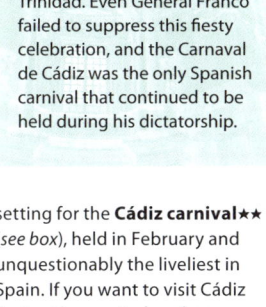

setting for the **Cádiz carnival★★** *(see box)*, held in February and unquestionably the liveliest in Spain. If you want to visit Cádiz during the carnival, make sure you reserve accommodations several months in advance. If you're in the mood to try something special, sample some of the local **mackerel**, sold on the streets of the Barrio de la Viña.

Torre Tavira★

Calle Marqués del Real Tesoro 10.
Open daily May–Sept 10am–8pm,
Oct–Apr 10am–6pm. Closed 1 Jan,
25 Dec. €5. 956 21 29 10.
www.torretavira.com.
This tower, in the highest part of the city, was designated as the official watchtower in 1778, monitoring the arrival and departure of seagoing ships through a complex system of semaphores. The very first **camera obscura** in Spain, an ingenious device capturing real-time images of the city's movements, was installed in the tower in 1995.

CÁDIZ

Plaza de las Flores

Plaza Topete is located behind the brick Correos (the main post office). Locals refer to this charming square as the plaza de las Flores (Square of the Flowers), and numerous flower and plant stands, cafés and shops contribute to the square's delightful atmosphere. A number of important shopping streets, including Calle Columela and Calle Compañía, branch off from here.

MUSEUMS

Museo de Cádiz★

Plaza de Mina. Open Tue–Sat 10am–8:30pm (Jun–mid Sept, 9am–3:30pm), Sun and public holidays 10am–5pm. Closed Mon. €1.50 (free for EU citizens). 956 20 33 68. www.museosdeandalucia.es. The city museum is housed in a small neo-Classical palace with a sober façade built midway through the 19C. The archaeological displays are worthy of special note, in particular the section dedicated to the Phoenicians. Two **anthropomorphous sarcophagi★★** in white marble from the 5C BC imitate Egyptian models and were almost certainly carved by Greek craftsmen. In the fine arts section, the star exhibit is the collection of nine **panels★** painted by Zurbarán between 1638 and 1639 for the sacrarium in the Cartuja monastery in Jerez. Note the artist's mastery of light and shade.

© Nito/Shutterstock.com

Cádiz in 1777

In 1777 Carlos III commissioned a 1:250 scale **model★** of the city of Cádiz, a royal whim that resulted in this magnificent 25m2/270sq ft maquette made from mahogany, ebony and marble. The model is so carefully wrought and precise that even the smallest details are visible. Most of the buildings standing today are identifiable on the model, which also provides insight into the development of several open spaces within the city, such as the plaza de Mina and the plaza de la Catedral. The model is on display at the **Museo de las Cortes de Cádiz** (*calle Santa Inés, 956 221 788, same opening hours and website as Museo de Cádiz, see above*).

FOR FUN

TAPAS & CAFÉS

See map pp80–81.

Aurelio

Calle Zorrilla 1 (B1). 956 22 10 31.
Next to plaza de Mina, you'll find a cervecería-marisquería that specializes in seafood and is famous for its tapas.

El Café de Levante

Calle Rosario 23 (A5). 956 22 02 27.
Located in one of the most characteristic streets in the historical quarter, this buzzing café attracts artists and a youthful, trendy crowd.

Taberna La Manzanilla

Calle Feduchy 19 (A5). 956 28 54 01. www.lamanzanilladecadiz.com.
This typical eatery has been open for business since 1900. Here you can try the white wine known as "Manzanilla" in each of its five distillation phases. The taberna also offers a vast range of wines from all over Andalucía.

NIGHTLIFE

During the winter, social life is concentrated around the city's commercial center. In summertime, action is at the beach area of **Playa de la Victoria** and its **Paseo Marítimo**. The most popular bars are in **calle General Muñoz Arenillas**. Another lively area is **Punta de San Vicente**, at the other end of the city.
The **Gran Teatro Falla** (*plaza Falla; 956 22 08 34*) organizes theater and concerts throughout the year.

See map pp80–81.

La Cava

Calle Antonio López 16 (C1). 956 21 18 66. www.flamencolacava.com.
Flamenco shows by local artists in a characteristic locale.

La Mirilla

Plaza Asdrúbal 7–8 (off map, C2). 956 25 17 12.
Consult La Mirilla's extensive list to select a drink or coffee to enjoy while taking in the ocean view.

SHOPPING

Shops in the old quarter sell traditional cakes and pastries. Try local specialties like *pan de Cádiz* at **Horno Compañía** (calle Compañía 7). **Arts and crafts markets** are regular events in the city. Head to the Sunday market near the **Arco de Pópulo**, or the market known as **El Piojito** (Little Flea) on avenida de la Bahía on Monday mornings.

Playa de la Barrosa

The delightful **Playa de la Barrosa★★**, an 8km/5mi stretch of fine sand, is just 7km/4.5mi away from **Chiclana de la Frontera** (*25km/15.5mi southeast of Cádiz*). The beach has a number of excellent recreation facilities, particularly in Sancti Petri and Novo Sancti Petri.

STRAIT OF GIBRALTAR★

More than a little bit Brit, complete with warm dark beer and prices in Sterling (though Euros are widely accepted), Gibraltar is synonymous with its Rock, a gargantuan limestone promontory rising 423m/1,388ft above the sea and visible from all over the bay.

A Bit of History

The history of Gibraltar is all about location. **Tarik-ibn-Ziyad**'s army of Moors landed here in 711. In antiquity, the Rock was known by its Latin name *Calpe*, or more colloquially one of the Pillars of Hercules. Its present name derives from "Tariq's Mountain" (in Arabic *Djebel Tarik*). Christians and Moors fought over the Rock, and ultimately the Duke of Medina Sidonia conquered it in 1462. The British took permanent but disputed control during the 18C **War of the Spanish Succession**.

GIBRALTAR★★★
Map of Andalucía.

Gibraltar Museum

18-20 Bomb House Lane. Open year-round Mon–Fri 10am–6pm, Sat 10am–2pm. Closed Sun. £2. +350 200 74 289. www.gibmuseum.gi.
Housed in a simple colonial

building above 14C **Moorish baths★**, the museum includes exhibits that cover the history of the Rock, ranging from the 1848 discovery of the **Gibraltar skull** (a Neanderthal woman), to Gibraltar's role in the Second World War. Don't miss the enormous **model★** (1865).

Main Street and the Lower Rock

Gibraltar's main thoroughfare is lined with shops and bars, many with a distinctly British feel. Visit **St Mary's Catholic Cathedral**, built above the former main mosque, and the **Convento**, the residence of Gibraltar's governor since 1728, where the changing of the guard occurs several times daily. On Rosia Road you'll find **Nelson's Anchorage** and the **100-tonne gun** (*open daily year-round 9:30am–6:45pm. £1 (free with Upper Rock ticket*). Built in 1870, the gun boasts a barrel length of over 9.7m/32ft, and could fire 13km/8mi.

Upper Rock of Gibraltar

©Bernd Haak/Fotolia.com

Practical Information

Location

Gibraltar lies at the southern tip of mainland Spain (122km/75.7mi southeast of Cádiz), just above North Africa, at opposite ends of a wide bay.

Getting There and Around

Gibraltar is a British Crown Colony and you'll need a passport for entry. EU nationals require only a valid national identity card.

◆ **By Air** – Regular flights to **Gibraltar airport** (www.gibraltar airport.gi) are available from London, Manchester and Birmingham.

◆ **By Car** – Visitors are advised to check the entry situation before arrival as long lines (1hr or more) sometimes form at the border both in and out of Gibraltar. On these occasions, it is worth leaving your car on the Spanish side and walking across the border.

◆ **By Bus** – Transportes Generales Comes serves Cádiz province and Sevilla. Buses from Algeciras (calle San Bernardo 1; 902 19 92 08; siu. ctas.ctan.es) reach La Línea de la Concepción, the town across the border, in 45min. The bus station is only a 5-minute walk from the frontier.

Visitor Information

Tourist offices in Gibraltar (Cathedral Square; +350 20 07 49 50; www.visitgibraltar.gi); La Línea de la Concepción (Avenida del Ejército; 956 78 41 35).

Upper Rock★

The top of the rock is accessible via cable car, car or taxi. Open daily year-round 9:30am–7:15pm (World War II Tunnels may close earlier Sat–Sun). Last cable car return 7:45pm. Cable Car, Apes, Viewpoint, Multimedia €11.90 (including all Nature Reserve Attractions €25.90). +350 200 72 735. www.gibraltarinfo.gi.

The Upper Rock hosts Gibraltar's most interesting sights and offers splendid **panoramic views★**. The **Great Siege Tunnels** originated during the Great Siege of 1779–82 when Spain and France besieged Gibraltar. Attacking forces dug into trenches right beneath the Rock to avoid British gunfire. In response, the British began to dig tunnels by hand in order to descend to a point where

Touring Tip

The Straits and Bay of Gibraltar are two of the best places in Europe for **dolphin and whale watching**. There are two operators in Marina Bay, Gibraltar: **Dolphin Adventure** *(+350 200 50 650; www.dolphin.gi)*; **Dolphin Safari** *(+350 200 07 19 14; www.dolphinsafari.gi)*.

they could fire on French and Spanish forces. The dust created by the tunneling was so stifling that air vents were created on the sides of the Rock. Only then did the British realize that these vents made excellent gun embrasures. The **World War II Tunnels** were built in 1940 to house barracks and offices, as well as a fully equipped hospital complete with

GIBRALTAR

an operating theater and X-ray equipment. Operation Torch, the November 1942 Allied invasion of French North Africa, was coordinated here.

Filled with giant stalactites and stalagmites, the spectacular natural caverns of **St Michael's Cave** begin about 350m above sea level and descend into the Rock. The cavern forms a huge auditorium, home to a spectacular sound and light show, staged twice daily (weekdays only). Concerts and live shows are also performed here (*visit www.philharmonic.gi for concert information*). The Upper Rock is also a designated nature reserve, home to the famous **Barbary apes**, brought here by British troops from North Africa at the end of the 18C. They roam freely and are quite tame. Visitors are forbidden to approach them directly or feed them (they are fed twice a day). According to legend, if the apes leave Gibraltar it will cease to be British.

EXCURSIONS

FROM ALGECIRAS TO VEJER DE LA FRONTERA
Map of Andalucía.

Algeciras
23.3km/14.5mi west of Gibraltar.
Its strategic location opposite the Rock of Gibraltar has exerted a major influence on Gibraltar since Moorish troops landed in the 8C. Today Algeciras bustles with commerce and is Spain's leading passenger port.

The road to Tarifa
This 21km/13mi road, the southernmost in Europe, offers stunning **views★★★** of North Africa. Cars can stop at the **Mirador del Estrecho**, though views are better near Algeciras.

Tarifa
22.5km/14mi southwest of Algeciras.
Tarifa is the southernmost town on the Iberian Peninsula, just 13km/8mi from the North African coast. Converging Atlantic and Mediterranean air masses and pristine beaches have made it one of Europe's most important **windsurfing** and **kitesurfing** destinations. The town's charming historic center, popular with an alternative crowd, exudes tranquillity and easy living.

The road from Tarifa to Punta Paloma
Follow the N 340 toward Cádiz.
This short stretch parallels the sea (**Playa de los Lances**). Campsites and hotels line the road, and there are numerous spots where you can pull over for a swim.
After 4km/2.5mi, a road to the right leads to the **Santuario de Nuestra Señora de la Luz**, named for Tarifa's patron saint. A little further along you'll find two delightful beaches, the **Playa de Valdevaqueros★** and the **Playa de Punta Paloma**, as well as impressive **sand dunes**.

Ruinas Romanas de Baelo Claudia★
22.5km/14mi northwest of Tarifa. Open Tue–Sat 9am–6:30pm

(Apr–May, 8pm; Jun–mid Sept, 3:30pm), Sun and public holidays 10am–5pm. Closed Mon. €1.50 (free for EU citizens). 956 10 67 97.
The Roman city of Baelo Claudia was founded in the 2C BC as a salt factory (*see box*). Emperor Claudius made it a municipality in the 1C AD and most of the remains visible today, including sections of its large fortified wall and gate, date from this period.

Vejer de la Frontera★
40km/25mi northwest of Baelo Claudia.
Vejer is perched on a rocky crag dominating the Barbate River valley, just a few kilometers from the Atlantic coast. One of Andalucía's most picturesque pueblos blancos, it has very strong Moorish roots, reflected in its maze of narrow, cobbled streets and whitewashed houses, enclosing verdant patios and crowned by flat terraced roofs.

Parque Natural La Breña y Marismas de Barbate★
Access from Vejer de la Frontera along the A 5206 or from Barbate.
The main attractions of this nature reserve are its lovely coves, nestled between rocky cliffs, and beaches bordered by umbrella pines, the most famous of which is the **Playa de los Caños de Meca★★**.

PARQUE NATURAL DE LOS ALCORNOCALES★
Map of Andalucía.

Several roads crisscross the park, including the A 375, the CA 503 from Arcos de la Frontera, and the A 369 from San Roque.

Rife with wild olive trees and cork oak, this nature park boasts many **paths and trails**. Two of the best walks include the path to La Sauceda (*about 5hrs*) and the more strenuous **El Picacho** ascent (*about 3hrs*).

Castillo de Castellar★
31.3km/19.5mi north of Algeciras.
The Nasrids built this village-fortress in the 13C to protect the recently-created kingdom of Granada. For two centuries, Castellar de la Frontera (as it was known) endured frontier battles until it was reconquered in 1434. In the early 1970s, following the construction of the **Embalse de Guadarranque**, a reservoir that flooded the local area, most inhabitants moved to "Nuevo Castellar," 7km/4mi to the south. The road to old Castellar winds up past whitewashed houses through an extraordinarily beautiful landscape.

Garum

Phoenicians and Romans fished schools of tuna as they moved into the Mediterranean during spawning season in May and June. Many of the Roman cities along the Andalusian coast, such as Baelo, were originally outposts dedicated to salting the catch. **Garum** was this industry's best-known and most expensive product: a sauce produced from the fish's head, entrails, blood and other remains, used as a condiment or even a main dish.

COSTA DEL SOL★★

The Sun Coast stretches along the Mediterranean from Tarifa to the Cabo de Gata, a headland east of Almería. Visitors are drawn to the area's warm climate, sandy beaches, whitewashed towns and villages and leisure activities, including a boom in golf course construction that has earned the coast the tongue-in-cheek moniker: Costa del Golf. Tourism is deeply rooted in the economy of the Costa del Sol, and you'll find accommodations of all tastes and sizes, from uninspiring concrete high-rises to luxurious holiday complexes.

FROM SOTOGRANDE TO TORREMOLINOS
Map of Andalucía.

Sotogrande
22.2km/13.8mi north of Gibraltar.
These luxury housing complexes and elegant homes lie alongside the famous ⛳ **Real Club de Golf Sotogrande**, often voted among the top ten golf courses in Europe.

Gaucín
39km/24mi north of Sotogrande.
The whitewashed houses and narrow streets of Gaucín, another of the region's classic *pueblo blancos*, lie on a rocky hill in the heart of the Serranía de Ronda. The **views**★ from the remains of the old castle are particularly impressive. Gaucín is well known for its unfermented **grape juice** (*mosto*) and its *aguardiente*, a fiery **brandy**.

Casares★
20km/12.5mi south of Gaucín.
The houses in this small, captivating settlement seem suspended above a promontory in the Sierra Crestenilla. The **approach**★★ to the village is stunning and this classic *pueblo blanco* vista is one of the most photographed sites in all Spain. Casares was one of the last mountain strongholds of the Moors in Málaga province. You'll find the birthplace of Andalusian nationalist **Blas Infante** (1855–1936) at no 51, calle Carrera. The old **Moorish quarter**★ retains its labyrinthine plan and low houses with reddish-colored roofs. The remains of a former Moorish fortress stand above the old quarter, alongside the 16C **Iglesia de la Encarnación**, badly damaged during the Spanish Civil War.

Casares

© Csp/Shutterstock.com

Practical Information

Location

The Serranía de Ronda mountain range protects the coast from weather inland. For this chapter we've covered a roughly 200km/124mi stretch of the Costa del Sol, extending from Sotogrande to Salobreña and passing through Marbella and Málaga.

Getting There and Around

♦ **By Air** – The Costa del Sol is served by **Málaga airport** (www.aena.es), 10km/6mi southwest of Málaga along the coastal road. Buses and a suburban train line serve coastal resorts. A hired car is also a good choice, given the coastal sprawl and excellent roads.

♦ **By Car** – The A 7-N340 is the main coastal highway.

♦ **By Train** – Long-distance trains only depart from the station in Málaga (Explanada de la Estación; 902 24 02 02). You can reach Málaga from Sevilla in 1hr 55min on the Avant trains; in 2hr 37mins on the less expensive MD trains. The suburban train line (*tren de cercanías*; www.renfe.com/viajeros/cercanias) connects Málaga with Fuengirola, Torremolinos, Benalmádena and other local towns. For information and reservations, 902 32 03 20, www.renfe.com.

♦ **By Bus** – Málaga's bus station (Paseo los Tilos; 952 35 00 61; www.estabus.emtsam.es) is right next to the train station. Avanza-CTSA Portillo company (902 02 00 52; www.avanzabus.com) runs buses to major towns (Málaga, Benalmádena, Estepona, Fuengirola, Marbella, Torremolinos, Cádiz and Tarifa), as well as many points between. To see all the bus connections available in the Málaga region, visit siu.ctmam.ctan.es. For information on local Málaga buses: 902 52 72 00; www.emtmalaga.es

♦ **By Taxi** – In Málaga, Unitaxi: 952 33 33 33; Taxi Union: 952 04 08 04 / 00 90. In Marbella, Marbella Taxis: 951 24 71 49; Taxi-Sol: 952 77 44 88 / 82 35 35.

♦ **By Boat** – Every major resort has a marina for recreational vessels. The main ones are in Puerto Banús (6km/3.6mi from central Marbella; 915 moorings) and Puerto Marina (in Benalmádena; 1,000 moorings). Additional marinas can be found in Estepona, Marbella and Fuengirola.

Visitor Information

Tourist offices in: **Málaga** (Avenida Cervantes 1, 951 92 72 05; Plaza de la Marina 11, 951 92 60 20; www.malagaturismo.com), **Marbella** (Plaza de los Naranjos, 952 82 35 50; www.marbellaexclusive.com), **Puerto Banús** (Plaza Antonio Banderas, 952 81 85 70), **Nerja** (Calle Carmen 1, 952 52 15 31), **Salobreña** (Plaza Goya, 958 61 03 14).

Manilva

13.7km/8.5mi south of Casares.
Surrounded by vineyards, Manilva is just a few kilometers from the Mediterranean. The town's 18C **Iglesia de Santa Ana** has an unusual arch over the portal. **Beaches** to the south include Playa de la Paloma, Playa del Salto de la Mora and Playa Negra between San Luis de Sabinillas and **Puerto Duquesa**.

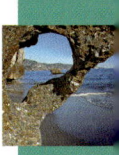

Estepona★

16.5km/10.3mi northeast of Manilva.
Estepona, at the foot of the Sierra Bermeja range, is one of the Costa del Sol's major resort areas, with hotels and beaches stretching out over 20km/12mi. There is a 900-boat marina, a golf course, a scuba-diving center, and the usual nightclubs and boutiques. You can visit watchtowers from the 15C and 16C located along the coast near the town.

Despite modern encroachments, the **old quarter★** preserves the charm of an Andalusian village, with narrow streets lined by whitewashed houses adorned with wrought-iron balconies and flowers. The picturesque **plaza de las Flores★** is one of Estepona's most famous sights. Its **castle ruins** include two towers, the Torre del Reloj and El Vigía. The 18C **Iglesia de Nuestra Señora de los Remedios** highlights colonial influence. Its most outstanding feature is its Baroque **portal★★**, with unusual decoration representing the sun, moon and stars.

San Pedro de Alcántara

23km/14mi northeast of Estepona.
What was once a town built for local plantation workers has been turned into a major resort location. Remains from the past include **Las Bóvedas**, unusual thermal baths with an octagonal floor plan and vaulted rooms.
A winding **road★★** links San Pedro de Alcántara with **Ronda★★** (*see RONDA AND PUEBLOS BLANCOS*).

Puerto Banús

3.7km/2.3mi east of San Pedro de Alcántara.

This superb marina shelters some of the world's most expensive sailing vessels. Alongside the moorings (and an impressive collection of luxury cars), are some of the region's most fashionable bars, restaurants and boutiques. The marina attracts all kinds of visitors on summer evenings for drinks, dinner and a little late night shopping.

Marbella★

7.8km/5mi east of Puerto Banús.
Marbella is the Costa del Sol's most exclusive resort town. A magnificent climate, superb beaches and leisure facilities have transformed a simple fishing port into a playground of seafront apartment blocks and inland holiday complexes. It is a shoppers' paradise, particularly for luxury goods, and has developed a reputation for its exclusive nightlife, health clubs and spas. Superb sporting facilities include famous **golf courses** and its cosmopolitan appeal means there are mosques and even a synagogue.

Traditional Andalucía still survives in the **old quarter★**, with typical whitewashed houses, flowers, twisting alleyways and plenty of shops, bars, cafés and restaurants.

Plaza de los Naranjos★

This enchanting square in the old quarter is perfect for unwinding at an outdoor café facing the 16C stone fountain, delightful floral displays and orange trees. Buildings around the square include the 16C **town hall**, with its wrought-iron balconies and handsome Mudéjar doorway, the 17C **Casa del Corregidor**

(Magistrate's Mansion), with a monumental stone **façade**★ and elegant balcony, and the 15C **Ermita de Nuestro Señor Santiago**, the first Christian church erected in Marbella.

Museo del Grabado Español Contemporáneo★

Calle Hospital de Bazán. Open Tue–Fri 11am–9pm, Sat 9am–2pm. Closed Mon, Sun and public holidays. €3. 952 76 57 41. www.mgec.es.
The Contemporary Spanish Print Museum, the only one of its kind in Spain, is located in the 16C former Hospital de Bazán. Works by Tàpies, Alberti, Chillida and Maruja Mallo are on display.

Fuengirola

30km/18.5mi east of Marbella.
Fuengirola is another of the Costa del Sol's major resort towns, with hotels, restaurants, leisure facilities and 7km/4.5mi of beaches drawing visitors year-round. The merloned towers of the 10C **Castillo de Sohail** dominate the town from on high. The **Santa Fe de los Boliches** district includes archaeological remains – some 1C AD baths and the vestiges of a Roman villa – as well as the **Museo Abierto**, an outdoor gallery with murals by well known artists like Sempere, Rafael Peinado, Elena Asins and others.

Mijas★

8.3km/5mi north of Fuengirola.
Picturesque Mijas, set high on a hill amid pines, offers stunning **views**★ of the Costa del Sol. Its winding streets, charming nooks and crannies, flower-decked houses and numerous tiny squares attract thousands visitors every year. The **old quarter**★ is photographer's paradise: a network of bright streets lined by low-roofed houses decorated with wrought-iron balconies and grilles. Boutiques and souvenir shops can be found in calle de Charcones, calle de San Sebastián and calle de Málaga.

Torremolinos

21.2km/13.2mi east of Mijas.
Torremolinos has experienced phenomenal growth since it first attracted artists in the 1950s. **Calle de San Miguel** is the commercial hub, but also where you'll find the last of the windmills for which the town was named. The **paseo Marítimo**, an attractive tree-lined promenade along the beach, boasts dozens of restaurants.

Estepona

MÁLAGA★
Map pp98–99.

This bustling gateway to the Costa del Sol is characterized by elegant promenades, impressive monuments, an active marina and port, and residential neighborhoods with fine 19C villas. Málaga's skyline is dominated by the Gibralfaro, or Lighthouse Hill, crowned by a Moorish fortress. Though surrounded by tourist-oriented seaside resorts, Málaga remains a resolutely Spanish enclave. Central Málaga has some delightful narrow streets and alleyways – much of the central area is pedestrianized – including pasaje Chinitas, a lively shopping area near calle Marqués de Larios, the old city's main street.

A Bit of History
Phoenicians founded *Malaca* around the late 8C /early 7C BC. Greek and Carthaginian trading posts followed. The Romans created a colony here in the 3C BC that exported wine, oil, raisins, cereals, salted meat and fish. Christianity arrived in the 4C. After 716, Málaga was ruled from Córdoba, then became part of the kingdom of Granada. The fortress (*alcazaba*) was built in the 11C, when the city developed its textile industry. Following periods of Almoravid and Almohad dominion, Málaga became the chief port of the Nasrids in Granada. In the 14C, the Gibralfaro fortress was rebuilt and extended by Yusuf I. The Genoese developed the city's commerce and opened new trade routes. In the 16C, under Felipe II, a new port brought renewed prosperity, and the city experienced further expansion in the 18C when trade was liberalized.

Cathedral★
Calle Molina Lario 9. Open Mon–Fri 10am–6pm, Sat 10am–5pm, Sun free entrance 2pm–6pm. Closed public holidays. €5. 952 22 03 45.
Construction took place between the 16C and 18C, hence the mix of styles: Renaissance predominates, while the ground plan is Gothic, and the ceilings and façade Baroque. The main façade faces plaza del Obispo. The tower on the right is unfinished, hence the nickname "La Manquita"

Málaga

© Tupungato/Shutterstock.com

(Missing One). Note the relief of the Incarnation (the Cathedral's name) on the middle portal. *Enter through the garden on the left side of the cathedral.*

The proportions are monumental: a hall-church ground plan with three aisles, side chapels and an ambulatory. The lofty naves rest on layers of columns, and are crowned by attractively-decorated **oven vaulting**★. Handsome 17C choir **stalls**★ were partly carved by Pedro de Mena. Note the two magnificent 18C Baroque organs, large choral stands, and the 17C marble pulpits with ecclesiastical escutcheons. Behind the choir is a lovely *Pietà* (1802) in Carrara marble by the Pisan brothers. The Capilla de Santa Bárbara has an impressive early-15C **Gothic retable**★★.

Museo

Enter from the ticket offices, downstairs.

This small museum exhibits religious paintings, anonymous 16C and 17C sculpture, and silver and gold objects.

El Sagrario

Calle Santa Maria 22. Open 9:30–12:30am and 6–7:30pm. 952 21 59 17.

This unusual 16C rectangular church in the cathedral gardens has a superbly sculptured Isabelline Gothic **side portal**★ *(opening onto calle Santa María)*. The single-nave Baroque interior dates from an 18C renovation. The superb sculpted **altarpiece**★★ in the apse is Mannerist in style and crowned by an impressive Calvary.

Alcazaba★

Calle Alcazabilla 2. Open in Summer daily 9am–8:15pm, in Winter daily 8:30am–7:30pm (Mon, 6pm). Closed 1 Jan, 28 Feb, 24, 25 and 31 Dec. €2.20 (free entrance Sun starting at 2pm; €3.55, including Castillo de Gibralfaro). 952 22 72 30.

Construction of this Moorish hilltop fortress began in 1040. One of the largest Muslim military installations preserved in Spain, it consists of a double enclosure with rectangular towers that were originally connected to the city walls. Access is via a zig-zag ramp from calle Alcazabilla past sections of brick and masonry walls and through gateways, some of which re-used Roman columns. The Arco de Cristo (Christ's Arch), where Mass was celebrated after the reconquest, leads to the Moorish gardens. The **views**★ from atop of the walls take in the city and port. In the second enclosure is the former palace, Nasrid in style.

Teatro Romano

The terraces on the slope of the hill are all that is left of this Roman theater at the foot of the Alcazaba (west side). Close by, the neo-Classical **Aduana** (Customs House) now houses provincial offices and an exhibit hall.

Beaches

Málaga is blessed with many beautiful beaches, from La Malagueta and Las Acacias to Playa del Palo, 5km/3mi east of the city. All have excellent facilities and a wide choice of bars and restaurants.

MÁLAGA

CÓRDOBA, GRANADA
↑ Finca de la Concepción

Map labels:

CENTRO CULTURAL PROVINCIAL

Museo del Vidrío y Cristal

la Regente

Ventura Rodríguez

Don Juan de Austria

Francisco Monje

Trinidad

Jara

Zamorano

Jaboneros

Mármoles

Pulidero Puente

Mota

Agustín

de la

Cerrojo

Calvo

Cristian

Hilera

Armengual

Av. de Andalucía

Puente de Tetuán

Av. de la Aurora

Ancha del Carmen

Cuarteles

Salitre

San Andrés del

Pasillo

Av. Comandante

Benítez

Alameda de Colón

Matadero

POL.

Guadalmedina

Av. de la

Carretería

Rosaleda

Puente de la Aurora

Pasillo de Santa Isabel

Pº de Guimbarda

Pº de Sto Domingo

Pl. de la Arriola

Pasillo Atocha

Hoyo de Espartero

Alameda

San Trinidad

Casas

Barroso

Lorenzo

Tomás

Grund

Heredia

Campos

de Córdoba

Av. Manuel Agustín Heredia

Principal

Plaza de la Marina

Fatima

Fajardo

Compañía

Cisneros

Museo Carmen Thyssen

Andrés Pérez

Los Mártires

Sta Lucía

Comedias

Tejón y Rodríguez

Pl. del Teatro

Pl. de la Constitución

Especerías Moreno Monroy

Museo de Artes y Costumbres Locales

Sebastián Souvirón

Pl. de Félix Sáenz

Herrería del Rey

Mercado Central

Museo interactivo de la Música

Marín García

Pza del Mar

Martínez

Sancha de Lara

Marqués de Larios

Pasaje de las Chinitas

Sta María

Granada

Calderería

Núñez

Sánchez Pastor

Palacio Episcopal

CATEDRAL

Strachan

Molina Larios

Postigo de los Abades

Cortina

Museo del Vidrío y Cristal

Madre de Dios

Mariblanca

Álamos

Cárcel

Ramón Franq

Museo C de Muñe

Casapalm

El Sagra

CAC Málaga

Museo Automovilístico

Castillo de Gibralfaro

Camino de Gibralfaro 11. Access: bus no 35. Get off at paseo del Parque. Open in Summer 9am–8pm, in Winter 9am–6pm. €2.20 (free entrance Sun starting at 2pm; €3.55, including Alcazaba). 952 22 72 30.

The path around the hilltop remains of the 14C Gibralfaro Castle, built to protect the *alcazaba*, provides magnificent **views★★** of the city and the port. The walled corridor connecting the Alcazaba with the castle was built in the 14C. The castle armory is now a visitor center.

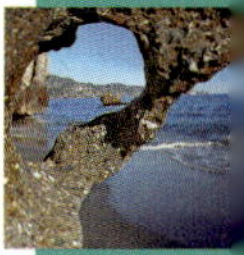

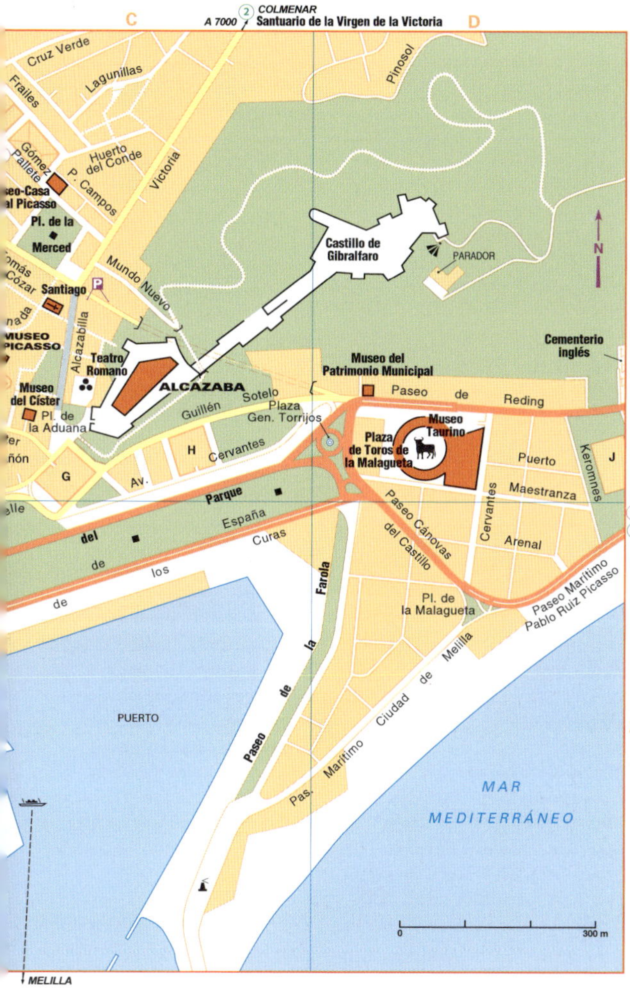

MÁLAGA

Cruz Verde
Lagunillas
Frailes
Gómez Pallete
Huerto del Conde
P. Campos
Victoria
Pinosol
seo-Casa el Picasso
Pl. de la Merced
Tomás Cózar
Santiago
Mundo Nuevo
MUSEO PICASSO
Teatro Romano
ALCAZABA
Alcazabilla
Museo del Císter
Pl. de la Aduana
Sotelo
Guillén
Plaza Gen. Torrijos
Cervantes
Av.
Parque
del
Espáña
de
Curas
los
de
Castillo de Gibralfaro
PARADOR
N
Museo del Patrimonio Municipal
Paseo   de   Reding
Cementerio inglés
A 7 · E 15 ALMERÍA / CALETA EL PALO
Plaza de Toros de la Malagueta
Museo Taurino
Puerto
Keromnes
Maestranza
Cervantes
Arenal
Paseo Cánovas del Castillo
Pl. de la Malagueta
Paseo Marítimo Pablo Ruiz Picasso

1

J

6
1

Farola

PUERTO

Paseo   de   la

Pas.   Marítimo   Ciudad   de   Melilla

2

MAR
MEDITERRÁNEO

0   300 m

MELILLA

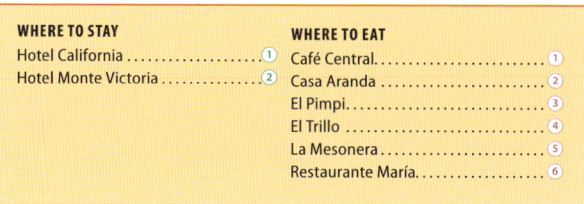

Fish and soup

If you are in Málaga in summer, make sure you try fried fish (*pescaíto frito*), as well as traditional local dishes like *ajoblanco*, a refreshing chilled soup made from almonds, garlic, breadcrumbs, salt and olive oil that is usually served with Moscatel grapes.

Paseo del Parque

This botanical garden provides a haven amid the urban bustle. In **paseo de la Farola**, to the east, is the **statue of the Cenachero**, a fish peddler and local legend. The **La Malagueta** quarter, beyond, marks the beach area.

Mercado Central

The main market is a 19C iron structure on the site of the old Moorish dockyards.

Museums

Museo Picasso★★

Calle San Agustín 8. Open Mon–Thu 10am–8pm, Fri–Sat 10am–9pm, Sun and public holidays 10am–8pm. €6. Closed Mon except Jun–Aug, 1 Jan, 25 Dec. 902 44 33 77. www.museopicassomalaga.org.
The Picasso Museum opened in 2003, in the 16C Renaissance Palacio de Buenavista. The permanent collection comprises more than 200 works from the collections of the artist's niece and grandson, Christine and Bernard Ruiz-Picasso. Displayed chronologically, oils, sketches, engravings, sculptures and ceramics illuminate the artist's development. Significant canvases include *Olga Kokholva with Mantilla* (1917, note the penetrating gaze); *Mother and Child* (1921–1922); the *Portrait of Pau with White Cap* (1923); *Bust of Woman with Arms Crossed Behind Head* (1939), an expressive work with surrealist influences; and *Woman in Armchair* (1946).

Museo-Casa Natal Picasso

Plaza de la Merced. Open year-round daily 9:30am–8pm. Closed public holidays. €2. 951 92 89 76. www.fundacionpicasso.es.
Picasso was born in the mid-19C building at no 15. The museum displays a number of his drawings and ceramics well as photos and memorabilia.

Museo de Artes y Costumbres Populares★

Pasillo de Santa Isabel 10. Open Mon–Fri 10am–5pm, Sat 10am–2pm. Closed Sun and public holidays. €4. 952 21 71 37. www.museoartespopulares.com.
The charming and informative Museum of Popular Arts and Traditions is set in the Mesón de la Victoria, an attractive 17C inn, and provides insight into traditional rural and urban life.

CAC Málaga

Calle Alemania 2. Open year-round Tue–Sun 10am–2pm and 5–9pm. Closed Mon. Free. 952 12 00 55. www.cacmalaga.org.
The former wholsale market is now the Centro de Arte Contemporáneo de Málaga (modern art center). It holds 400 works donated from private collections, shown on a rotating basis. Notable are 20C Spanish paintings by Sicilia, Broto, Barceló and others.

Museo Interactivo de la Música

Calle Beatas 15. Open year-round daily 10am–2pm and 4–8pm. Closed Mon afternoon. €4. 952 21 04 40. www.musicaenaccion.com.

This lively new museum has an entertaining and well-presented collection of over 300 musical instruments from different eras and regions, and showcases musical styles from Eminem to Mozart. Emphasis throughout the museum is "se ruega tocar" ("please play").

Finca de la Concepción★

7km/4.5mi north of Málaga. Camino del Jardín Botánico 3. Open year-round 9:30am–8:30pm (Oct–Mar, 5:30pm). Last admission 90mins before closing. Closed Mon, 1 Jan, 25 Dec. €5.20. 952 25 21 48. www.laconcepcion.malaga.eu.

This magnificent botanical garden was created in the middle of the 19C by Jorge Loring and his wife, Amalia Heredia, who brought tropical and subtropical species to Málaga on ships owned by her father. The delightful estate is a forest of greenery and small streams, embellished with lakes, waterfalls, fountains, footbridges and Roman ruins.

ROAD TO SALOBREÑA

Map of Andalucía.

Frigiliana★

59km/36.5mi east of Málaga.

This charming *pueblo blanco* extends across the southern slopes of the Sierra de la Almijara. Its **Morisco-Mudéjar quarter★★** is a superb ensemble of meticulously maintained whitewashed houses. Flowers add an extra dash of color. Panels of *azulejos* on several walls recall battles fought here between Moors and Christians.

Nerja★

9km/5.5mi south of Frigiliana.

Nerja is a charming town of Moorish origin perched above the Mediterranean. The coast below the Sierra de Almijara is characterized by steep cliffs and delightful beaches.
Numerous bars, outdoor cafés, restaurants and nightclubs have made Nerja one of the most popular summer resorts along the

Beach near Nerja

© SueC/Shutterstock.com

eastern Costa del Sol, though it is nowhere near as brash as its rivals to the west.

Balcón de Europa★

This magnificent *mirador* (viewpoint) in old Nerja is on the site of the old castle. On a clear day you can see all the way to Africa. The whitewashed 17C Iglesia del Salvador, with its impressive bell tower, stands alongside.

Cueva de Nerja★★

4.5km/3mi east toward Motril. Admission by guided tour only (45 mins) year-round daily Jun–Aug 10am–7:30pm, the rest of the year 10am–2pm, 4–6:30pm. Closed 1 Jan and 15 May. €8.50. 952 52 95 20. www.cuevadenerja.es.

Discovered in 1959, this enormous cave yielded pottery, ceramics, human remains and wall paintings that indicate the caves were inhabited as far back as the Palaeolithic era. The cave is hugely impressive in the scale of its chambers and its spectacular stalactites and stalagmites, one of which is reputedly the biggest in the world.

The **Sala de la Cascada** (Cascade Chamber), also known as the **Sala del Ballet** (Ballet Chamber), takes its name from the formations you can see on the right-hand side. An annual **Festival of Music and Dance** is held here in July.

Salobreña★

32.8km/20.5mi east of Nerja.

Whitewashed Salobreña is the most attractive town on this stretch of coast. Visit the imposing **castle**, the **Iglesia de la Virgen del Rosario**, and splendid beaches like **Playa de El Peñón**.

Salobreña Castle (*open summer, 10:30am–2pm, 5pm–9:30pm; winter Tue–Sun 10:30am–2pm, 4pm–7pm; €2 (€2.55 including entry to museum); 958 61 27 33/ 03 14*) is a famous landmark, best viewed from the Almuñécar road. The original 10C castle was transformed into a luxurious residence – and royal prison – under the Nasrids. Access is via a corner doorway to the first enclosure. Continue to the *alcazaba* (fortress), with its two underground caverns, where prisoners were kept in total darkness, and keep.

The Three Princesses of Salobreña

In his *Tales of the Alhambra* **Washington Irving** wrote that the princesses Zaida, Zoraida and Zorahaida, daughters of King Mohammed IX of Granada, were confined to the sumptuous palace of Salobreña for many years by their father. Heeding advice from his astrologers, the king decided to protect them from everyday temptation, not least the risk of running into undesirable suitors. The three princesses lived here surrounded by luxury, their every need attended to, until their father decided to take them to his palace at the Alhambra. Destiny intervened on the journey to Granada, when the party ran into three Christian prisoners who immediately fell in love with the young princesses, thereby making the astrologers' predictions come true.

FOR FUN

TAPAS & CAFÉS

FUENGIROLA

Bodega Charolais

Calle Larga 14. 952 47 54 41.
www.bodegacharolais.com.
Located next to the restaurant
of the same name, this bar has
its own separate entrance. The
contemporary look is accentuated
by tables and stools of differing
heights. Creative tapas and wines
by the glass.

MÁLAGA
See map pp98–99.

 Café Central

Plaza de la Constitución 11 (D1).
952 22 49 72. www.cafecentral
malaga.com.
A century-old coffee house
frequented by faithful regulars.
There is a pleasant terrace on the
square, but make sure you don't
miss the large tea room.

Casa Aranda

Calle Herrería del Rey 2 (D2). 952
22 28 12. www.casa-aranda.net.
First opened in 1932, this lively café
has taken over every building on
its street. Great place for chat over
chocolate with *churros*.

La Mesonera

Calle Gómez Pallete 11 (E1).
952 22 59 65.
This small bar fills up with stars
before and after flamenco
performances at the Teatro
Cervantes opposite. Delicious
tapas and a colorful Andalusian
atmosphere.

NIGHTLIFE

ESTEPONA

Calle Real, in the town center, and
the **Puerto Deportivo** (marina)
are the main centers of activity
after the sun goes down. In the late
afternoon and evening the port is
pleasant for a quiet drink on one of
the many terraces. Later, the action
tends to move to the bars on calle
Real, then on to harborside bars.
Pop and rock concerts are organized
on the beach in summer.

FUENGIROLA

Plaza de la Constitución is
the epicenter of local nightlife.
Other popular areas nearby
include calle Miguel de Cervantes,
calle Emancipación and the Paseo
Marítimo Rey de España.
The town organizes a number

Málaga by night

Pius Koller/imagebrok/Age Fotostock

of activities between July and September, including art shows, concerts and theater.

🏛 El Piso

Avenida de la Estación. 649 90 65 23.
Cosy, warm ambience and old-style decoration with flamenco and Latin music nights.

Mahama

On the ring road, in Mijas Costa. 952 58 86 05.
Discoteca Mahama is laid out in Andalusian style out around a patio filled with plants and fountains, quiet areas, an enormous dance floor and an all-night grill. Locals of all ages drop in, getting younger as the night deepens.

MARBELLA

Marbella is queen of the Costa del Sol, and buzzes with activity year-round. Marbella's teenagers hang out near the **marina** (*puerto deportivo*). The trendiest, most lively areas are in **Puerto Banús**, and caters to all ages and tastes. Some of the best-known night-spots, however, are along the main coast road (*autovía*). For more highbrow nightlife and the performing arts, visit the **Auditorio** in Parque de la Constitución, a venue for concerts and theater.

Olivia Valère

On the Istán road. 952 82 88 61. www.oliviavalere.com.
Designed as a Moorish palace, complete with patios, terraces and gardens offering a variety of different atmospheres for a quiet drink or dinner, this is one of the most exclusive and luxurious venues on the Costa del Sol.

Suite

Hotel Puente Romano, Bulevar Principe Alfonso von Hohenlohe. 952 82 09 00. www.suiteclubs.com.
Boasting a restaurant featuring Lebanese and Moroccan cuisine, in the summertime the evenings are extended with a lounge bar, disco and DJ set.

MÁLAGA
See map pp98–99.

The central area around the cathedral and calle Larios has numerous lively old bars, mainly frequented by Málaga's younger generations and foreign visitors, as well as quieter cafés and tea shops (*teterías*). In summer, locals tend to spend more time along the paseo Marítimo. You'll find more exclusive bars and clubs in the upscale El Limonar district at the foot of the mountains. The **Teatro Cervantes** (*calle Ramos María; 952 22 41 09; www.teatrocervantes.com*), which opened in 1870, offers an extensive theater program and concerts.

El Pimpi

Calle Granada 62 and Jardines Alcazabilla (C1). 952 22 89 90. www.bodegabarelpimpi.com.
This traditional tavern in the old town is good for tapas in the afternoon and early evening; and for lively nights after sunset when the volume is cranked up. Recently this *bodega* has been joined by another, newer Pimpi: **El Pimpi Marinero**, a naval-themed locale that offers seafood and cocktails.

🍵 La Tetería

Calle San Agustín (B1). 952 21 53 86. www.la-teteria.com.
A small bar, located on a pedestrian street. The Moorish feel and aroma of the many teas offered add to its atmosphere.

Siempre Así

Calle Convaleciente 5 (C1).
This centrally-located bar is a favorite of the city's jet set. From midnight onwards the dance floor fills with people dancing to rumbas, *sevillanas* and the latest latino hits.

TORREMOLINOS

The town hall organizes shows and concerts year-round. Most bars and nightclubs are concentrated in calle San Miguel, plaza Costa del Sol and avenida Palma de Mallorca, although locals and tourists head to the nearby marina (Puerto Marina) in **Benalmádena** for a wider variety of entertainment and greater sophistication.

FIESTAS & EVENTS

Film Festival

Málaga is home to the **Festival of Spanish Film**, the most important of its kind.

Semana Santa

Málaga celebrates Holy Week to the full, with processions rooted in 16C traditions. Huge floats, known as *tronos* (thrones), are erected in the open. The moment when these floats are lifted up and "rocked" is one of the most spectacular of the entire week.

The most important **processions** during Holy Week are: Señor de los Gitanos (Easter Monday), El Cautivo (Wednesday), Cristo de la Buena Muerte and Esperanza Perchelera (Maundy Thursday). For more details visit www. semana-santa-malaga.com.

🍵 Málaga Feria

This annual fair, commemorating the reconquest of Málaga, is held the middle week of August.

It includes entertainment booths, copious eating and drinking, dancing, and general merriment for both locals and visitors.

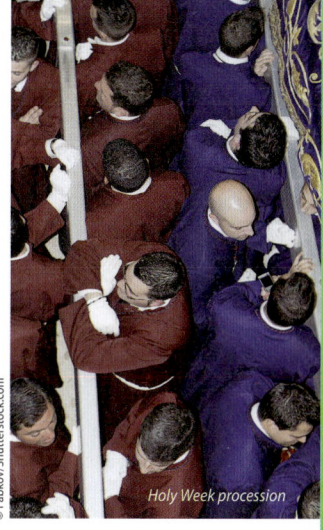

© Pabkov/Shutterstock.com

Holy Week procession

RONDA★★ AND PUEBLOS BLANCOS★★

Ronda stands at the heart of the Serranía de Ronda, split by the famous Guadalevín River ravine, or Tajo. Once a favorite destination for 19C Romantic writers, today visitors flock to this striking, isolated town year-round. Take a tour of the Pueblos Blancos to enjoy some of the most beautiful whitewashed villages in Andalucía, traversing what many consider the most beautiful part of the Iberian Peninsula.

RONDA★★

Map p108.

A Bit of History

Ronda under the Moors
Invaders under Tarik-ibn-Zeyad followed the Roman route from Gibraltar and founded Izna-Rand-Onda, today Ronda, some 20km/12mi from old Roman Acinipo. Under the Umayyads, Ronda was the capital of a Moorish region (cora), becoming a taifa capital after the fall of the Caliphate. Ronda prospered under the Almohads and into the Nasrid era, and fell to Christians in 1485.

La Ciudad★★

Located south of the Tajo, this Moorish quarter is filled with narrow alleys, churches, mansions and whitewashed houses with iron balconies, and provides fine views of the surrounding countryside.

Puente Nuevo★

The New Bridge, a magnificent feat of 18C engineering, is the best place to start your visit. Take the path to the coffee shop of the parador for a superb view of the bridge, the Guadiaro valley, and the Sierra de Grazalema. A chamber under an arch, once a jail, now houses the **Centro de Interpretación del Puente Nuevo** (*open year-round Mon–Fri 10am–7pm, Sat–Sun and public holidays 10am–3pm; €2; 649 96 53 38*).

Casa del Rey Moro

According to legend, this was the mansion of Almonated, king of Ronda, who drank wine from the

Ronda's New Bridge

© Allylondon/Shutterstock.com

Practical Information

Location

Stretching from Ronda to Arcos de la Frontera, this region is formed by four sierras: Grazalema, Ubrique, Margarita and Ronda. Ronda is 102km/68mi west of Málaga. Arcos de la Frontera is 33km/20.5mi east of Jerez de la Frontera and 91km/56.5mi south of Sevilla.

Getting There and Around

◆ **By Air – Málaga airport** (www.aena.es) is the nearest to Ronda (109km/67.7mi). But you can also reach Arcos de la Frontera (36km/22.3mi east), the western gateway to the White Villages, quite quickly from the **aeroporto di Jerez** (www.aena.es).

◆ **By Car** – You can reach Ronda from Málaga (102km/63.3mi), or more quickly from San Pedro de Alcántara (48km/29.8mi south, near Marbella; see COSTA DEL SOL). Arriving from Sevilla or Jerez de la Frontera will make it easier to start your tour of the area, using Arcos de la Frontera as a departure point.

◆ **By Train** – The only train connections available are between Ronda and Málaga (1hr 47mins). For information and reservations, 902 32 03 20, www.renfe.com.

◆ **By Bus** – Buses depart from Ronda for Setenil de las Bodegas (Sierra de las Nieves company), Grazalema and Olvera (Los Amarillos company), Zahara de la Sierra (Comes company). Check connections and timetables at www.turismoderonda.es. Visit siu.cmtbc.es for buses to Arcos de la Frontera from the Cádiz province. There are also bus connections from Arcos to Pueblos Blancos (inquire at the Arcos tourist office).

Visitor Information

You can find out more about organized excursions by inquiring at tourist offices in **Ronda** (Paseo de Blas Infante, 952 18 71 19; www.turismoderonda.es) and **Arcos de la Frontera** (Cuesta de Belén 5; 956 70 22 64; www.turismoarcos.es). Buy a tourist pass (bono turistico, €7) valid for four of Ronda's attractions, available from participating attractions and the tourist office.

---

skulls of his vanquished enemies. The current 18C building has Mudéjar-style brick towers and wooden balconies. A 200-step Moorish staircase, **La Mina**, descends to the river.

La Mina and Jardines de Forestier★

Open year-round daily 10am–7pm. €4.
In 1912 the French landscaper **Forestier** (who later designed María Luisa Park in Sevilla) was commissioned to design these lovely gardens. Turning the narrowness of the terrain to his advantage, Forestier created a multicultural landscaping masterpiece: three terraces combine Moorish features (fountains, water and *azulejos*) with European pergolas and parterres.

Palacio del Marqués de Salvatierra

Interior closed to visitors.
This small mansion is typical of noble 18C architecture. Note the

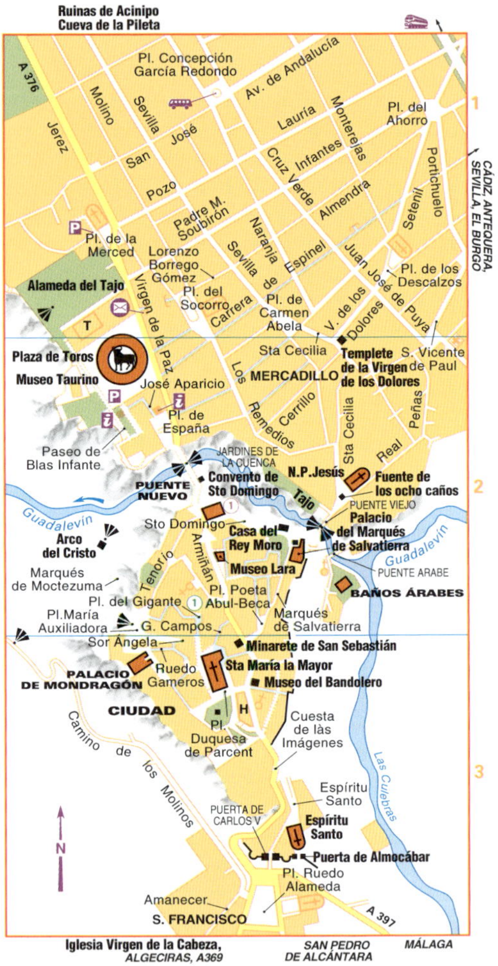

Ruinas de Acinipo
Cueva de la Pileta

A 376

Molino

Jerez

Sevilla

San

Pozo

José

Pl. Concepción
García Redondo

Av. de Andalucía

Lauría

Cruz Verde

Infantes

Montejaras

Almendra

Padre M.
Soubirón

Naranja

Sevilla

de

Espinel

Juan José de Puya

Portichuelo

Senil

Pl. del
Ahorro

1

CÁDIZ, ANTEQUERA,
SEVILLA, EL BURGO

1

Pl. de la
Merced

Lorenzo
Borrego
Gómez

Pl. del
Socorro

Carrera

Virgen de la Paz

Alameda del Tajo

T

Pl. de
Carmen
Abela

V. de los Dolores

Pl. de los
Descalzos

Sta Cecilia

Sta Cecilia

**Plaza de Toros
Museo Taurino**

José Aparicio

Pl. de
España

Los Remedios

MERCADILLO

Cerrillo

**Templete
de la Virgen
de los Dolores**

S. Vicente
de Paul

Peñas

Real

Paseo de
Blas Infante

JARDINES DE
LA CUENCA

**PUENTE
NUEVO**

**Convento de
Sto Domingo**

Tajo

N.P. Jesús

**Fuente de
los ocho caños**

2

2

Guadalevín

**Arco
del Cristo**

Sto Domingo

Armiñán

Tenorio

**Casa del
Rey Moro**

Museo Lara

PUENTE VIEJO

**Palacio
del Marqués
de Salvatierra**

Guadalevín

PUENTE ÁRABE

Marqués
de Moctezuma

Pl. del Gigante

**Pl. Poeta
Abul-Beca**

Marqués
de Salvatierra

BAÑOS ÁRABES

Pl.María
Auxiliadora

G. Campos

Sor Ángela

**PALACIO
DE MONDRAGÓN**

Ruedo
Gameros

Sta María la Mayor

Minarete de San Sebastián

Museo del Bandolero

CIUDAD

Pl.
Duquesa
de Parcent

H

Cuesta
de làs
Imágenes

Las Cumbres

3

3

Camino

de

los

Molinos

N

PUERTA DE
CARLOS V

Espíritu
Santo

**Espíritu
Santo**

Amanecer

S. FRANCISCO

Puerta de Almocábar

Pl. Ruedo
Alameda

A 397

Iglesia Virgen de la Cabeza,
ALGECIRAS, A369

SAN PEDRO
DE ALCÁNTARA

MÁLAGA

WHERE TO STAY	WHERE TO EAT
Hotel San Gabriel .... ①	Casa Santa Pola...... ①

extraordinary **portal**★★, flanked
by pairs of Corinthian columns
topped by an architrave decorated

with medallions. Above, human
figures with strong pre-Columbian
influence substitute for columns.

Moorish/Arab Baths★

Open year-round Mon–Fri
10am–7pm (Nov–Mar, 6pm),
Sat–Sun and public holidays
10am–3pm (Nov–Mar, 1pm). €3.
649 96 53 38.

These 13C baths are some of the
best preserved on the Iberian
Peninsula. They were built close
to the river along Las Culebras,
a stream in the Arrabal Viejo, a
district then popular with artisans
and tanners. The first, roofless part
of the building leads to the baths,
extending over three transversal
rooms topped with barrel vaults
and illuminated by star-shaped
lunettes. The middle room, divided
by horseshoe arches and brick
columns, is the most impressive.
Additional areas open for display
include the boiler area and a
tannery established following
Christian conquest of Ronda.

Minarete de San Sebastián★

Plaza del Poeta Abul-Beca.
This graceful minaret is the only
remnant of a 14C Nasrid mosque,
which victorious Christians
converted to a church, and the
smallest minaret still standing in
Andalucía. The lower stone section
is Moorish; the upper brick section
is Mudéjar. Note the horseshoe
arch doorway.

Palacio de Mondragón (Museo de la Ciudad)★★

Open year-round Mon–Fri
10am–7pm, Sat–Sun and public
holidays 10am–3pm. €3 (Wed,
free entrance). 952 87 08 18.

The palace foundations are
from a 14C Moorish residence.
The present building mixes
Mudéjar (towers and patios)
and Renaissance styles, the
latter best seen on the doorway.
The charming **Mudéjar patio**★★
retains traces of *azulejos* and
stuccowork between its arches.
The palace houses the town
museum, with exhibits on history,
ethnography and the environment,
including the Serranía de Ronda.

◗ Follow the path heading
down to the 18C Arco de Cristo
(Christ's Arch), from where there is
a magnificent view★★ of the ravine
(tajo) and bridge.

Plaza del Socorro

© AllyJondon/Shutterstock.com

RONDA

109

El Mercadillo

This district, founded in the 16C, connects to **La Ciudad** by the **Puente Nuevo** (New Bridge) and the Puente Viejo (Old Bridge). El Mercadillo is a commercial area, with pedestrianized streets like calle Nueva, **calle Remedios**, calle Ermita and the **plaza del Socorro**, as well as a square with attractive 19C and 20C buildings.

Bullring (Museo Taurino)★

Open year-round daily 10am–8pm (Mar and Oct, 7pm; rest of the year, 6pm). €6.50. 952 87 15 39. www.rmcr.org.

Built in 1785 by the Real Maestranza de Caballería (Royal Institute of Knights), this bullring is one of Spain's most beautiful. At 66m/216ft, it is the widest bullring anywhere.

The twin-tier interior is neo-Classical with Tuscan columns and a stone barrier, but the overall effect is one of great simplicity. Note the statues immortalizing Ronda's most honored bullfighting dynasties, the Romero and Ordóñez families.

The bullring also houses a colorful **museum** that displays old bullfighting posters and photographs of Orson Welles and Ernest Hemingway, both regular visitors.

Templete de la Virgen de los Dolores★

Built in 1734, this small temple is crowned by a plain vault resting on two columns and two pilasters. Each column is adorned with four strikingly expressive half-human, half-fantasy **figures**★, their arms interlinked and attached at the necks.

From Ronda to Costa del Sol★★

The **A 376** (49km/30.5mi) was built in the 1970s to connect the Serranía de Ronda with the Costa del Sol (*see p 94*). Although it does not pass through any towns or villages, it runs between two of the most spectacular mountain ranges in Málaga province: to the left the Parque Natural de la Sierra de las Nieves and to the right, the Sierra Bermeja. The road climbs gradually though a landscape of pines and Spanish fir to the Alijar Pass (410m/1,345ft), then descends steeply toward the coast.

Iglesia Rupestre de la Virgen de la Cabeza★

2.7km/1.7mi south of Ronda via the A 369. Follow the signposted road to the right (approx 700m/770yd outside town) leading to the chapel. Contact Ronda tourist office for opening times, 952 18 71 19.

This small Mozarabic cave chapel was probably founded by Hispano-Visigoths in the 9C. It sits on the opposite bank of the River Guadalevín, affording one of the best **views**★★ of Ronda. The interior is split into three parts: the store, the monastic quarters and the church. The frescoes were painted in the 18C. In the middle of August every year the Virgen de la Cabeza (Virgin of the Head) is ceremoniously taken from the collegiate church to the chapel next to the monastery.

PUEBLOS BLANCOS DE ANDALUCÍA★★

Map of Andalucía.

Setenil★

19km/11.8mi north of Ronda.
This is the only village in this region with troglodyte dwellings built into the rock. Unlike at Guadix (*see p 134*), no chimneys are visible, just rows of houses that appear to support the weight of the rock above. Fine examples include the **Cuevas del Sol** (Caves of the Sun) and **Cuevas de la Sombra** (Caves of the Shade). The **tourist office** is in an impressive building with a 16C *artesonado* ceiling (*calle Villa 2; 956 13 42 61*). Nearby Olvera is visible from atop a keep in the upper town.

Olvera

16km/10mi northwest of Setenil.
The triangular-shaped 12C **castle** (*open Tue–Sun 10:30am–2pm and 4–6:30pm; 7pm Mar–Oct. €2. 956 12 08 16*) overlooking Olvera defended the Nasrid kingdom until its conquest by Alfonso XI in 1327. If you're in the mood for a culinary treat, pick up a bottle of Olvera's **olive oil**, considered some of Spain's finest.

Zahara de la Sierra★

28km/17.3mi southwest of Olvera.
Even by Pueblo Blanco standards Zahara de la Sierra enjoys a splendid hilltop **setting**★★. The view from the castle encompasses the **Zahara Dam**, neighboring Algodonales and extends as far as Olvera. Note the 16C clock tower and Baroque, 18C **Iglesia de Santa María de Mesa**.

Arcos de la Frontera★★

57km/35.4mi southwest of Zahara.
Arcos enjoys a remarkable clifftop **setting**★★, poised as if hovering above the deep Guadalete river valley. Its Renaissance and Baroque mansions and whitewashed houses are adorned with classic Andalusian wrought-iron grilles and balconies, many trimmed with red geraniums.

A Bit of History

The Roman colony on this site was Arx-Arcis, "fortress on high ground," though some claim that the town's name derives from Arcobrigán, the arch of Brigus, grandson of Noah. Arcos was the capital of a taifa kingdom in the 11C. Following an initial incursion by Fernando III, it was finally conquered by Alfonso X in 1264.

Walking tour

Ascend the cuesta de Belén, a hill that connects the bustling 19C heart of Arcos with what was once the nucleus of the medieval city, making your way up steep, narrow alleyways. Pass through the Puerta de Jerez, one of the gateways to the walled Moorish city. Beyond **callejón de Juan del Valle** note the 15C Gothic-Mudéjar **façade★** of the **Palacio del Conde del Águila** and its magnificent doorway to the right. The tower of the **Iglesia de Santa María** dominates Plaza del Cabildo, where you'll find the town hall, the parador, housed in the former magistrate's house (Casa del Corregidor), and the castle, now privately owned.

Arcos de la Frontera

©Cristofori/age fotostock

Basílica de Santa María de la Asunción★

Calle de Deán Espinosa. Open Mon–Fri 10am–1pm and 4–7pm (Winter, 3:30–6:30pm), Sat 10am–2pm.

This splendid church was built around 1530 above an earlier 14C church, in turn erected on the site of a mosque. Its **west façade★**, the work of Don Alonso de Baena, is an extraordinary example of Plateresque art. The interior, accessed via the neo-Classical south façade, has a basilical plan with three aisles separated by robust columns supporting star vaults with tiercerons. In the high altar, a 17C **retable** by Jerónimo Hernández and Juan Bautista Vázquez represents the Ascension of the Virgin. Hidden behind the high altar is the polygonal apse of the earlier Mudéjar church. The **frescoes★** *(The Coronation of the Virgin)* which decorated the earlier high altar were transferred to the wall of the Evangelist nave (to the left of the altar) in the 1960s..

Grazalema

49km/30.4mi east of Arcos de la Frontera.

The approach to the beautiful village of Grazalema (Moorish *Ben-Zalema*) runs through Los Alamillos Pass, revealing **Peñón Grande**, a peak rising to 1,000m/3,328ft behind the village. Many are surprised to discover that Grazalema is Spain's wettest village, despite being located in the middle of one of the country's drier territories. This quirk of nature is due to the **föhn effect**, whereby warm clouds full of moisture from the Atlantic penetrate inland areas. Inside the town, the tower of the **Iglesia de San Juan** is of Moorish origin. The tower of the 16C **Iglesia de la Encarnación** is Mudéjar in style. If you're in the mood for a little souvenir shopping, Grazalema is famous for its **basketwork** and **woollen blankets**.

EXCURSIONS

OSUNA★★

This elegant Andalusian town, built on a hill at the heart of the Sevillian countryside, has preserved the beauty it achieved as a former ducal seat. The dukedom was created in 1562 and the House of Osuna eventually became one of the most powerful on the Iberian Peninsula. The prosperity that Osuna enjoyed in subsequent centuries is reflected in the town's fine examples of civil and religious architecture.

A Bit of History

Initially inhabited by the Iberians, who named it Urso, this elegant town was subsequently conquered by the Romans, under Caesar. Following the period of Moorish occupation, it was reconquered by Fernando III the Saint in 1239, and then ceded to the Order of Calatrava by Alfonso X the Wise in 1264. However, its period of greatest splendor is inextricably linked with the House of Osuna, under whose control it passed in 1562, when Felipe II granted the title of Duke of Osuna to the fifth Count of Ureña.

La Colegiata★★

Plaza de la Encarnación. Guided tours (45mins), Tue–Sun 10am –1:30pm and 4–7pm (Oct–Apr 3:30–6:30pm). Closed Sun afternoons in Jul–Aug and Mon. €2. 954 81 04 44.
This imposing 16C Renaissance-style collegiate church dominates the town. The façade is adorned with a finely sculpted Plateresque doorway.

Interior

The **church** is composed of three elegant Renaissance aisles opening out onto several chapels and a Baroque apse with an interesting retable in the same style, bearing the coat of arms of the House of Osuna. The organ dates from the 18C. The church contains several important works of art: *Jesus of Nazareth* by the "divine" Morales; a *Christ of Mercy* by Juan de Mesa; the superb tenebrist canvas, **The Expiration of Christ★★**, by **José Ribera**, "lo Spagnoletto." The **sacristy** is adorned with 16C **azulejos** and some original **artesonado** work. Exhibits include several books of Gregorian chants dating from the 16C, and four more **paintings by Ribera★★** from the early 16C. Additional works of art on view in other rooms include an *Immaculate Conception* by Alonso Cano, a silver processional cross (1534) and Flemish paintings.

Panteón Ducal★★

The ducal pantheon was built in Plateresque style in 1545 as the burial place for the Dukes of Osuna. The chapel stands just below the Colegiata's main altar, and despite its tiny dimensions (8m/26ft long, 4.5m/15ft wide and 2.5m/8ft high), it comprises three aisles and a choir. It is crowned by a blue and gold polychrome coffered ceiling.

Monasterio de la Encarnación★★

Plaza de la Encarnación. Open Tue–Sun 10am–1:30pm and 4–7pm (Oct–Apr 3:30–6:30pm).

PUEBLOS BLANCOS / EXCURSIONS

Closed Sun afternoons in Jul–Aug and Mon. €2.50.

This convent of discalced nuns was founded by the fourth Duke of Osuna in the 17C. Its outstanding feature is the magnificent **dado**★ of 17C Sevillian *azulejos* in the patio, dedicated to the five senses. The convent hosts a large collection of paintings, statuary and other artistic objects. Like many convents in Andalucía, the nuns produce and sell several types of delicious cookies and **pastries**.

Torre del Agua

Plaza de la Duquesa, on the way down to plaza Mayor. Open daily 10am–1:30pm and 4–7pm (Oct–Apr 3:30–6:30pm). Closed Sun afternoons in Jul–Aug and Mon. €2.50. 954 81 12 07.

This medieval defensive tower dates from the 12C–13C, although its origins can be traced to the Carthaginians. Nowadays, it is home to the town's **Museo Arqueológico**, displaying a range of Iberian and Roman objects discovered in Osuna, as well as reproductions of Iberian bulls and Roman bronzes (the originals can be seen in the Museo Arqueológico Nacional, Madrid).

Palaces★

The center of Osuna has some fine examples of civil architecture, including an impressive array of Baroque **palaces and seigniorial residences★★**. In addition to several interesting town houses and churches, **calle San Pedro**★ contains two magnificent 18C Baroque palaces: **Cilla del Cabildo** and **Palacio de los Marqueses de la Gomera**.

LAGUNA DE LA FUENTE DE PIEDRA★

40km/25mi southeast of Osuna. Take the A 92 to Fuente de Piedra, then follow the signposts. www.fuentedepiedra.es.

This large lagoon is home to one of Europe's largest ⚘ **flamingo** colonies, but you'll also see storks, gulls, cranes and egrets. Catching a glimpse of these birds in flight or massed on the water is a remarkable experience, particularly in the late afternoon. The lagoon also hosts a wide variety of flora, including saltwort, *suaeda vera*, rushes and more.

VALLE DEL GUADALHORCE★★

Antequera is 23.5km/14.5mi southeast of Fuente de Piedra.

The Guadalhorce River meanders through the Serranía de Ronda and the Montes de Málaga on its way to the Guadalteba-Guadalhorce Reservoir (*embalse*), traversing a landscape of olive groves, plains, mountains, fields, hills dotted with whitewashed houses, vegetable plots and rocky walls that provides superb **views**. From **Antequera**, follow this **road** as it winds through delightful landscapes, passing through the Abdalajís Valley before heading south to Álora.

Álora★

39km/24mi southwest of Antequera.
The traditional home of the haunting fandango-style *malagueña* song, Álora perches on a hillside along the River Guadalhorce, at the foot of Monte Hacho. It is a maze of narrow

RONDA AND PUEBLOS BLANCOS

MUST SEE

streets lined by low, whitewashed houses, overlooked by a castle, with fine views.

Desfiladero de los Gaitanes★★

23km/14mi west of Álora. Given the dangerous nature of the gorge, we recommend that you go no farther than the metal bridge suspended high above the El Chorro defile.

A **winding road**★ crosses superb mountain scenery to the astonishing Garganta del Chorros gorge. Leave your car at the **El Chorro campsite** and continue on foot along a tarmac  **track** *(30min there and back)* which climbs to a metal bridge offering magnificent **views**★★★ and the sensation of being suspended in mid-air far above the riverbed. A flimsy catwalk of wood and rope, the Camino del Rey, skirts the rockface to join a bridge in a worse state of disrepair.

Embalse del Guadelteba-Guadalhorce★

21km/13mi north of Desfiladero de los Gaitanes.

This reservoir *(embalse)* is in the heart of the Parque de Ardales, an area of dark woods, light-colored stone rocks and plentiful camping areas. **Footpaths** skirt the reservoir and crisscross landscapes that let you feel like you're the only person on earth. Silence, particularly in winter, pure air and a perfect clime are the area's main attractions. The views from the hills overlooking the reservoir are spectacular.

Cueva de Ardales★

Visits by guided tour only (3hrs), which must be booked in advance (up to 3 weeks). Closed Mon. €8. 952 45 80 46.
www.cuevadeardales.com.
This cave, running 1,600m/5,250ft, contains evidence of occupation from the Paleolithic period to the Bronze Age. It has exceptional wall paintings (54 representations of animals and 130 symbols). Note the painting of a female deer, its legs and heart painted bright red.

PARQUE NATURAL DE EL TORCAL★★

From Antequera, take the A 7075 toward Villanueva de la Concepción (17km/10.5mi south), then bear right onto a signposted road. Visitor Center open Apr–Sept 10am–7pm, Oct–Mar 10am–5pm. 952 24 33 24. www.torcaldeantequera.com

The park's 12ha/30 acres hold some of Spain's most unusual scenery, including chasms, obelisks and other strange limestone formations created by erosion. The native flora, including Spanish squill and Venus's navelwort, is particularly impressive in spring, when the color and scent of wild flowers and plants are a botanist's delight. Two signposted **walks** start at the reception center. The shorter (*1hr there and back*) La Losa footpath leads to the Maceta corrie (*torca*), passing the Ventanillas viewpoint. **Views**★★ are quite exceptional. The longer walk (*3hr return*) traverses the Chamorro chasm (*sima*), Pizarro Rock (*peñón*) and the Los Topaderos trail (*vereda*).

GRANADA★★★

"Give him alms, woman, for there is no greater grief than to be blind in Granada." This saying, inscribed in the Alhambra, evokes the beauty of this city, from its delightful setting to its spectacular monuments. The Alhambra is its crown jewel, one of the most magnificent artistic creations on the planet. Set on a verdant plain and extending up and over three large hills – the Albaicín, Sacromonte and Alhambra – Granada is at once Moorish and Christian; a perfect symbiosis of art and history framed by the snow-capped ridge of the Sierra Nevada.

A Bit of History

Initially settled by the Iberians, Romans founded Illiberis here on the Albaicín hill. The city remained little more than an outpost until the Moors arrived in the early 8C.

Moorish Granada

In 713, Tarik's troops conquered the city, which extended across the Alhambra and Albaicín hills, and Granada became part of the Córdoban Caliphate.

In 1013, it became the capital of a kingdom (*taifa*). The **Zirite dynasty** strengthened its defences and built the El Bañuelo baths and a bridge, the Puente de Cadí.

In 1090, Granada fell to the **Almoravids**, then in the mid-12C to the **Almohads**. Despite frequent conflicts, the city experienced considerable development, as drainage and sewer systems were built and its fortifications strengthened.

Nasrid kingdom

The ascendancy of the Nasrids in 1238 heralded the city's Golden Age. Mohammed ibn Nasar, the dynasty's founder, acknowledged his position as the vassal of Christian monarch Fernando II, ensuring peace and stability for the city. The kingdom now encompassed Almería and Málaga, as well as part of Cádiz, Sevilla, Córdoba and Jaén. Granada prospered, expanded and grew increasingly beautiful. Yusuf I (1333–53) and Mohammed V (1353–91), under whose rule the Alhambra's Nasrid palaces were built, transformed Granada into one of the leading cities of the period.

The **15C** was marked by infighting. Territory was gradually yielded to the Christians. Following a long siege, the Catholic Monarchs took Granada on 2 January 1492, bringing to a close eight centuries of Moorish domination on the Iberian Peninsula.

Nasrid Palaces in the Alhambra

© Jane Rix/Shutterstock.com

Practical Information

Location
Granada is 139km/86mi northeast of Málaga.

Population
240,099.

Getting There
♦ **By Air** – The nearest international airport is **Federico García Lorca Granada-Jaén** (www.aena.es). Buses are available at the airport for downtown Granada (17km/10.5mi east, roughly 40 mins) run by Autocares Jose Gonzalez (958 49 01 64; www.autocaresjosegonzalez. com). The airport in **Málaga** (www.aena.es) is nearby as well, where buses run by Alsa (902 42 22 42; www.alsa.es) leave for Granada (2hr 15mins).

♦ **By Car** – You can reach Granada by traveling along the Costa del Sol, leaving from Málaga and following highways A 45 and A 92, or by taking the A 44-E 902 near Motril; or arriving from further inland, passing through Antequera to the west or Jaén to the north.

♦ **By Train** – The station is on avenida de Andalucía. Service to the province, Almería (2hr 24mins), Córdoba (2hr 20mins) and Sevilla (3hr 12mins). For information and reservations, 902 32 03 20, www. renfe.com.

♦ **By Bus** – Buses run by Alsa (902 42 22 42; www.alsa.es) connect Granada to Almería, Almuñecar, Córdoba, Jaén, Málaga, Salobreña and other cities in Andalucía. Autocares Bonal (958 46 79 86) and Alsa (902 42 22 42; www.alsa.es) run connections across the Sierra Nevadas. For connections within the Granada province, visit siu.ctagr. com. The bus station is in avenida Juan Pablo II.

Getting Around
♦ **By Car** – Getting around by car and finding parking is difficult, especially for those unfamiliar with local restrictions. Use public transportation or taxis, or walk.

♦ **By Bus** – Transportes Rober serves all of Granada's major monuments and suburbs. 900 71 09 00. www.transportesrober.com.

♦ **By Taxi** – Radio Taxi G. S. L., 958 13 23 23. Tele-Radio-Taxi, 958 28 06 54.

Visitor Information
You'll find local tourist offices in Plaza del Carmen, 958 24 82 80, and calle Virgen Blanca 9, 902 40 50 45; www.granadatur.com. Information for the entire Granada province is available in Plaza Mariana Pineda 10 bajo, 958 24 71 28; www.turgranada.es. You'll find the Oficina de turismo de la Junta de Andalucía in calle Santa Ana 2, 958 57 52 02.

Christian Granada
Under Christian rule, the city's *morisco*, or Moorish population was concentrated on the Albaicín. By the end of the 15C the first conflicts broke out, after a decree was issued forcing Muslims to be baptized. In 1568 rebel leader Abén Humeya fled to the Alpujarras mountains, where he was subdued by Don Juan of Austria, on the orders of Felipe II.

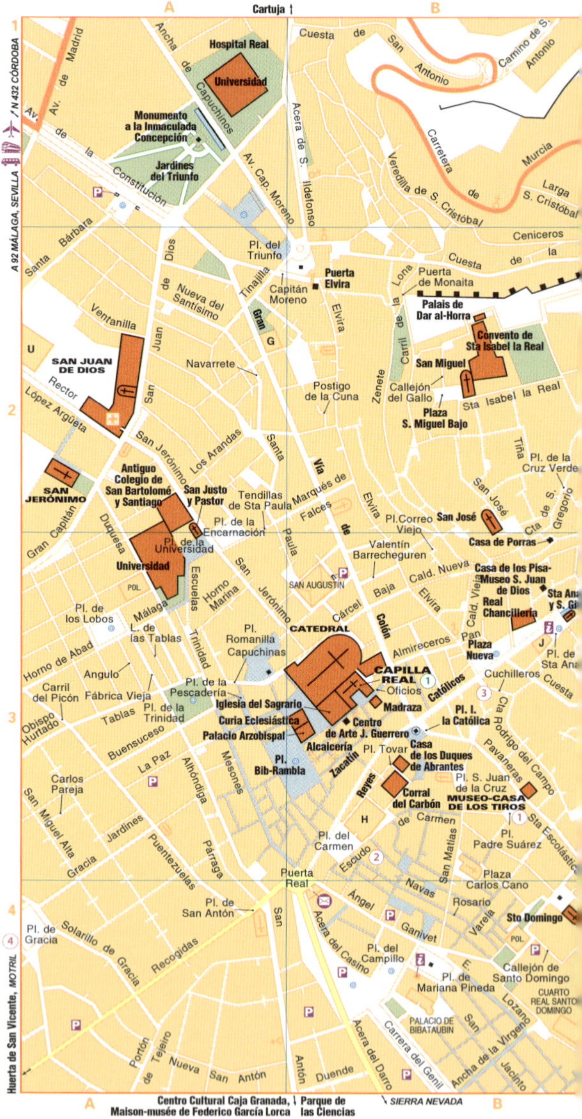

Cartuja ↑

A   B

A 92 MÁLAGA, SEVILLA / N 432 CÓRDOBA

Av. de Madrid

Ancha de Capuchinos

Cuesta de San Antonio

Camino de S. Antonio

Hospital Real
Universidad

Monumento a la Inmaculada Concepción

Jardines del Triunfo

Av. de la Constitución

Av. Cap. Moreno

Acera de S. Ildefonso

Carretera

Verdeja de S. Cristóbal

Murcia

Larga
S. Cristóbal

Santa Bárbara

Pl. del Triunfo

Puerta Elvira

Cuesta de la

Ceniceros

Puerta de Monaita

Dios

Nueva del Santísimo

Tinajilla

Capitán Moreno

Gran

Elvira

Palais de Dar al-Horra

Ventanilla

San Juan de Dios

Navarrete

Convento de Sta Isabel la Real

San Miguel

Sta Isabel la Real

SAN JUAN DE DIOS

López Argüeta

Rector

Postigo de la Cuna

Callejón del Gallo

Plaza S. Miguel Bajo

Pl. de la Cruz Verde

Gran Capitán

SAN JERÓNIMO

Antiguo Colegio de San Bartolomé y Santiago

San Justo y Pastor

Tendillas de Sta Paula

Marqués de Falces

Pl.Correo Viejo

San José

Casa de Porras

Pl. de la Encarnación

Universidad

de la Universidad

Pl. de los Lobos

Málaga

Horno Marina

Jerónimo

SAN AUGUSTIN

Baja

Cald. Nueva

Casa de los Pisa- Museo S. Juan de Dios
Real Chancillería

Sta Ana y S. Gi...

Cárcel

CATEDRAL

Pl. Romanilla Capuchinas

Almireceros

Plaza Nueva

Horno de Abad

Angulo

Carril del Picón

Fábrica Vieja

Pl. de la Pescadería

CAPILLA REAL

Oficios

Madraza

Cuchilleros

Pl. de Sta Ana

Obispo Hurtado

Tablas

Pl. de la Trinidad

Iglesia del Sagrario

Curia Eclesiástica

Palacio Arzobispal

Centro de Arte J. Guerrero

Alcaicería

Católicos

Pl. I. la Católica

Ca Rodrigo del Campo

Pavaneras

Buensuceso

La Paz

Zacatín

Pl. Tovar

Casa de los Duques de Abrantes

Carlos Pareja

Almibdiga

Mesones

Pl. Bib-Rambla

Reyes

Corral del Carbón

Pl. S. Juan de la Cruz

MUSEO-CASA DE LOS TIROS

San Miguel Alta

Jardines

Puentezuelas

Párraga

de Carmen

Pl. Padre Suárez

Gracia

Pl. del Carmen

San Matías

Plaza Carlos Cano

Puerta Real

Escudo

Navas

Rosario

Sto Domingo

Pl. de San Antón

Acera del Casino

Angel

Ganivet

Varela

Pl. de Gracia

Pl. de Solarillo de Gracia

Recogidas

San

Pl. del Campillo

E.

Callejón de Santo Domingo

Pl. de Mariana Pineda

Lozano

CUARTO REAL SANTO DOMINGO

PALACIO DE BIBATAUBÍN

Portón de Tejeiro

Nueva

San Antón

Antón

Duende

Carrera del Darro

Carrera del Genil

Ancha de la Virgen

Jacinto

Huerta de San Vicente, MOTRIL

Centro Cultural Caja Granada,
Maison-musée de Federico García Lorca

Parque de las Ciencias

SIERRA NEVADA

A   B

WHERE TO STAY

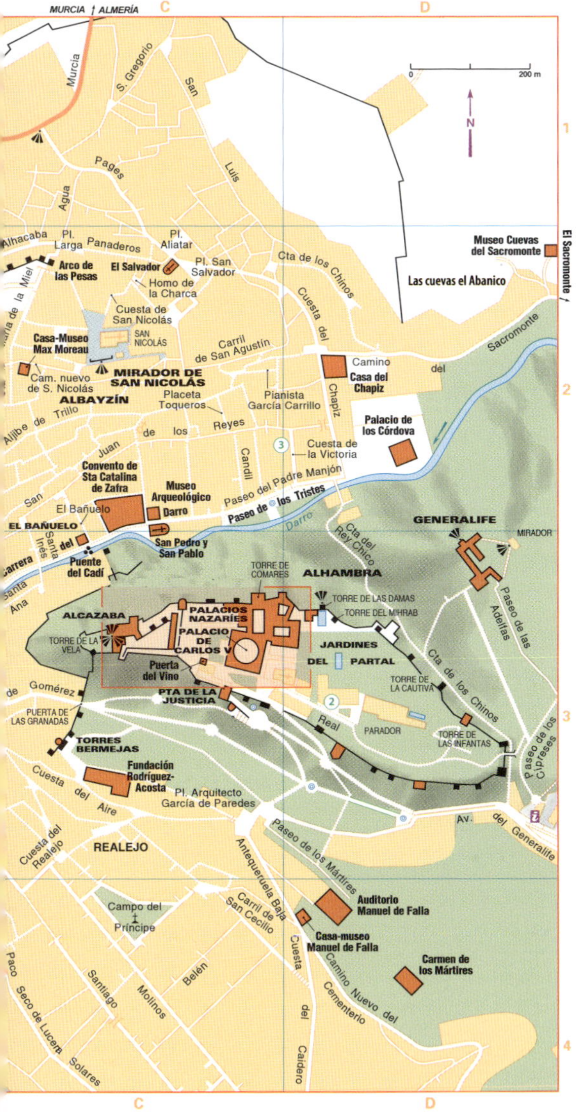

Map Labels

MURCIA ↑ ALMERÍA

Murcia

S. Gregorio

San

Pages

Agua

de la Miel

Alhacaba

Pl. Larga Panaderos

Arco de las Pesas

El Salvador

Pl. San Salvador

Homo de la Charca

Casa-Museo Max Moreau

Cuesta de San Nicolás

SAN NICOLÁS

Cam. nuevo de S. Nicolás

MIRADOR DE SAN NICOLÁS

ALBAYZÍN

Aljibe de Trillo

Placeta Toqueros

Pianista García Carrillo

Juan

de los Reyes

Candil

Cuesta de la Victoria

San

El Bañuelo

Museo Arqueológico

EL BAÑUELO

del

Darro

Convento de Sta Catalina de Zafra

Carrera

Santa Ana

Senés

Puente del Cadí

San Pedro y San Pablo

de Gomérez

PUERTA DE LAS GRANADAS

ALCAZABA

TORRE DE LA VELA

PALACIOS NAZARÍES

PALACIO DE CARLOS V

Puerta del Vino

PTA DE LA JUSTICIA

TORRES BERMEJAS

Cuesta del Aire

Fundación Rodríguez-Acosta

Pl. Arquitecto García de Paredes

REALEJO

Cuesta del Realejo

Campo del Príncipe

Paseo Seco de Lucena

Solares

Santiago

Molinos

Belén

Antequeruela Baja

Carril de San Cecilio

Cuesta

del

Caldero

Camino Nuevo del Cementerio

Auditorio Manuel de Falla

Casa-museo Manuel de Falla

Carmen de los Mártires

Paseo de los Mártires

Cta de los Chinos

Cuesta del Chapiz

Camino del Chapiz

Casa del Chapiz

Museo Cuevas del Sacromonte

Las cuevas el Abanico

El Sacromonte

Sacromonte

Palacio de los Córdova

Carril de San Agustín

Paseo del Padre Manjón

Paseo de los Tristes

Darro

Cta del Rey Chico

GENERALIFE

MIRADOR

ALHAMBRA

TORRE DE COMARES

TORRE DE LAS DAMAS

TORRE DEL MIHRAB

JARDINES DEL PARTAL

TORRE DE LA CAUTIVA

Real

PARADOR

TORRE DE LAS INFANTAS

Cta de los Chinos

Paseo de las Adelfas

Paseo de los Cipreses

Av. del Generalife

N

0 — 200 m

WHERE TO EAT

Alacena de las Monjas .... ①   La Trastienda .... ③

El Retiro Taberna .... ②   Mariquilla .... ④

Following this episode, all *moriscos* were expelled from Granada. The city was transformed during the **16C** and **17C**. Its maze of Moorish lanes gave way to wider streets and spacious squares. The cathedral, Chapel Royal, Charles V's palace, Exchange, Royal Hospital, chancery and Carthusian monastery were built.

In the **18C**, and particularly the **19C**, Granada bewitched numerous visitors, becoming the darling of Romantic writers. Its beauty, mysticism and exoticism became literary themes for Victor Hugo, Alexandre Dumas and Washington Irving, who penned a collection of imaginative stories, *Tales of the Alhambra,* during his stay in Granada.

In the 19C the French sacked Granada and even tried to raze the Alhambra, but only succeeded in destroying some towers and wall sections.

The city today

Granada is the capital of an agricultural and ranching province, busy all year round. It has a lively, youthful atmosphere generated by the students of its respected university and the thousands of visitors the city receives. *Granadinos* believe that their city has the perfect location: set at the foot of the sun-blessed ski slopes of the Sierra Nevada and an hour's drive from sparkling Mediterranean beaches.

ALHAMBRA AND GENERALIFE★★★

Map pp118–119.

Open year-round daily mid Mar–mid Oct 8:30am–8pm (and 10–11:30pm Fri–Sat); mid Oct–mid Mar 8:30am–6pm (and 8–9:30pm Fri–Sat). Closed 1 Jan and 25 Dec. €13, garden only €7, evening visits to the Nasrid Palaces €8, to the Generalife €5; ticket sales stop

---

Touring Tip

There are a limited number of tickets allocated daily to visit Alhambra and Generalife. Purchase tickets in advance (at least one week) to make sure you get in and avoid long lines. Tickets can be bought by phone (from Spain 902 88 80 01; abroad 958 92 60 31) or online at www.alhambra-tickets.es.

If tickets to Alhambra have sold out and you are unable to purchase, another possibility is to buy a Granada City Pass (**Bono Turístico**), valid for 3 (Bono Básico, €33.50) or 5 days (Bono Plus, €37.50). This pass includes entrance to the Alhambra and major sights (Cathedral, Royal Chapel, the Cartuja, Monastery of San Jerónimo, Science Park and Museum Memoria de Andalucía), 5 (Básico) or 9 (Plus) trips on any municipal buses and minibuses and (Plus only) 1 day on the City Sightseeing tourist bus. You can buy the pass at the Science Park, the tourist office in Plaza del Carmen, Caja Granada office in Plaza de Isabel la Católica 6, or the THIS IS Kiosk in Plaza Nueva. There is also a **Children's City Pass** (3-11 years old, €10.50). These are linked to an adult city pass and provide the same services as the type of adult pass purchased. For further information, visit www.turgranada.es.

1hr before last entry. Tickets for Alhambra and Generalife gardens specify entry time to the Nasrid palaces. 958 02 79 71. www.alhambra-patronato.es.

Access on foot is along cuesta de Gomérez, from plaza Nueva. Enter by the Puerta de Granadas (Pomegranate Gate, built by Machuca under Charles V), to reach the **shrubbery**★.

Alhambra★★★

The Calat Alhambra (Red Castle) is one of the most remarkable fortresses ever built, and the finest Moorish palace still standing. It sits atop the highest hill in the city; "La Sabika (as the hill was called) is the crown on Granada's head… and the Alhambra is the ruby on the crown" wrote the poet Ibn Zamrak (1333–93).

Visitors are spellbound by the splendor of its architecture, set amid delightful gardens and running water in what feels like a Koranic Eden on earth. But its beauty is full of contradictions. Sumptuous appearances belie the poverty of the materials. It is also curious that not only should a power in decline build such a masterpiece but that the Alhambra would be so respected by its usurpers.

Nasrid Palaces (Palacios Nazaríes)★★★

These palaces are the nucleus of the Alhambra. Nothing on their exterior presages their rich and original *mocárabe* vaults, domes, friezes and stuccowork.

The buildings are set around three courtyards: the Patio del Cuarto Dorado (Courtyard of the Golden Room), the Patio de los Arrayanes (Myrtle Courtyard) and the Patio de los Leones (Lion Courtyard). The use of small interconnected passageways heightens the impact as visitors pass from one architectural masterpiece to the next.

The Mexuar

The tour begins in the rectangular **Mexuar**. Four columns support a stucco-adorned entablature. A frieze of *azulejos* and a calligraphic border cover walls decorated with coats of arms. This room was most likely a council chamber. Note the small oratory leading off the room to the rear.

Patio de Los Leones

© Kutlayev Dmitry/Shutterstock.com

GRANADA

Patio del Cuarto Dorado

The magnificent south wall is a compendium of Nasrid art. This wall-façade comprises *azulejos* with geometric decoration, panels with vegetal features, calligraphic borders, a *mocárabe* frieze, a carved wood cornice and a large eave, all arranged around two doors and five windows. Opposite is the Cuarto Dorado, with tiled paneling, fine stuccowork and a beautiful wooden ceiling. Its windows provide a magnificent **view★** of the Albaicín.

Patio de los Arrayanes

The entry to the Myrtle Courtyard is to the left of the south wall. This delightful patio has a long, narrow pool. A myrtle border reflects the mass of the **Torre de Comares**. Slender porticoes give onto the **Sala de la Barca**, where walls are adorned with the coats of arms of the Nasrids and calligraphy. This room leads to the **Salón de Embajadores** (Hall of Ambassadors), an audience chamber. The decoration is exquisite: magnificent lustre *azulejo* paneling, delicate stucco with plant and geometric motifs, and calligraphic strips with religious and poetic inscriptions. The remarkable **dome**, rising above latticework windows and comprising over 8,000 pieces of multicolored wood, represents the seven heavens of the Koran.

Patio de los Leones

The Lion Courtyard dates from the reign of Mohammed V. The 11C fountain at its center, supported by 12 rough stone lions, is surrounded by arcades of slender columns leading to sumptuous state apartments. Two elegant columned pavilions project over the sides of the courtyard.

The **Sala de los Abencerrajes** to the south is where the Abencerrajes were slaughtered and their heads piled in the fountain. The room has a stalactite ceiling and a splendid star-shaped lantern cupola illuminated by 16 windows.

The **Sala de los Reyes**, or Kings' Chamber, on the east side, comprises three square sections covered with *mocárabe* cupolas. The vaulting in the alcoves depicts pastimes of Moorish and Christian princes. It probably dates from the late 14C.

The **Sala de Dos Hermanas** (Hall of Two Sisters), is famed for a honeycomb cupola, fine *azulejos* and stuccowork. According to legend, the hall was given this name because two sisters who were imprisoned within its walls. Beyond are the **Sala de los Ajimeces** and the **Mirador de Lindaraja**, both resplendent with stuccowork and honeycomb decoration.

A corridor passes the cupolas

Key Dates

The most accepted chronology for the construction of the Alhambra and Generalife is as follows:

- late 12C: external walls;
- 14C: the Generalife, then the Nasrid palaces, built during the reigns of Yusuf I (1333–54) and Mohammed V (1354–59 and 1362–91).

GRANADA

MUST SEE

of the **Royal Baths** to the left (*Baños Reales*, ***only open certain days, inquire at the tourist office***). Continue to an open gallery with delightful **views**★ of the Albaicín; descend the stairs to the Patio de la Reja and the 16C Patio de Lindaraja.

Gardens and perimeter towers★★

To the east are the **Jardines del Partal**, terraced gardens that descend to towers punctuating the walls. The first is the **Torre de las Damas** (Ladies' Tower), built by Yusuf I at the beginning of the 14C, preceded by a graceful *artesonado* portico. The Torre del Mihrab and the former Nasrid mosque (*mezquita*) are to the right. The Torre de la Cautiva (Captive's Tower), also dating from the reign of Yusuf I, and the later Torre de las Infantas (Infantas' Tower), have sumptuous internal decoration.

Charles V's palace (Palacio de Carlos V)★★

Emperor Charles V commissioned Pedro Machuca, who had studied under Michelangelo, to build this palace in 1526. The simplicity of its Classical plan – a circle in a square – and the harmony of its lines confer a majestic beauty.
On the main doorway of the lower level of dressed stone, note the medallions and superb bas-reliefs representing the triumph of peace (at the center) and battles (to the side). The upper storey bears the escutcheon of Spain.
The palace's most outstanding feature is its circular patio (31m/102ft in diameter), fronted by Doric and Ionic (upper tier) columns. The patio's simplicity and

beautiful proportions combine to create a masterpiece of the Spanish Renaissance.
The palace contains two museums.

Museo de la Alhambra★

Entrance to the right of the vestibule. This pleasant museum exhibits ceramics, wood carvings, panels of *azulejos* and *alicatados*, stuccowork, bronzes, fabric and more. Outstanding objects include the Pila de Almanzor, a 10C ablutions basin decorated with lions and stags; the famous **blue** or **gazelle amphora**★, a delicate 14C masterpiece; as well as unusual ceramics representing animals.

Museo de Bellas Artes (Fine Arts Museum)

Entrance on the upper storey. Paintings from the 15C and 16C include religious works by renowned artists such as Sánchez Cotán, Siloé, Alonso Cano and Pedro de Mena, and a magnificent still life, *Thistle and Carrots*★★, by Sánchez Cotán. 19C and 20C galleries contain works by Rodríguez Acosta, Muñoz Degrain, López Mezquita and Manuel Ángeles Ortiz, as well as more avant-garde exhibits.

Puerta del Vino

The Wine Gateway, built by Mohammed V, is purely monumental.

Alcazaba★

To the left of the Plaza de los Aljibes (Cistern Court) stands the Alcazaba, the oldest part of the Alhambra. Three towers overlook the courtyard: the Torre del Adarguero, the Torre Quebrada and the Torre del Homenaje (keep).

View the Alhambra wood from the Jardín de los Adarves on the south side. At the remains of the **Torre de la Vela** (Watchtower) the Catholic Monarchs first hoisted their flags. The tower provides a magnificent **panorama**★★ of the palace, Granada and the Sierra Nevada. To the west are the **Torres Bermejas** (Red Towers). These were built in the late 8C and early 9C, and subsequently modified.

Puerta de la Justicia★

Built by Yusuf I, the massive Justice Gateway is set in a tower in the outer walls. It comprises a large horseshoe arch and a wide strip of delightful *azulejos* with an image of the Virgin and Child from the 16C.

Generalife★★

The name Generalife derives from *Yannat al-Arif*, possibly "most noble of gardens." Terraced **gardens** filled with running water surround a palace. An avenue of cypress trees leads to the new gardens and an auditorium – the setting for Granada's annual Festival of Music and Dance. The central **Patio de la Acequia**, a long pool *(acequia)* lined with water jets, has a pavilion at either end. A *mirador* alongside affords superb views of the Alhambra. The Sala Regia in the rear pavilion (reached through a portico) boasts fine stuccowork. The Patio de la Sultana is enclosed on one side by a 16C gallery. In the gardens above you'll find the ingenious **escalera del agua**, or water staircase, protected by overarching laurel trees: water from the Royal Canal flows down inverted pan tiles along the stairway parapets.

CATHEDRAL QUARTER★★
Map pp118–119 (A-B 3).

Cathedral★

Entrance on Gran Vía de Colón. Open Mon–Sat 10:45am–1:30pm and 4–8pm (Nov–Mar, 7pm), Sun afternoons only. €*4. 958 22 29 59.*
Construction of the cathedral began at the center of the Moorish city in 1518 and continued for almost two centuries. Original plans called for a Gothic cathedral to be built, but Diego Siloé, who replaced Enrique Egas as head of the project in 1528, introduced Renaissance styles into its construction.

Interior

Five lofty aisles lead to an ambulatory. Enormous square pillars support large sections of entablature, thereby considerably increasing the overall height. Note the Gothic vaulting overhead. The **high altar**★ *(capilla mayor)* is richly decorated, circular and unusually high. Note the **silver tabernacle** in the center of the presbytery, and the pulpits at each side. The right transept arm opens to the **north portal of the Chapel Royal**★, dominated by a Gothic-style Virgin and Child, by Enrique Egas. Above, Fernando and Isabel's emblems, the yoke and arrow, flank their coat of arms.
The large marble retable in the **Capilla de la Virgen de las Angustias** (Chapel of the Virgin of Anguish) shows the Virgin with the dead Christ in her arms. The **Capilla de Nuestra Señora de la Antigua** contains a fine 15C statue of the Virgin and Child in a magnificent early-18C Baroque

altarpiece by Pedro Duque Cornejo. The ambulatory contains an interesting collection of choir books from the 16C to 18C.

Museo Catedralicio

The small **museum** exhibits silverware, tapestry, vestments, an image of the Virgin of Bethlehem, a bust of St Paul by Alonso Cano, and a bust of the Virgin and Child by Pedro de Mena. In the **sacristy** you'll find a delightful image of the Virgin, also by Alonso Cano.

Exterior

Exit the cathedral onto calle Cárcel Baja, where there are two doorways by Siloé. On the lower section of the **Puerta del Perdón** (Pardon Doorway), Faith and Justice hold a tablet. Two magnificent royal escutcheons, of the Catholic Monarchs and Emperor Charles V, adorn the buttresses. The **Portada de San Jerónimo** (St Jerome portal) has a semicircular arch between Plateresque pilasters. The façade facing plaza de las Pasiegas was designed by Alonso Cano in 1667.

Madraza

In calle Oficios, opposite the Chapel Royal.

The Madraza (Muslim university) was built in the 14C by Yusuf I. The Catholic Monarchs installed Granada's civil administration here. The Baroque façade, with adorning escutcheons, is from an 18C reconstruction. On the opposite side of the inner patio you'll find the Moorish **oratory**, an attractive hall of polychrome stuccowork, *mocárabe* decoration and an octagonal dome adorned with a lantern.

Capilla Real★★

Calle Oficios 3. Open Mon–Sat 10:15am–1:30pm and 4–7:30pm (Winter, 6:30pm), Sun and public holidays 11am–1:30pm and 3:30–6:30pm. Closed 1 Jan, Good Fri, 25 Dec. €4. 958 22 92 39. www.capillarealgranada.com.

The Catholic Monarchs commissioned the Chapel Royal as their burial place. Enrique Egas began the project in 1506 and completed it 15 years later, producing a masterpiece of the Isabelline Gothic style.

Outstanding **exterior** features include the fine pinnacles and elegant **cresting**. The lower section is adorned with the letters F and Y, for Fernando and Ysabel. Access is via the old **Lonja** (Exchange), a graceful 16C Plateresque building. The city's coat of arms is on the lower section of the Lonja, while the upper floor gallery bears the emblems of the Catholic Monarchs and Charles V on the carved sills.

The **interior** consists of a single nave with side chapels, and ribbed vaults. A blue fringe with a gilded inscription adorns the upper walls. Heraldic features on the walls and wrought-iron grilles are profuse. A spectacular 16C **screen★★★** by Master Bartolomé de Jaén encloses the chancel. Note the escutcheon and yoke and arrow of Fernando and Isabel, and scenes of the life of Christ on the upper section.

The two double **mausoleums★★★** in the chancel, one of the Catholic Monarchs, the other of their daughter, Juana la Loca (Joan the Mad), and her husband, Felipe el Hermoso (Philip the Handsome), are outstanding. The first, by Domenico Fancelli, was carved in Genoa in 1517 from Carrara marble,

and is decorated with reliefs of Apostles and medallions. The second was carved by Bartolomé Ordóñez in 1519 on a pedestal decorated with religious scenes. The royal remains are in four simple coffins in the chapel's crypt.

The magnificent Plateresque **retable★** with lifelike figures from the Gospels was sculpted by Felipe Vigarny between 1520 and 1522. The lower register of the predella depicts the siege of Granada. Note the statues of the Catholic Monarchs at prayer.

Museum

Objects of priceless historical value include **Queen Isabel's scepter and crown**, **King Fernando's sword**, plus an outstanding **collection of paintings★★** by Flemish (Rogier van der Weyden, Memling), Italian (Perugino, Botticelli) and Spanish (Bartolomé Bermejo, Pedro Berruguete) artists. In the rear of the museum you'll find the **Triptych of the Passion** by the Dirk Bouts and two sculptures of the Catholic Monarchs at prayer by Felipe Vigarny.

Centro de Arte José Guerrero

In calle Oficios.
This magnificent late 19C building is a center of modern art. Its galleries show works by Spanish and foreign artists. The third floor is devoted to Granada painter José Guerrero (1914–1991), associated with the abstract movement.

Plaza Bib-Rambla

This central square with its Neptune fountain is the setting for a number of colorful flower stalls, *cafeterías* and restaurants.

Alcaicería

The restored area of the Moorish silk market, with winding alleyways, arches and oriental decoration, is now a center for crafts and souvenir shops.

Plaza de Isabel la Católica

Mariano Benlliure's monument to the Santa Fe Agreement (1892) stands in this square, showing Columbus presenting his plans to Queen Isabel.

Casa de los Tiros

This mid-16C palace has an unusual stone façade displaying five sculpted figures in warrior dress. It houses a museum of 19C Granada. The Cuadra Dorada salon has a splendid Renaissance **artesonado ceiling★** with famous figures in relief.

CARRERA DEL DARRO★
Map pp118–119 (C 2-3).

This delightful street runs along the River Darro through an older, village-like area. Simple stone bridges provide access to Granada's legendary hills, the Alhambra and Albaicín. Start with a look at **plaza Nueva** and **plaza de Santa Ana**.

Chancillería

The former 16C chancery on plaza Nueva now houses Andalucía's High Court of Justice. The Classical façade combines elements that presage the Baroque. The balustrade is an 18C addition. The harmonious **patio★** is attributed to Siloé.

Carrera del Darro

© Javi Indy/Shutterstock.com

El Bañuelo★

Carrera del Darro 31. Open Tue–Sat 9am–2pm. 958 02 78 00.
The Moorish baths are opposite the ruins of 11C **Puente del Cadí** (bridge). Part of a tower and horseshoe arch remain. The 11C baths are some of the best preserved in Spain. Note the star-pierced vaults with octagonal skylights. The arcades in the last two rooms have Roman, Caliphal and Visigothic capitals.

Casa Castril

The **archaeological museum** (*see Museums*), housed in the Casa Castril (1539), has a **Plateresque doorway★** adorned with heraldic motifs, shells, animals and more.

Paseo de los Tristes

This avenue offers unforgettable nighttime **views★★** of the illuminated Alhambra rising above. Grab a table at one of the many café terraces for the perfect vantage point.

ALBAICÍN★

Map pp118–119 (C-D 2).

This hilly district is Granada's most famous quarter, and offers magnificent views of the Alhambra at every turn. A maze of narrow alleyways winds up between the palisades of small Moorish-style villas known as *cármenes*, through delightful squares and past picturesque street corners.

Palacio de los Córdova

An avenue of cypress trees in the garden leads to the Municipal Archives, a palace with a Renaissance doorway.

Casa del Chapiz

Cuesta del Chapiz 22, entrance along camino de Sacromonte. Open Summer 9am–2pm, Winter 9am–6pm. 958 22 22 90.
Now the School of Arabic Studies, this is a combination of two Moorish houses from the 15C and 16C, including patios and galleries. The gardens offer fine Alhambra **views★**.

Mirador de San Nicolás

This terrace in front of the **Iglesia de San Nicolás** enjoys magnificent **views★★★** of the breathtaking ochre-colored Alhambra and, further out, the outline of the Sierra Nevada.

UNIVERSITY TO THE ROYAL HOSPITAL★
Map pp118–119 (A 2-3).

University

On plaza de la Universidad you'll find the Baroque building that served as the university's headquarters in the 18C. The statue of founder Charles V is in the center of the square. The building, with Solomonic columns, now houses the Faculty of Law.

Monasterio de San Jerónimo★

Entrance on calle López Argüeta. Open year-round 10am–1:30pm and 4–7:30pm (Sun, from 11am). 958 27 93 37.

Construction of the monastery began in 1496 under the direction of Jacopo Fiorentino (Jacopo l'Indaco), and continued under Diego Siloé from 1526 onward. Note the **façade** of the church. The upper section shows the coats of arms of the Catholic Monarchs. A fine window is flanked by medallions and grotesque animals. Plateresque and Renaissance doorways open onto the large **cloisters** completed in 1519 to plans principally by Diego de Siloé. The church wall has a Plateresque window and the magnificent escutcheon of El Gran Capitán.

Church★★

Past the fine Siloé-designed **Plateresque doorway** are surprisingly rich interior elements: vaults and domes with high reliefs, a magnificent main retable and murals all combine to create an ensemble masterpiece of Spanish Renaissance architecture. Construction began during the Gothic period. The transept and apse were completed under Siloé in Renaissance style. The vault above the high altar depicts Christ accompanied by Apostles, angels and saints.

The large **retable★★** of the Granadine School portrays God the Father above clouds on the crowning piece.

Iglesia de San Juan de Dios★

This is one of Granada's main Baroque churches, dating to the early 18C. On the **façade★**, between the bell towers, the lower niches hold images of archangels Gabriel and Raphael, while the upper section features St. John of God, St. Ildefonsus and St. Barbara. The **interior**, reached through a carved mahogany doorway, has a Latin-cross ground plan, elevated cupola and chancel. The massive Churrigueresque altarpiece is of gilded wood. The **camarín** (chapel) behind is accessed via a door to the right of the altar.

Hospital Real

The 16C former Royal Hospital is now the university Rectorate, designed by Enrique Egas in the form of a cross in a square with four patios. Plateresque windows adorn the upper storey. Note the yoke and arrows – emblems of the Catholic Monarchs – over the 17C marble doorway; above it a Virgin and Child is flanked by statues of Fernando and Isabel, crafted by Alonso de Mena. Stairs lead from the right-hand patio to the library (*biblioteca central*), which has an open framework and a wooden coffered dome at its center.

MUST SEE GRANADA

OTHER SIGHTS

La Cartuja★

Off map, 3km/1.8mi north of the Hospital Real. Bus no. 8. Paseo de Cartuja. Open daily 10am–1pm, 4pm–8pm (Nov–Mar, 3–6pm). 958 16 19 32.

Construction of the Carthusian monastery began early in the 16C. Enter the atrium through a Plateresque portal.

Church

The church is filled with Baroque stucco (1662) and paintings. The Assumption, below the baldaquin, is by José de Mora. Note the exuberant early 18C Baroque **sacrarium**, decorated by Francisco Hurtado.

Sacristy★★

This Baroque masterpiece (built 1727–1764) masks its structure in a sea of stucco, and cornices are all arranged to create an extraordinary interplay of light and shadow. Lanjarón marble is used extensively. The magnificent door and cedarwood furnishings, inlaid with tortoiseshell, mother-of-pearl and silver, are by a Carthusian monk, José Manuel Vázquez.

🚲 Parque de las Ciencias★

Off map, 2.4km/1.5mi south of the Cathedral. Avenida del Mediterraneo. Bus no. 5. Open year-round Tue–Sat 10am–7pm, Sun and public holidays 10am–3pm. Closed Mon, 1 Jan, 1 May, 25 Dec. €6.50 Museum, €2.50 Planetarium. 958 13 19 00. www.parqueciencias.com.

This open-air complex features over 270 interactive stations set up in two exhibition buildings (with pavilions dedicated to the human anatomy, the scientific legacy of al-Andalus, technology, physics, chemistry, geology and more), as well as a Planetarium, Tropical Butterfly House, Observation Tower and Astronomy Garden. There is a dedicated area for younger (3- to 7-year-old) explorers.

MUSEUMS

Museo Manuel de Falla

Paseo de los Mártires. Open year-round Tue–Fri 9am–2:30pm and 3:30–7pm, Sat–Sun 9am–2:30pm. Closed Mon and public holidays. €3. 958 22 21 88. www.museo manueldefalla.com.

Manuel de Falla (1876–1946), often called the greatest Spanish composer of the 20C, was a passionate admirer of Granada, a city he didn't discover until he was in his forties. This 16C house, where de Falla lived from 1919 to 1939, has remained unchanged since his day.

Museo Arqueológico

Carrera del Darro 43. Closed at the time of publication. 958 57 54 08.

The archaeological museum is in the Casa Castril (1539), a Renaissance palace with a fine **Plateresque doorway★**. It exhibits 9C BC Egyptian alabaster vases found in Almuñécar, numerous Roman artifacts and Moorish decorative objects.

FOR FUN

TAPAS & CAFÉS
See map pp118–119.

Café Central
Calle Elvira 3 (plaza Nueva, B3).
A classic Granada café that's good for breakfast or a break, serving coffees and teas.

El Retiro Taberna
Calle Piedra Santa 19 (B3). 958 22 54 37. www.elretirotaberna.es.
The tapas served here are prepared with delicious jamones and Spanish meats, cheeses, baccalà and much more. The atmosphere is warm and welcoming, with tables set amid enormous wine barrels. Excellent wine selection as well.

La Trastienda
Calle Cuchilleros 11 (B3). 958 22 69 65.
Descend a couple of steps to this 1836 grocery with a tapas counter. Enjoy a wide selection of tapas served in a simple, welcoming atmosphere.

Tea Houses
Calderería Nueva (B3).
Calle Calderería Nueva transports you to an Arab souk full of *teterías* (Moorish tea houses). **Kasbah** (no. 4, 958 22 79 36), for example, has carpets and cushioned seating befitting a Moorish guest.

NIGHTLIFE
See map pp118–119.

Calle Pedro Antonio de Alarcón (popular with students), and the carrera del Darro, close to the Alhambra and Albaicín district,

attract a younger crowd. Events are programmed year-round. Look out for first-class quality concerts at the **Auditorio Manuel de Falla** (Paseo de los Mártires, 958 22 21 88; www.manueldefalla.org). Shows and exhibitions are listed in the city's cultural guide, available at tourist offices.

Flamenco Caves
Many of Spain's finest flamenco singers, musicians and dancers have been of gypsy (gitano) stock. Consequently the cave dwellers of Sacromonte have turned their homes into flamenco nightspots for tourists, through unfortunately these have earned a reputation for fleecing foreign visitors in particular. One reputable flamenco show in Sacromonte (on the Camino del Sacromonte) is the **Zambra Museo Flamenco** cave, also known as La Cueva de María "la Canastera" (607 57 87 51): flamenco shows every night at 10:30pm (around 1hr 15mins). Another good place to catch authentic flamenco is **Peña Platería** (Placeta de Toqueros 7, Albaicín, 958 21 06 50; www. laplateria.org.es).

Bohemia Jazz Café
Plaza de los Lobos 11 (A3). bohemiajazzcafe.blogspot.it
Perfect for a drink and chat while jazz plays in the background. The pianos are collectors' items and bands often play live.

SHOPPING

Gran Vía de Colón, calle Reyes Católicos and calle Recogidas offer a mix of traditional shops, modern boutiques and the occasional shopping center. The former Moorish silk market, the Alcaicería, is a maze of alleyways in the same area located near the cathedral, where you'll find souvenir and craft shops. Traditional Granada crafts include inlaid wood, particularly on small objects such as boxes and jewelery cases, and pottery. Every Sunday a **market** selling all sorts of wares is held at the Campo de la Feria on the carretera de Jaén.

Pastry Shops

The Alcaicería has a number of pastry shops (*pastelerías*) selling *piononos*, a traditional Granada delicacy. Pastelería **Flor y Nata**, in calle Reyes Católicos, is one of the very best.

FIESTAS & EVENTS

Toma de Granada

The first important festival in the busy Granada calendar, on 2 January, commemorates Boabdil's surrender to the Catholic Monarchs. A procession climbs to the Alhambra, where the bell in the Torre de la Vela is rung. According to local legend, young women who take part will be wed within the year.

San Cecilio

The day of St. Cecil (1 Feb), Granada's patron saint, is celebrated by a pilgrimage (*romería*) to the Sacramonte district, where locals serve wine and broad beans (habas), sing songs and perform traditional *sevillanas* dances.

Semana Santa

Granada's Holy Week is a time of restraint. Processions file along steep, cobbled streets. Valuable Baroque statues by masters such as Diego de Siloé and Pedro de Mena test the *costaleros* (carriers), who kneel and struggle to squeeze floats into the cathedral. Be sure to try some of the traditional dishes that accompany these religious celebrations, like sweetmeats (roscos, pestiños, leche frita and empanadillas) and stewed codfish.

Las Cruces de Mayo

Flower-decked crosses adorn local streets in May.

Corpus Christi

Granada's annual *feria* is the biggest Corpus Christi celebration in Andalucía, with bullfights and a wide variety of entertainment. Alongside it you'll see the solemn Corpus Christi procession make its way through streets carpeted with flowers.

Festivals

Annual celebrations include the International **Theater Festival** (May, Teatro Manuel de Falla); the International **Music and Dance Festival** (Jun–Jul, Alhambra; www.granadafestival.org); and the International **Jazz Festival** (Oct–Nov).

SIERRA NEVADA★

Literally "snow-covered mountain range," the Sierra Nevada are Europe's second-highest peaks. Perpetually covered with snow, the mountains' many attractions include a superb ski resort and magnificent mountain landscapes, characterized by steep valleys and breathtaking ravines.

A TRULY GREAT OUTDOORS

Snow and ice have sculpted this young mountain chain into a striking, twisted profile. Fourteen of the Sierra Nevada's 70 or so peaks are over 3,000m/9,840ft high. The very highest peaks, Mulhacén (3,482m/11,424ft), Veleta (3,394m/11,132ft) and Alcazaba (3,371m/11,057ft) are all in the western part of the range. The range covers 170,000ha/420,070 acres, just over half of which are protected as the Parque Nacional de Sierra Nevada. Winter options include downhill skiing, various excursions and treks to some of the highest snow-capped peaks. In summer, hiking and horse riding are popular. Snow can start to fall in October and continue even into June; despite

this, the Sierra Nevada is gloriously sun-drenched for two-thirds of the year, when sun, snow and blue sky combine to create a scene of almost unparalleled beauty. Head for the visitor center to obtain information on **walks**. The most popular departure points are: from the El Dornajo visitor center in Güéjar Sierra, and the **Albergue Universitario**. The most interesting routes are the climb to the Laguna de las Yeguas lagoon and the ascents to Pico Veleta and Mulhacén.

Sol y Nieve★

In Pradollano, 37km/23mi southeast of Granada. 902 70 80 90. www.sierranevada.es. Sierra Nevada's ski resort was built in 1964 and hosted a World Cup downhill race in 1977, but

The peaks of Sierra Nevada

© Lledo/Shutterstock.com

Practical Information

Location

The Sierra Nevada lie immediately southeast of Granada.

Getting There and Around

♦ **By Air** – The nearest international airport is **Federico García Lorca Granada-Jaén** (www.aena.es).

♦ **By Car** – The fastest route from Granada is along the A 395. In Pradollano visitors must leave their vehicles in the underground car park. The best way to explore the mountains is by following one of the designated routes by car.

♦ **By Train** – The nearest train station to Sierra Nevada's ski resort is in Granada (32km/20mi). Guadix station is on the line that connects Sevilla and Almería, passing through Osuna and Granada as well. Other towns in the Sierra Nevada are not accessible by train. For information and reservations, 902 32 03 20, www.renfe.com.

♦ **By Bus** – Autocares Bonal (958 46 79 86) operates several daily services from Granada to Pradollano. The Alsa company (902 42 22 42; www.alsa.es) connects Guadix and La Calahorra to Granada and Almería; it also links with towns in the Alpujarras (the Granada-Trevélez line makes stops in Lanjarón, Pampaneira e Busquístar), as well as towns in the Lecrín valley (Dúrcal, Nigüelas, Restábal, Melegís and Saleres).

Visitor Information

For information on Sierra Nevada National Park, including its biodiversity, visit the **Centro de Visitantes "El Dornajo"** (Carretera de Sierra Nevada, Km 23, Güéjar Sierra; 958 34 06 25) or the National Park information point in **Pampaneira** (plaza de la Libertad): from here the **Nevadensis agency** (958 76 31 27; www.nevadensis.com) organizes activities in the Sierra Nevada and Alpujarras. There is also a tourist office in **Guadix** (Plaza de la Constitución, 958 66 28 04).

struggled financially thereafter. The situation has improved as protective measures for the Sierra Nevada were enacted, and investments made for the 1996 World Skiing Championships transformed Sol y Nieve. Today the resort can boast 84km/43.7mi of skiable trails, 80 runs and over 20 lifts, and offers weekend night skiing. In the event nature fails to deliver, over 400 snow canons provide its 32km of slopes with artificial snow. You can find a full range of apartment and hotel accommodations in Pradollano.

Pradollano ski resort

© Nick Stubbs/Shutterstock.com

SIERRA NEVADA

FROM GRANADA TO EL DORNAJO

Itinerary of approx. 27km/16.5mi. Road open only in summer.

Leave Granada on the old mountain road (*carretera de la Sierra*). After 8km/5mi turn toward Pinos Genil. The road skirts the Canales Reservoir (*embalse*) to reach **Güejar-Sierra**. After Maitena, the road crosses and then follows the Genil, twisting sharply up to the Hotel del Duque, now a seminary, and the **El Dornajo** visitor center.

FROM EL DORNAJO TO THE BORREGUILES CROSSROADS

Itinerary of approx. 29km/18mi.

From the El Dornajo Visitor Center take the left fork to climb to the Collado de las Sabinas pass, a steep ascent punctuated by sharp turns that will provide you with views of native pines and the Genil Valley. Continue to **Pradollano**, and the **Borreguiles** crossroads.

FROM GRANADA TO LA CALAHORRA

Map of Andalucía.

Guadix★

54km/33.5mi northeast of Granada.

Guadix is perfectly framed by clay hills, with the Sierra Nevada as a backdrop. A forest of white chimneys poking up from an underground world hints at the secrets hidden below within troglodyte dwellings. Guadix sits at a crossroads between eastern and western Andalucía, an area that has been settled by a succession of peoples. It reached its peak during Moorish rule; its fortress (*alcazaba*) survives from those days, though most buildings you will see today in the old quarter date from the 17C and 18C.

Barrio de Santiago★

This is one of the most characteristic districts, rife with seigniorial mansions like the **Palacio de Peñaflor**, where you can view an unusual, wood-decorated **balcony** and beautiful Renaissance patio. The seminary (*seminario menor*) next door provides access to the former Arab **alcazaba** (fortress) dating from the 11C. Although the fortress is in poor condition, a tour of it provides the best views of Guadix and the town's troglodyte district. Back in calle Barradas, flights of steps lead to **plazuela de Santiago**. At the end of this small square is the **Iglesia de Santiago**, its lovely Plateresque **doorway★** crowned with the shield of Charles V, recognizable by the two-headed eagle and the Golden Fleece. The Mudéjar ceiling inside is especially impressive (*visits by prior arrangement; 958 66 10 97/08 00)*. **Calle Ancha**, which leads off this square, boasts a number of fine 19C seigniorial mansions.

Barrio de las Cuevas★

The cave district is situated in the highest part of Guadix, amid a landscape of streams, gullies and small brown hills. The caves are built on different levels, so that those dwellings hollowed into the side of hills often have their entrance on top of a different cave roof. A **cave museum of popular arts and traditions** (*Centro de Interpretación Cuevas de Guadix: Plaza Padre Poveda,*

*open year-round Mon–Fri
10am–2pm and 4–6pm (Summer,
5–7pm), Sat and public holidays
10am–2pm; closed Sun; €2.50; 958
66 55 69)* re-creates life in a cave
dwelling during the 19C. Several
rooms exhibit local farming and
shepherds' tools.

Barrio de Santa Ana
The town's Moorish quarter is
a network of narrow alleyways,
lined by whitewashed houses
embellished with flowers and
aromatic plants.

La Calahorra★
19km/12mi south of Guadix.
Hidden behind the peaks of the
Sierra Nevada and surrounded
by almond trees, La Calahorra
has retained much of its historic
past. One of the most spectacular
approaches is the route across
the Sierra Nevada via the **Ragua
Pass★★**, along which you can
appreciate the contrast between
Sierra and Altiplano. This isolated
village, crowned by an impressive
fortress, stands much as it did
back when it was the capital of the
Marquisate of Zenete.
The desolate landscape of the
Minas del Marquesado, mines
which were abandoned in 1997, is
visible 4km/2.5mi from the village.

Castillo de la Calahorra★★
*Visit by guided tour only, Wed 10am–
1pm and 4–6pm. 958 67 70 98.*
Despite the castle's robust military
appearance, enhanced by four
cylindrical towers, it contains
one of Spain's most beautiful
Renaissance patios★★. The patio
was built at the beginning of the
15C in the artistic style of the
Italian *quattrocento*, and is laid out

in a square plan with two sections
joined by a splendid **staircase★★**
comprising three flights of stairs.
Note the extensive decoration,
particularly on the doorways and
capitals.

VALLE DEL LECRÍN★
*Head south from Granada along
the A 44-E 902, then turn off the
main road in Dúrcal (32km/20mi
south of Granada).*
The little-known Lecrín Valley is
a delight of orange groves and
hillside villages. Make your way
through small towns like **Dúrcal**,
Nigüelas – one of the prettiest
settlements in the Sierra Nevada
– **Mondújar**, Murchas, Restábal,
Melegís and **Saleres**.

LAS ALPUJARRAS★★
*Map of Andalucía. This rugged
and varied region extends across
the southern slopes of the Sierra
Nevada, inland from the Costa
Tropical and Motril.*
The Alpujarras (from the Arabic
al-bucharrat, or "pastures") is a
region of whitewashed villages,
rugged mountains and fertile
valleys straddling Granada and
Almería provinces. It was the
final stronghold of the Nasrids.
This magnificent range was
rediscovered by 19C Romantic
travelers, and is now one of the
most popular destinations in
Andalucía.

Lanjarón
19km/12mi east of Saleres.
Lanjarón is the gateway to the
Alpujarras from Granada. Famous
for its medicinal waters, it attracts
thousands of visitors every year.
Its other attraction is a 16C **castle**,
guarding the valley entrance.

Village in Las Alpujarras

©J.I. Pascual/Age Fotostock

Pampaneira★★

22km/13.5mi east of Lanjarón.
Located in the **Poqueira Valley★★**, Pampaneira has preserved its traditional atmosphere. The main street, where shops offer only local products, leads to **plaza de la Libertad**, dominated by the 17C Baroque Iglesia de la Santa Cruz. Stroll the narrow streets to appreciate the town's charms, and stop at a traditional loom where Alpujarras rugs (*jarapas*) are made. The **NEVADENSIS Center** (*see Practical Information*), can organize 🚶 **excursions**.

Busquístar

10km/6mi east of Pampaneira.
This quiet, Mozarabic village of gleaming white houses is the first in the spectacular **Trevélez Valley★**. The road continues on all the way to Trevélez.

Trevélez★

10km/6mi north of Busquístar.
Trevélez is the highest town in Spain (1,600m/5,250ft in the *barrio alto*). Towering above the town you'll see **Mulhacén**, the highest peak on the Iberian Peninsula (3,482m/11,424ft).

Puerto de la Ragua★★

64km/39.5mi northeast of Trevélez.
The road ascends gently to the summit (2,000m/6,559ft) amid a high mountain landscape, then narrows and descends abruptly to the Guadix Plateau, offering magnificent views of the **Castillo de la Calahorra★★** (*see p 135*).

Trevélez cured ham

Ever since **Queen Isabel II** first extolled the virtues of the town's cured ham (*jamón*) in the 19C, the name Trevélez has been synonymous with this culinary delicacy. The secret of its drying sheds (*secaderos*) lies in their special climatic conditions (dry and cold) and the exclusive use of sea salt. White-colored pigs are bred to produce these large (up to 10kg/22lb), gently-rounded hams.

THE GREAT OUTDOORS

Unlike the Doñana National Park, access to the Sierra Nevada is unrestricted. This is Spain's most mountainous area and the highest peaks in Europe after the Alps. The Sierra Nevada's snow-covered crest is contrasted by the foothills of the Alpujarras, where gentle slopes are cultivated with terraces of almond trees and vegetables.

🎿 Winter sports

Sierra Nevada has 84km/43.7mi of marked runs and all the facilities expected of a major ski resort. Snow permitting, the season generally runs from late November/early December to April. (Avoid the last week in February, when the resort is crowded with families on school holidays). Information on skiing in the Sierra Nevada (plus other year-round activities) is available from the resort operator **Cetursa** (Plaza de Andalucía, Monachil; 902 70 80 90; www.cetursa.es).

🪂 Paragliding

Sierra Nevada Mountains are a popular venue for this exhilarating pastime (*parapente* as it is called locally). For more information on *parapente* in the Granada region visit www.flygranada.com.

The Route of the Alpujarras

This route links Almería and Granada via a series of mountain passes. It stretches north to the peaks of Sierra Nevada and south to the Mediterranean. This region is partially characterized by its traditional isolation, the source of its ethnological and historical peculiarities. It was a center of resistance against the advance of Islam and was the last redoubt of the Moriscos, the Christianized Spanish Moors. Numerous remains of old medieval fortifications (watchtowers, castles, forts and towers) can be found here, along with a valuable archaeological heritage from Muslim times. Towns and villages along the route include: Benahadux, Alhama de Almería, Laujar de Andarax, Ugíjar, Válor, Juviles, Trevélez, Pitres, Capileira, Pampaneira, Bubión, Cádiar, Torvizcón, Orgiva, Lanjarón, Dúrcal, Otura, Dílar, Gójar, La Zubia, Cájar and Huetor Vega.

🪂 Activities

The **Centro de Interpretación del Parque Nacional de Sierra Nevada** (Nevadensis) in Pampaneira (Plaza de la Libertad, 958 76 31 27; www.nevadensis.com) organizes hikes, climbing trips and horseback rides. Cross-country skiing and dog-sledding can be arranged at **Consorcio Estacion Recreativa Puerto de La Ragua** (Plaza de la Constitución 3, Laroles, 958 76 02 23; www.puertodelaragua.com).

Shopping

Local rugs (*jarapas*) were originally created from different brightly colored sections, but are now woven whole. Two workshops in Pampaneira are: **Hilacar** (2km/1.2mi N; 956 76 32 26) and **La Rueca** (Avenida de la Alpujarra 2; 958 76 30 14).

COSTA DE ALMERÍA ★

With wide beaches, coves kissed by crystal-clear waters, fishing villages, modern vacation resorts and great stretches of undeveloped natural beauty, the Costa de Almería is swiftly making a name for itself as a tourist destination. Add warm weather, little rainfall and what sometimes feels like eternal sunshine and you're left no good reason not to spend some time in this corner of Spain.

FROM ADRA TO ALMERÍA ★★

Map of Andalucía.

Adra

62km/38.5mi east of Salobreña.
Set on a fertile plain, Adra has a fishing port, marina, beach and several 17C/18C mansions.

Berja

16km/10mi northeast of Adra.
Set at the foot of the Sierra de Gádor, the Roman Virgi (which evolved into *vergel*, meaning "orchard"), has a number of handsome noble Renaissance mansions and fountains, and the remains of a Roman amphitheater.

Roquetas de Mar

38km/23.5mi southeast of Berja.
This fishing village has been transformed into a lively resort. The remains of the old castle can be seen by the lighthouse (*faro*). Roquetas has a fishing port and marina, **golf course** and a water park. The **Urbanización Roquetas de Mar** *(3.5km/2mi)* has attractive beaches and a long palm-lined promenade with views of the Gulf of Almería and Cabo de Gata. In addition to the beach there is also an interesting **Aquarium** (*open Jun–Sept daily 10am–9pm; Oct–May Wed–Fri 10am–6pm, Sat–Sun 10am–7pm; €14.95; 950 16 00 36, www.aquariumroquetas.com*) filled with sharks, rays, tropical fish, freshwater tanks and a touch tank that kids (and not only) will enjoy.

Aguadulce

8km/5mi north of Roquetas de Mar.
This large and popular Blue Flag beach resort is set in an area of abundant vegetation just 11km/7mi from Almería.
The **nature reserve of Punta**

Almería

© Tupungato/Shutterstock.com

Practical Information

Location

The Costa de Almería runs along the southeastern Iberian Peninsula from Adra to Mojácar, and includes the provincial capital, Almería, which is 172km/107mi southeast of Granada. Most development is between Adra – including the immense sandy beaches of Balanegra and Balerma, and the resort town Almerimar – and Aguadulce. The stretch from Aguadulce to Almería comprises an impressive series of steep cliffs. To the east of the provincial capital, the Mediterranean is bordered by the Parque Natural de Cabo de Gata, boasting superb beaches, and San José, an attractive small resort town.

Getting There and Around

♦ **By Air** – Almería airport (www. aena.es) is located 9km/5.5mi east of the city center along the N 344. Bus no. 22 (Surbus: 950 62 47 35; www.surbus.com) connects the airport with train and bus stations (Estación Intermodal) in the city center in roughly 35 mins.

♦ **By Car** – The A 7-E 15, just off the coast, is the principal highway.

♦ **By Train** – Trains connect Sevilla to Almería (approx. 5hr 40mins), passing through Granada (2hr 24mins along the route) and Guadix (1hr 12mins). The Intermodal Station (trains and buses) is in Plaza de la Estación.

♦ **By Bus** – Bus company Alsa (902 42 22 42; www.alsa.es) connects Almería to Córdoba, Granada, Jaén, Málaga and towns along the Costa de Almería (Adra, Berja, Roquetas de Mar, Aguadulce, Níjar, Mojácar). To reach San José from the Intermodal Station in Almería, take one of the buses run by Autocares Bernardo (950 25 04 22; www.autocaresbernardo.com). For connections in the Almería region, you can also visit www.siu.ctal.es.

♦ **By Taxi** – In Almería: Tele Taxi: 950 25 11 11; Radio Taxi: 950 22 61 61.

Visitor Information

In **Almería** there are city tourist offices in Plaza de la Constitución (950 21 05 38 / 27 08 48; www. turismodealmeria.org), and in Parque Nicolás Salmerón, corner of Calle Martínez Campos (950 17 52 20). You'll find information on the entire region in Plaza Bendicho (95 08 81 178, www.turismoalmeria. com). You can also visit the Parque Natural Cabo de Gata Information Center in Níjar (Avenida San José 27, 950 38 08 99).

Entinas–Sabinar, an area of sand dunes and marshland, lies to the southeast. Juniper bushes, bulrushes and canes predominate this unusual landscape.

Road to Almería

The road follows the coast, hugging cliff tops and tunneling through rock. The approach to Almería offers views of the city, the bay, the port and the fortress.

Almería

11km/7mi east of Aguadulce.
The whitewashed town of Almería spreads out between the sea and the arid hill of its impressive fortress (*alcazaba*). Spanish agriculture flourishes here, and the

139

area's hot, dry climate is attracting an increasing number of tourists.

Alcazaba★

Calle Almanzor. Open Tue–Sat 9am–3:30pm and 6:30–10pm in mid Jun–mid Sept (1–15 Jun, 9am–3:30pm; Apr–May, 9am–8pm; mid Sept–Mar 9am–6:30pm), Sun and public holidays 10am–5pm. Closed Mon, 1 Jan and 25 Dec. €1.50 (free for EU citizens). 950 80 10 08.

Abd ar-Rahman III had this superbly-sited hilltop fortress built in the 10C. It was enlarged by Almotacín, and by the Catholic Monarchs. The **first enclosure** (*recinto*) holds gardens and a cistern. The bell tower was used to warn of pirate attacks. Walls connect the fortress with San Cristóbal hill. The **second enclosure** housed the Caliphal residence, and includes the cistern room (now an exhibition hall), a Mudéjar hermitage, a pool and baths for the troops. The baths of the Caliph's wife are in one corner. In the **third enclosure**, to the west, you'll find the castle of the Catholic Monarchs. The large parade ground is dominated by an imposing keep with a Gothic doorway. The impressive **view★** from the battlements takes in city and port, as well as the working-class district of **La Chanca**, all set against a backdrop of arid hills and the shimmering azure sea.

Cathedral★

Plaza de la Catedral. Open year-round Mon–Fri 10am–1:30pm and 4–5pm, Sat 10am–1:30pm. €5. 950 23 48 48.

This fortress-like cathedral was built on the site of a mosque in the 16C, when Barbary pirates were frequent, though unwelcome visitors. The large 17C tower is crowned by a small belfry.

The Renaissance **main doorway★** contrasts with the austere façade. Before entering the cathedral, admire the unusual relief of the **Portocarrero sun★** – an animated sunburst, the city's symbol – at the east end. The chancel, tabernacle, retable and ambulatory arches were renovated in the 18C.

The Renaissance **choir stalls** have exceptional profile medallions in the upper stalls and full-bodied lifelike reliefs. Note the neo-Classical back wall, in multi-hued marble, which was designed by Ventura Rodríguez.

The **ambulatory** has three chapels: the Gothic axial houses the venerated statue of Cristo de la Escucha, while St Indalecio, patron of Almería, can be seen in the right-hand Renaissance chapel, and various canvases by Alonso Cano are in the chapel to the left. The late-19C Palacio Episcopal (Bishop's Palace) and the Iglesia de las Puras, part of an old convent founded in the 16C, look out onto the **plaza de la Catedral**.

Plaza Vieja

The **town hall** dominates this lovely, arcaded 19C square where Moorish bazaars once stood.

Iglesia de Santiago

This 16C church, one of the city's smallest, is located in the narrow calle de las Tiendas ("street of shops"). A **Renaissance portal★**, similar to the cathedral doorway, depicts St James the Moorslayer *(Santiago Matamoros)*.

Puerta de Purchena

This is the heart of Almerían life. Many of its manorial buildings date from the late 19C.

Paseo de Almería

The city's main avenue is lined with a mixture of 20C buildings and modern tower blocks. The **Círculo Mercantil**, with 1920s ceilings, stuccowork and *azulejo* paneling, is one of its most attractive structures. Behind it, the landmark **Teatro Cervantes** opened in 1921. The nearby **Basílica de Nuestra Señora del Mar** houses the remains of Almería's venerated patron saint; its 18C cloister is now home to the city's **Arts and Crafts School**.

Parque Nicolás Salmerón

This pleasant strip of greenery, fountains and pools runs parallel to the port in a former warehouse district.

PARQUE NATURAL DE CABO DE GATA-NÍJAR★★

Map of Andalucía.

Cabo de Gata–Níjar park offers visitors cliffs, wild beaches, delightful coves and azure skies. The landscape is sprinkled with prickly pears, agave and other species able to survive a region that registers the lowest rainfall in Spain.

Níjar

North of the park. 39km/24mi northeast of Almería.

The whitewashed houses and cobbled alleyways of this old Moorish town are the essence of Andalucía. It sits on the southern slopes of the Sierra de Alhamilla, in view of the agricultural plain of **Campo de Níjar** below. Irrigation has transformed the surrounding landscape. The town is known for its handicrafts: blue and green **pottery** and *jarapas*, colorful cotton and wool rugs and blankets. Walk from the 15C **parish church** to the **market square** (*plaza del Mercado*), where you'll discover a 19C ceramic fountain and hundred-year-old elm trees. Next ascend a steep and stony path to the hilltop watchtower for a commanding **view** of the Níjar plain, with Cabo de Gata and the Mediterranean in the distance.

Cabo de Gata

© Greg Blok/Shutterstock.com

Cabo de Gata

30km/18.5mi south of Níjar.
The road winds up to the lighthouse and volcanic formations called **The Finger** (*El Dedo*) and **Mermaids' Reef** (*Arrecife de las Sirenas*). A viewpoint (*Mirador de las Sirenas*) and an information point adjoin the lighthouse. The nearby **visitor center** provides detailed park information.

San José

22km/13.5mi east of Cabo de Gata.
The whitewashed houses of this small resort town line the slopes above an attractive beach and small marina.

Beaches

There are two superb beaches on the edge of San José. **Playa de los Genoveses★** lines a wide bay 2km/1.2mi; the **Playa de Monsul★** (2.5km/1.5mi from San José) nestles between mountain spurs descending to the sea, with a sand dune at one end, a rock in its center, and a cove beyond.

Mojácar at sunset

© Fotomicar/Shutterstock.com

ROAD TO MOJÁCAR

Map of Andalucía.

Agua Amarga

40km/25mi northeast of San José.
The houses of this seaside village appear after a bend in the road. The resort's attractive and well-maintained beach is framed by two rocky promontories.

Mojácar Playa

The Mojácar municipality includes 17km/10.5mi of **beaches** and coves. Mojácar Playa is a modern resort of whitewashed tourist developments.

Mojácar★

30km/18.5mi northeast of Agua Amarga.
This enchanting town enjoys a superb **setting★** on a promontory, with delightful views of the Mediterranean just to the east and unusual rock formations in the surrounding plain. The old hillside quarter has a Moorish character, with narrow, cobbled streets lined by whitewashed houses adorned with floral arrangements. A significant foreign community, particularly from northern Europe, gives Mojácar a cosmopolitan feel. The town's numerous restaurants, cafés and craft shops attract tens of thousands of visitors every year, particularly in summer.
If you're in the mood, you can also visit the popular water park **Parque Acuático Vera** (*open mid May–mid Sept 11am–6pm; Jul–Aug, 7:30pm; €23; 950 46 73 37. www. ociovera.com*), located along the road between **Vera** and **Garrucha** (*10km/6mi north of Mojácar*), a former fishing village with excellent beaches and a marina.

FOR FUN

TAPAS & CAFÉS

Casa Puga

Calle Jovellanos 7 (old town). 950 23 15 30. www.barcasapuga.es.
Almería is teeming with tapas bars, of which Casa Puga is the oldest. Here you'll get to choose from an enormous range of tapas, excellent wines and sausages.

El Quinto Toro

Calle Juan Leal 6. 950 23 91 35.
Located near the central market, this locale is a classic tapas destination. Make sure you try their speciality, *patatas a lo pobre*.

ACTIVITIES

🚲 Boat trips

Contact Garrucha tourist office for further information, Paseo del Malecón 42, 950 13 27 83.
Excursions to Mojácar Bay, Carboneras and the Parque Natural de Cabo de Gata-Níjar are all available from Garrucha.

🚲 Mountain-biking

Biking amid the landscapes of the Cabo de Gata-Níjar Nature Park, you can follow a route recognized as one of the most breathtaking, starting in the old mining village of Rodalquilar (*16km/10mi northeast of San José*) and leading to Cerro del Cinto Hill.

🚲 Scuba-diving

Tranquil, crystal-clear waters, pleasant temperatures, numerous different species, fascinating caves, basalt columns and breathtaking underwater scenery have made Parque Natural de Cabo de Gata one of Europe's most important marine reserves and a paradise for scuba divers. Underwater enthusiasts can choose from several sites, including Cala San Pedro, Playazo de Rodalquivar, Cala del Embarcadero (in Los Escullos) and others. Authorization is not required for scuba diving; however, solo divers need a permit from the Consejería de Medio Ambiente of the Junta de Andalucía. Contact a local scuba diving center for further information.

🚲 Oasys Parque Tématico (Mini Hollywood)

27km/16.5mi north of Almería on the A 370-N340A toward Tabernas. Open daily Holy Week–Oct; rest of the year weekends or long weekends only; consult the website for opening times. P22, 3-11 years old P12.50. 902 53 35 32. www.oasysparquetematico.com.
This unusual complex is part zoo, boasting bears, giraffes, elephants, kangaroos and other animals, and touches on bio-biodiversity themes. But almost everyone visits to see "Mini Hollywood," the set where *A Fistful of Dollars* was filmed. As you walk the dusty streets past the saloon and bank you'll be transported to another era (and continent) against a backdrop of bare rocky mountains. There are staged brawls and shoot-outs in the best Wild Western tradition, and the complex includes a small film museum as well.

NORTHEAST ANDALUCÍA★★

From the imposing Renaissance cathedral towering over Jaén to architectural treasures that have earned Úbeda World Heritage Site status, northeastern Andalucía offers visitors a wide range of attractions. And if you're in the mood for something more than man-made, make sure you explore the wealth of flora and fauna on display in the Parque Natural de las Sierras de Cazorla, Segura y Las Villas.

JAÉN★

Map of Andalucía.

Jaén, recognized as the **olive** capital of Spain, rises onto Cerro de Santa Catalina (St Catherine's Hill). The town is a storehouse of artistic heritage, from its Moorish castle to numerous Renaissance buildings, many designed by Andrés de Vandelvira.

Cathedral★★

Plaza de Santa María. Open year-round Mon–Sat 10am–2pm and 4–8pm (Sat, 7pm), Sun 9am–1:30pm and 6–8pm. €5. 953 23 42 33. www.catedraldejaen.org.
Towering over old Jaén, built in the 16C and 17C to plans by Andrés de Vandelvira, this is one of the most extraordinary Renaissance buildings in Andalucía. On the lower tier of the sumptuous **façade★★**, fine reliefs represent the Assumption of the Virgin, the archangel St Michael, and St Catherine. Sculptures on the full **balustrade★** represent King Fernando, the four Evangelists and the Doctors of the Church. The domed transept is a magnificent work by Pedro del Portillo and Juan de Aranda. Note the way light illuminates the building. The **choir stalls★★** are by José Gallego and Oviedo del Portal, disciples of Alonso Berruguete. The altarpiece includes the Gothic **Virgin of La Antigua★**. The **Veil of the Holy Face★**, used by Veronica to wipe the face of Christ on his way to Calvary, bears His features. Note the *Annunciation* by Cellini and a *Visitation* attributed to Titian.

View of Jaén

© E. Luider/Hemis.fr

Practical Information

Location

Jaén is 94km/59mi north of Granada via the A 44–E 902. Baeza is 50km/31mi northeast of Jaén. Úbeda stands at the center of the province of Jaén between the Guadalquivir and Guadalimar Valleys. The Parque Natural de las Sierras de Cazorla, Segura y Las Villas reserve is situated to the northeast of Jaén, covering the Cazorla, Segura and Las Villas ranges, at altitudes between 600m/1,950ft and 2,017m/6,616ft.

Getting There and Around

♦ **By Air** – Federico García Lorca Granada-Jaén airport (www.aena.es) is located 99km/61.5mi south of the city of Jaén, an hour or so along N 323. Buses will take you from the airport (Autocares Jose Gonzalez / 958 49 01 64; www.autocaresjosegonzalez.com) to downtown Granada, from which point you can travel to Jaén (1hr 10mins) on buses with the company Alsa (902 42 22 42; www.alsa.es).

♦ **By Car** – Úbeda and the Parque Natural de las Sierras de Cazorla, Segura y Las Villas are linked with Jaén, 57km/36mi southwest via the A 316, and Córdoba, 146km/91mi west, via the N 322 and A 4–E 5.

♦ **By Train** – Direct trains run from Sevilla, Córdoba and Cádiz to the station on Paseo de las Culturas in Jaén. Trains from Jaén, Sevilla, Córdoba and Granada arrive in the Linares-Baeza station (14km/8.5mi northwest of Baeza). For information and reservations, 902 32 03 20, www.renfe.com.

♦ **By Bus** – Jaén central station on Plaza de la Libertad has routes to every provincial capital in Andalucía. Alsa (902 42 22 42; www.alsa.es) connects Jaén, Úbeda, Baeza and Andújar via various bus routes running at different times daily, as well as connections with Cazorla in the Parque Natural de las Sierras de Cazorla, Segura y Las Villas.

Visitor Information

Tourist offices in: **Jaén** (Calle Maestra 8, 953 19 04 55 / 31 32 81; www.turjaen.org), **Úbeda** (Calle Baja del Marqués 4; 953 77 92 04; turismodeubeda.com), **Baeza** (Plaza del Pópulo; 953 77 99 82). Head to one of the **Parque Natural de las Sierras de Cazorla, Segura y Las Villas** information points in order to plan a route that will provide you views of the most breathtaking landscapes. The largest information point is at the **Torre del Vinagre** (Carretera del Tranco A 319, km 48, Coto Ríos, Santiago-Pontones; 953 713 017; www.sierrasdecazorlaseguraylasvillas.es); others can be found at **Cazorla, Segura de la Sierra** and **Siles**.

Capilla de San Andrés★

Calle de San Andrés. Open daily 10am–12:30pm. 953 24 03 21.
Perched along a steep street, this 16C Mudéjar chapel with Judaic features was commissioned by Gutierre González Doncel, treasurer to Pope Leo X. The **Capilla de la Purísima Inmaculada★★** (Chapel of the Immaculate Conception) is a Plateresque masterpiece. The gilded chapel

145

screen★ is by Maestro Bartolomé (16C), a native of Jaén.

Palacio de Villardompardo★

Plaza de Santa Luisa de Marillac. Open year-round Tue–Fri 9am–8pm, Sat–Sun 9:30am–2:30pm. 953 24 80 68.

This elegant 16C palace with an arcaded **patio★** was the residence of Fernando de Torres y Portugal, Viceroy of Peru and Count of Villardompardo. It houses the **Museo de Artes y Costumbres Populares** (Museum of arts and traditions); and the **Museo Internacional de Arte Naïf**.

Moorish Baths★

The *Baños Árabes*, situated deep below the palace, are the largest of their kind left in Spain. As you step into barrel-vaulted entrance hall with star-shaped skylight and alcoves at either end, note the 11C remains from its period of construction, now protected under glass. Visitors can view a cold room; a larger warm room, roofed with a handsome hemispherical cupola on pendentives; and a hot room alongside the boilers.

ÚBEDA★★

Map of Andalucía.

Úbeda is a town of gracious monuments, widely renowned as one of Andalucía's architectural treasure houses, celebrated by illustrious travelers and designated a World Heritage Site. Visitors come to view its austere palaces, elegant squares and fine details from when Andalusian art reached its zenith. The maze-like Moorish quarter (barrio de San Millán)

delightfully contrasts Úbeda's 16C masterpieces. Refering to this dichotomy between fine art and narrow streets, poet Antonio Machado (1875-1939) called Úbeda "a queen and gypsy."

A Bit of History

Although its origins are Roman, the Moors founded Ubbadat Al Arab, one of the major cities in Al-Andalus. In 1234, Fernando III (the Saint) reconquered the city. Úbeda enjoyed its greatest splendor in the 16C, during the reigns of Charles V and Felipe II. Its citizens held important positions in the Empire, magnificent Renaissance buildings were erected, and members of the nobility took up residence here.

Plaza Vázquez de Molina★★

This magnificent square is at the heart of the old quarter, lined with sumptuous buildings and delightful streets that transport visitors to another era. Here you'll see the **Palacio de las Cadenas**, **Capilla del Salvador**, **Iglesia de Santa María de los Alcázares** and the 16C **Casa del Deán Ortega**, now a parador.

Other noteworthy buildings include the **Palacio del Marqués de Mancera**, the Renaissance façade of which is crowned by a quadrangular tower; and the **Casa del Regidor**.

Palacio de las Cadenas★

Open year-round Mon–Fri 7:30am–3pm. Closed Sat-Sun. Free entrance. 953 75 04 40. turismodeubeda.com

This palace was built by Vandelvira in the middle of the 16C under orders from Don Juan Vázquez de Molina. In 1566 it was turned into a convent, then later used as a jail before finally becoming the town hall in 1868.

The name, Palace of the Chains, derives from the iron chains that once stretched across its entry. The **façade**★★, which bears the family coat of arms, is an unusual combination of decorative Andalusian features and classical architecture. Note the alternating bays and pilasters, replaced on the upper tier by caryatids and atlantes. Two elegant lanterns on the ends add a lighter touch. Inside is a delightful Renaissance patio with refined arcades and a central fountain. The basement houses the **Centro Municipal de Interpretación Turística**, (*953 75 62 34, www.renacentalia. net*) which illuminates Úbeda's heritage through models and panels, exhibiting local pottery and ceramics.

Iglesia de Santa María de los Alcázares★

This church was built in the 13C over the remains of a mosque. Its harmonious façade, crowned by two belfries, each with three large bells and a smaller one, is one of the most attractive features on the plaza Vázquez de Molina. The interior, badly damaged during the Spanish Civil War, contains several beautiful **chapels**★ adorned with sculptures and profuse decoration, in particular the Capilla de La Yedra and Capilla de los Becerra, both enclosed by impressive **grilles**★ designed by Master Bartolomé. The patio of the mosque was replaced in the 16C by handsome

Renaissance **cloisters** with elegant pointed arches and groin vaulting.

Capilla del Salvador★★
Open Mon–Sat 9:30am–2pm and 5–7pm (Apr–May, 4:30–6:30pm; Oct–Mar, 4–6pm), Sun 11:30am–2pm and 5–8pm (Apr–May, 4:30–7:30pm; Oct–Mar, 4–7pm). €5. 609 27 99 05.

Designed by Diego de Siloé in 1536 and built by Andrés de Vandelvira between 1540 and 1556, this chapel is one of the finest religious buildings of the Andalusian Renaissance. It was commissioned as a family pantheon by Don Francisco de los Cobos, secretary to Charles V, who, thanks to his vast fortune and artistic leanings, became a leading figure in 16C imperial Spain. The lavish **interior**★★ has a single nave, its vaulting outlined in blue and gold. The central part, intended for the tombs of Don Francisco de los Cobos and his wife, is separated from the rest of the chapel by a monumental grille attributed to Villalpando. The presbytery, by Vandelvira, is a rotunda in which an immense 16C altarpiece includes a baldaquin with a sculpture of the Transfiguration by Alonso Berruguete; only the carving of Christ remains. The **sacristy**★★, also by Vandelvira, is an architectural jewel, containing interesting decoration based on caissons, caryatids, atlantes and medallions, clearly influenced by the Italian Renaissance.

Iglesia de San Pablo★
Plaza 1º de Mayo.
The harmony of the main Gothic portal with its Plateresque bell

MUST SEE

tower, contrasts with the attractive Isabelline-style reliefs on the south doorway (1511). Two chapels stand out: the **Capilla de las Calaveras**, with an impressive arch by Vandelvira, and the Isabelline **Capilla de las Mercedes**, enclosed by extraordinary **grilles**★★ created in Úbeda. Note the highly imaginative scene of Adam and Eve.

Palacio de los Condes de Guadiana

Calle Real.
Built in the early 17C, the Palace of the Count of Guadiana is crowned by a fine **tower**★ with angular balconies divided by small columns and galleries on the third floor.

Calle Real

This attractive thoroughfare, one of the most elegant in Úbeda, provides visitors with an insight into the town's architectural splendor during the 16C, when Úbeda was at its economic and artistic zenith. It is lined by monumental buildings and typical local shops.

BAEZA★★

Map of Andalucía.

Baeza extends across a low hill, surrounded by fields of cereal crops and olive groves stretching to the horizon, a setting immortalized by poet Antonio Machado: "Oh land of Baeza, I shall dream of you when I cannot see you." Churches, monuments and splendid mansions of golden stone recall the splendor of this peaceful provincial town during the 16C and 17C. The best time to visit Baeza is during the solemn processions of Holy Week or Corpus Christi.

Plaza del Pópulo★

In the center of this small square you'll see the **Fuente de los Leones** (Fountain of the Lions), built using stones from the ruins of nearby Cástulo. The central figure is said to be Imilce, the wife of Hannibal. The square is fronted by the former abattoir (*carnicería*) and the Casa del Pópulo, a former court turned tourist office. The **Arco de Villalar** (arch) commemorates the victory of Carlos I (Holy Roman Emperor Charles V) over the

Baeza countryside

comuneros in 1521. Alongside, the **Puerta de Jaén** projects onto the Casa del Pópulo via an attractive quarter-circle balcony.

Plaza de Santa María

The fountain, decorated with caryatids and atlantes, is by Ginés Martínez. To one side stands the 17C Seminario de San Felipe Neri.

Cathedral★

Open year-round Mon–Fri 10am–2pm and 4–7pm (Winter, 6pm), Sat 10am–7pm, Sun 10am–6pm. €4. 953 74 41 57.
Fernando III ordered the cathedral built over a destroyed mosque. In mid-afternoon, its silhouette casts a mysterious shadow over the narrow cobbled streets behind. The Renaissance-style façade contrasts with the west side's 13C Gothic-Mudéjar Puerta de la Luna (Moon Doorway), and 14C Gothic rose window. In the south wall is the 15C Puerta del Perdón (Pardon Doorway).

Interior★★

The severity of Castilian architecture combines harmoniously with graceful Andalusian features.

© Sokolovsky/Shutterstock.com

Andrés de Vandelvira designed the 16C reconstruction. The fine **Capilla del Sagrario** (Sacrarium Chapel) at the end of the north aisle holds a Baroque silver **monstrance**, carried in procession on Corpus Christi. Note the polychrome metal **pulpit** (1580) in the transept, the Baroque retable, and the monumental iron **grille** by Maestro Bartolomé in the nave. Four Mudéjar chapels in the cloisters have decorative plant motifs and Arabic inscriptions.

Palacio de Jabalquinto★

Open year-round Mon–Fri 9am–2pm. Closed Sat–Sun. Free entrance. 953 74 27 75.
Once the Flamboyant Gothic residence of Juan Alfonso de Benavides, the Capitán de Lorca, this building boasts an exceptional **façade★★**, attributed to Juan Guas and Enrique Egas. It is best seen in late afternoon when shadows accentuate its details. Stylish features of the day include projecting pinnacles, stone fleurons and elaborate escutcheons.
Inside is a spacious Renaissance **patio** with marble Corinthian columns and a monumental Baroque staircase.

Plaza del Mercado Viejo (or Plaza de la Constitución)

This is the epicenter of town life, surrounded by the **Antigua Alhóndiga** (old corn exchange) and the 18C Baroque **Casas Consistoriales Bajas**, a former civic building. A number of traditional bars and cafés line its arcades.

PARQUE NATURAL DE LAS SIERRAS DE CAZORLA, SEGURA Y LAS VILLAS★★★

Map of Andalucía.

Covering over 214,000 hectares (529,500 acres), this is the largest park in Spain. It features cliffs, gorges and a complex river

🐾 Flora and Fauna Galore

Parque Natural de las Sierras de Cazorla, Segura y Las Villas is the largest protected area in all of Spain, and boasts one of the country's richest collections of flora and fauna. There are over 1,300 catalogued species present in the park, including unique flowers like the Cazorla violet, reputedly the smallest daffodil in the world.
Hiking amid black pine, holm and downy oak, hazel, holly and Austrian pine (an indigenous species that can be found above 1,200 meters), you'll find it easy to appreciate the abundant vegetation of Andalucía. Deer, wild boar and mountain goats are common, but there are also numerous predatory species present including the genet, stone marten, wildcat and fox, as well as acquatic fauna and fish like the otter, trout, barbel, carp and black perch. Birdlife includes the golden eagle, peregine falcon, kite, osprey and others. If you're lucky, you'll catch a glimpse of one of the park's rarer denizens, the Valverde wall lizard.

network. The Guadalquivir rises here (in Cañada de las Fuentes, at a height of over 1,300m) as well as the Segura. Altitude and humidity favor dense Mediterranean-type mountain vegetation. Many of the towns and villages in the park have preserved their traditional cultures and crafts.

Tíscar★

55km/34mi southeast of Úbeda.
Below a statue of the Virgin in the **Santuario de Tíscar** is the impressive **Cueva del Agua★** (*open for worship Jun–Sept 11am–1pm, 5pm–7pm; Oct–May 11:30am–1pm, 4:30pm–6pm; 953 71 36 06*), where a torrent emerges between rocks.

Quesada

15km/9.5mi north of Tíscar.
Set amid olive groves, Quesada was the birthplace of painter **Rafael Zabaleta** (1907–60). His work, shown in the Quesada **museum**, (*Plaza Cesáreo Rodríguez Aguilera 5; open Wed–Sat 10am–2pm and 5–8pm [Nov–Mar, 4–7pm], Sun and public holidays 10am–2:30pm; €6; 953 73 42 60; www.museozabaleta. org*) captures local light and character. The **Cañada de las Fuentes** ravine is the **source of the River Guadalquivir** (*access via a track off the A 315, to the north of Quesada*).

Cazorla★

17km/10.5mi northeast of Quesada.
Cazorla lies in the heart of the national park. The town's streets, lined by whitewashed houses with balconies replete with flowers, are perfect for a quiet stroll or whiling away time over drinks on a *terraza*.

Castillo de la Yedra

Open Tue–Sat 10am–8:30pm (Jun–mid Sept, 9am–3:30pm), Sun and public holidays 10am–5pm. Closed Mon, 1 Jan, 1 May, 25 Dec. €1.50 (free for EU citizens). 953 10 14 02.
You'll enjoy superb views from the keep of the Roman fortress above Cazorla. A chapel contains a life-size Romanesque-Byzantine image of Christ, surrounded by 12 paintings of the Apostles. The castle also hosts a traditional Guadalquivir arts and crafts **museum**.

La Iruela

1.5km/1mi north of Cazorla.
La Iruela was settled by Carthaginians in the 3C BC. The Iglesia de Santo Domingo, a Renaissance-style church designed by Vandelvira, stands at its center. The remains of a Templar castle offer superb **views★★** of the Guadalquivir Valley.

Iruela church

© Ana del Castillo/Shutterstock.com

Road to the Embalse del Tranco de Beas★

42km/26mi northeast of La Iruela.
The first 17km/10.5mi of the winding A 319 afford **spectacular views★★**. The Parador de **El Adelantado** is reached via a branch road winding 8km/5mi up through forests.

Embalse del Tranco de Beas

Several camping areas, hotels and **water sport** facilities are located near this reservoir on the Guadalquivir River. The ruins of a Moorish castle stand on **Isla de Bujaraiza** island.

Hornos

North of Embalse del Tranco de Beas.
The remains of the fortress of Hornos rise above a cliff. From here you can enjoy **views★** of the Tranco Reservoir and Guadalquivir Valley. An **arts and crafts market** is held on the first Saturday of every month.

Segura de la Sierra★

21km/13mi northeast of Hornos.
The village of Segura de la Sierra straddles a hill at 1,240m/4,067ft. There is a sweeping **panorama★★★** from the keep of its partially intact Mudéjar **castle**, home to the **Centro de Interpretación** (*open Apr–Oct Tue–Sun 11am–2pm, 5pm–8pm, Nov–Mar Wed–Sun 11am–2pm, 4pm–7pm; €3; www.ayuntamlento-seguradelasierra.com. 902 43 04 18*).
Explore the central maze of alleyways where you will find the **town hall**, with its fine Plateresque doorway; the **parish church**, containing an alabaster statue of the Virgin; and, most rewarding of all, at calle Baño Moro, the **Moorish baths** (*baños árabes*), with horseshoe arches and star-shaped vault lights.

EXCURSIONS

ANDÚJAR★
62km/38.5mi west of Baeza.

Situated in the center of Spain's olive-growing region, Andújar is a collection of narrow, winding streets, 15C and 16C churches and houses, and vestiges of monumental 9C Moorish walls

Iglesia de Santa María

Construction of this church most likely began in the 13C, but was not completed until the 17C, hence its eclectic mix of styles. Here you can view the magnificent **Christ in the Garden of Olives★★** by El Greco, in a chapel enclosed by a fine 16C **grille★** by Maestro Bartolomé. This enormous canvas depicts Christ in an elegant red tunic, illuminated from above, and the Apostles St Peter, St James and St John, who appear to be dozing at his feet.

🌲 PARQUE NATURAL DE LA SIERRA DE ANDÚJAR★

Leave Andújar to the north along A 1208. For information contact the Park visitor center (Carretera Andújar-Santuario Virgen de la Cabeza, km 13, 953 54 90 30).

The access road winds up through an impressive landscape of holm oaks, cork oaks, wild olives and arbutus, offering magnificent **views★★** of the surrounding area. This protected park in the low foothills of the Sierra Morena above the Guadalquivir Valley alternates from open pasture where fighting bulls graze to dark ravines rife with dense vegetation ideal for deer, lynx and wild boar.

🌲 PARQUE NATURAL DE DESPEÑAPERROS★

The Parque Natural de Despeñaperros in northern Jaén area is reached by the A 4-E 5 highway linking Madrid with Sevilla and Córdoba.

This natural gateway to Andalucía is a spectacular gorge (desfiladero) carved by the River Despeñaperros through the Sierra Morena. At 1,000m/3,300ft, it provides magnificent **views★★★** of vertical walls of slate and the deep precipices dividing the park. According to tradition, Christians threw vanquished Moors into the ravine after the Battle of Las Navas de Tolosa, hence its unusual name (*despeñaperros* translates as "where dogs are hurled"). The best way to enjoy the park's impressive natural beauty is to follow 🌲 **itineraries** by car or on foot, available at the **Puerta de Andalucía visitor center** (*Carretera N-IV, km 257, Santa Elena; 953 60 97 06*). The 6,000ha/14,800 acre park includes oak (holm, cork and gall) forests, umbrella pine, mastic and myrtle. Fauna include wolf, lynx, stone marten, genet, deer and wild boar, griffon vulture and the spectacular imperial eagle. The **Paraje Natural de la Cascada de Cimbarra** (*4km/2.5mi northwest of Santa Elena*) is famous for its spectacular waterfalls and canyons. The route from **Arroyo del Rey** passes through a landscape of vertical drops and strange formations like **Los Órganos**, where natural erosion has eaten away the rocks until they resemble gigantic organ pipes.

FOR FUN

🏂 Sports

Mountain-bikers, horse-riders and hikers can follow the extensive network of forest tracks and footpaths crisscrossing the **Parque Natural de las Sierras de Cazorla, Segura y Las Villas**. Head to one of the park information points (*see Practical Information*; www.sierrasdecazorlaseguraylasvillas.es) to learn more.

In the **Parque Natural de la Sierra de Andújar**, hikers can enjoy an extensive network of paths winding through forests and thickets carpeted with wild jasmine and mastic trees.

The **Parque Natural de Despeñaperros** is ideal for hiking and cycle-touring enthusiasts.

🏂 Aventura Sport

Carretera de Huesa 4, Quesada. 953 71 42 18. www.aventurasport.es.

Canoeing, canyoning, paintballing, quad bikes, archery, mountain biking, 4x4 driving and horseriding are just some of the many activities available here.

Parque Natural de las Sierras de Cazorla

© R. Mattes/Hemis.fr

SHOPPING

Jaén's main shopping streets are located around plaza de la Constitución. Calle Virgen de la Capilla, calle San Clemente and paseo de la Estación are the main commercial arteries, along with other adjoining streets lined by small shops and the odd department store. An open-air *mercadillo* (market) offering a wide selection of food, clothing and domestic items is held on Thursday mornings at the fairground (*recinto ferial*) near Alameda de Calvo Sotelo.

In **Úbeda**, you'll find local products including hand-embroidered esparto matting, rugs, pottery, and lanterns made of tin and glass. You can also check out artisan craftwork including local ceramics and wrought-iron items.

Local Specialties

In **Baeza**, try *bacalao al estilo de Baeza* (salt cod), *cocido mareado* (bean stew with garlic, onions and tomatoes), and *ochíos*, made from an oil and bread dough and sprinkled with paprika.

CÓRDOBA★★★

Magnificent and multicultural, Córdoba is a celebration of Roman, Moorish, Jewish and Christian influences. You'll be wowed by the *Mezquita*, the city's mosque-cathedral masterpiece, and enjoy getting lost in Córdoba's delightful Jewish quarter, or *Judería*. The city is a maze of narrow, romantic streets, tranquil squares, flower-filled patios and shrines illuminated by beautiful lanterns.

A Bit of History

Roman Córdoba

Córdoba became a Roman colony in 152 BC and was the capital of Baetica until almost the end of the Empire. Leading intellectual figures included **Seneca the Rhetorician** (55 BC–AD 39); his son, **Seneca the Philosopher** (AD 4–65); and the poet **Lucan**, Seneca the Philosopher's nephew, companion to Nero in his student days. Christian Córdoba produced **Bishop Ossius** (257–359), counselor to Emperor Constantine.

Muslim Córdoba

Emirs from Damascus established themselves as early as 719. Abd ar-Rahman I, sole survivor of the Umayyads, created an **independent emirate**. In the 9C, under Abd ar-Rahman II, the city underwent great cultural development, led by the Iraqi poet Ziryab.

The Caliphate

In 929, Abd ar-Rahman III proclaimed himself independent Caliph of Córdoba. Commerce, agriculture and the city expanded, enhanced by an extensive network of roads. Peace and prosperity during the 10C brought unprecedented cultural splendor, as Jewish, Christian and Muslim communities enriched the city. Córdoba became the capital of the Western world, with a population estimated to exceed 250,000 inhabitants,

The Mezquita

Practical Information

Location
Córdoba is 143km/89mi northeast of Sevilla.

Population
329,618.

Getting There
♦ **Airport** – For the moment, Córdoba airport is not connected internationally. The closest international connections are at **Sevilla airport** (902 40 47 04; www.aena.es).

♦ **By Train** – Córdoba Central (Plaza de las Tres Culturas, 902 43 23 43) is the stop for high-speed AVE trains that interconnect Madrid, Sevilla, Málaga, Barcelona and Valencia, though it's more convenient to take the less expensive but extremely fast AVANT trains (Sevilla–Córdoba in 45 mins), Talgo (Sevilla–Córdoba in 1 hour 15 mins). Altaría trains run to Granada (2 hours 21 mins). For information and reservations: Renfe, 902 32 03 20; www.renfe.com.

♦ **By Bus** – Inter-city buses in Plaza de las Tres Culturas (in front of RENFE-AVE train station). ALSA buses run routes between Sevilla, Granada, Málaga and other Andalusian cities (902 42 22 42; www.alsa.es). Socibus connects Córdoba with Ayamonte, Cádiz, Huelva and Jerez de la Frontera (902 22 92 92, www.socibus.es).

♦ **Parking** – You will find it difficult to park in the city center. If possible, park outside and walk in. If you are staying in the historic quarter, it may be best to ask your hotel about parking before you arrive.

Getting Around
♦ **By Bus** – In the city, Aucorsa (957 76 46 76; www.aucorsa.es). For Córdoba province, Carrera (957 50 03 02; www.autocarescarrera.es).

♦ **By Taxi** – Radio Taxi Córdoba, 957 76 44 44; www.radiotaxicordoba. com. Radio Taxi Córdoba, 957 78 97 89; cordoba.etaxi.es.

Visitor Information
Oficina de turismo de Córdoba: Plaza de las Tendillas, open 9am–2pm and 5:30–8 pm. 902 20 17 74. Additional tourist information points in the train station and in Campo Santo de los Mártires in front of Alcázar.

Oficina de turismo de la Junta de Andalucía: Calle Torrijos 10, open Mon–Fri 9am–7:30 pm, Sat–Sun and public holidays 9:30am–3pm. 957 35 51 79; www.turismodecordoba.org.

and may have numbered many more. The city had some 3,000 mosques, a multitude of markets and baths, and a complex sewer system. The university, the library (created by Al-Hakam II, the largest of the period) and Córdoba's many other sumptuous buildings amazed visitors and inspired artists.

A kingdom of taifas
The Caliphate dissolved amid power struggles in the early 11C, Al-Andalus fragmented into small warring kingdoms known as the **reinos de taifas**, and Córdoba remained a taifa until its reconquest in 1236. During this period astronomy, mathematics, medicine and

A — Las Ermitas — **B** — N 432 BADAJOZ, ALMADÉN

N

0 — 200 m

Av. de las Ollerías

Torre de la Malmuerta

Palacio de la Diputación

Pl. de Colón

Pl. del Conde de Priego

América

Monumento a Manolete

Santa Marina de Aguas Santas

Av. de Fernando de Córdoba

B. Pérez Galdós

JARDINES DE LA MERCED

Convento de Sta Isabel

Pl. de Gómes

PALACIO DE VIANA

Av. de Cervantes

La Bodega

del los Tejares

Cristo de los Faroles

Pl. Puerta del Rincón

Sta Isabel E Redel

Av. de los Mozárabes

Ronda de los

Gran Capitán

José Cruz Conde

Osario

Pl. de los Capuchinos

Alfaros

A 431 SEVILLA, HUELVA

Glorieta Aguilar Galindo

Argentina

SAN MIGUEL

San Zoilo

Pl. de San Andrés

San Andrés

Mausoleo Romano

Barqueros

Alfonso

San Pablo

Casa de la Luna

Palacio de los Villalones

Medina Azahara — A 431

Concepción

Conde de Gondomar

Pl. Mármol de Bañuelos

Pl. de las Tendillas

Templo Romano

XIII

Capitulares

Espartería

Rodríguez Marín

Av. de la República

Eduardo Dato

San Nicolás de la Villa

San Felipe

Jesús y María

Juan de Mena

Claudio

Marcelo

Diego de Córdoba

Pedró López

Tundidores

Pl. de la Corredera

La Trinidad

Pl. S. Juan

Santa Victoria

Lope de Hoces

Valladares

Barroso

MUSEO ARQUEOLÓGICO PROVINCIAL

San

Museo de Bellas Artes

Lineros

PUERTA DE ALMODÓVAR

S. de Feria

Pl. J. Páez

San Francisco

R. Barros

MUSEO J. ROMERO DE TORRES

Pl. del Potro

LA JUDERÍA

Rey

Lucano

Pl. de las Riber

Romero

Deanes

Calleja de las Flores

Heredia

Fernando

Pas. de la Riber

see plan II

Av. Dr. Fleming

MEZQUITA-CATEDRAL

Amparo

Isasa

Cardenal González

de

Puente Miraflores

GUADALQUIVIR

Av. del Conde de Vallellano

ALCÁZAR

Ronda

Puente Romano

Caballerizas Reales

Puerta de Sevilla

San Basilio

TORRE DE LA CALAHORRA

Santo Cristo

S. BASILIO

Av. del Alcázar

MOLINOS ÁRABES

Plaza Sta Teresa

Av. del Corregidor

Puente de San Rafael

Av. de la Confederación

Av. de Cádiz

A 4 - E 5 SEVILLA
N 432 GRANADA

philosophy flourished. The writings of **Averroës** (1126–98) had a major impact on the works of Aristotle, while **Maimónides** (1135–1204) stood out as a philosopher and physician. His *Guide of the Perplexed*, in which he establishes conciliation between faith and reason, influenced Christian scholars, particularly St Thomas Aquinas.

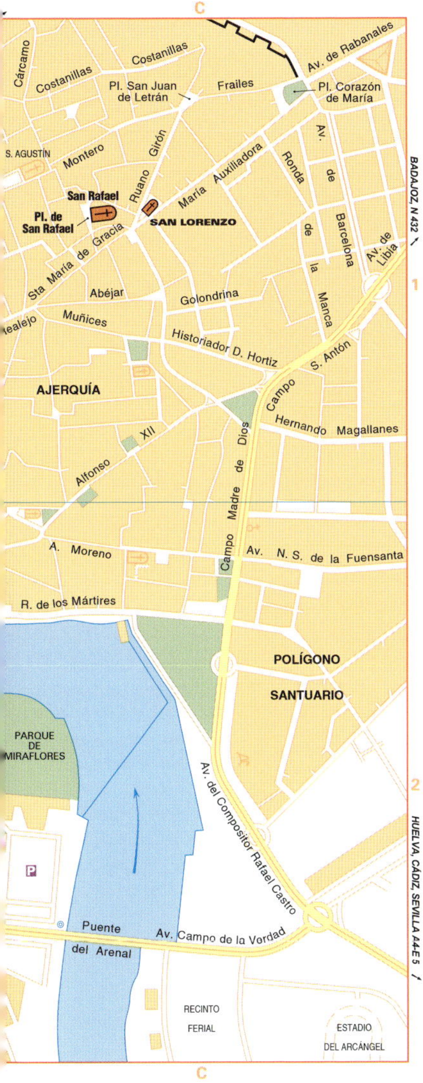

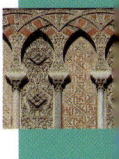

C
Cárcamo
Costanillas
Costanillas
Pl. San Juan de Letrán
Frailes
Av. de Rabanales
Pl. Corazón de María
S. AGUSTÍN
Montero
Girón
Ruano
María Auxiliadora
Ronda de Barcelona
Av. de la Manca
Av. de Libia
San Rafael
Pl. de San Rafael
SAN LORENZO
Sta María de Gracia
Abéjar
Golondrina
Muñices
Realejo
Historiador D. Hortiz
S. Antón
Campo
AJERQUÍA
Hernando Magallanes
Madre de Dios
Alfonso XII
A. Moreno
Campo
Av. N. S. de la Fuensanta
R. de los Mártires
POLÍGONO
SANTUARIO
PARQUE DE MIRAFLORES
Av. del Compositor Rafael Castro
Puente del Arenal
Av. Campo de la Verdad
RECINTO FERIAL
ESTADIO DEL ARCÁNGEL
BADAJOZ, N 432
HUELVA, CÁDIZ, SEVILLA A4-E 5
1
2
C

WHERE TO STAY

Hotel Casa de los Azulejos 1

Hotel & Hostal Maestre........... 2

WHERE TO EAT

Café Gaudí......... 1

Taberna Salinas 2

Taberna San Miguel – Casa El Pisto 3

Christian Córdoba

On 29 June 1236, **Fernando III the Saint** reconquered the city. The arrival of the Christians had a large impact on Córdoba's architecture, culimating in the construction of 14 parish churches. In 1486 **Columbus** presented Catholic Monarchs in Córdoba with his plans for an expedition to the Indies.

MEZQUITA-CATEDRAL★★★

Maps p160 and p163.

Open Mon–Sat 10am–7pm, Sun and holidays 8:30am–11:30am and 3pm–7pm. €8. 957 47 05 12. www.catedraldecordoba.es.

The Mezquita, a masterpiece of Islamic art, is one of the world's most extraordinary buildings. It was built between the 8C and 10C above the Visigothic basilica of San Vicente. Following the Reconquest of Córdoba in 1236, Christians erected a Gothic cathedral in the very heart of this Muslim place of worship. The result was a surprisingly harmonious piece of architecture that incorporates religious and architectural features of the two faiths in distinct, yet equally magnificent, parts.

The Mezquita was inspired by the house of the Prophet Muhammad in Medina. A crenellated square perimeter encloses a patio for ritual ablution, the prayer hall and the minaret. The first Muslims in Córdoba shared the Visigothic church of St Vincent with Christians. But around 780 Abd ar-Rahman I (758–88) razed the church and began the construction of a splendid mosque with 11 aisles, each opening onto the Patio de los Naranjos. Marble pillars and stone were removed from Roman and Visigothic buildings. Innovations included the superimposition of tiers of arches to gain height and space. In 848 Abd ar-Rahman II had the mosque extended to the present-day Capilla de Villaviciosa (Villaviciosa Chapel); in 961 Al-Hakam II built the *mihrab* (prayer-niche); and in 987, Al-Mansur added eight red brick aisles.

Exterior

The **minaret** built under Abd ar-Rahman III is enveloped in a Baroque tower dating from the late 16C and early 17C. To the side, the 14C Mudéjar **Puerta del Perdón** (Pardon Doorway) opens onto the street.

A small shrine to the **Virgin of the Lanterns** is set into the north wall, and is particularly beautiful to behold at night.

Take a moment to walk around the exterior of the Mezquita and admire the elegant decoration on its **entrance gates**, most of which have now been permanently sealed. Two in particular – the Puerta de San Esteban, created by Abd ar-Rahman I, and the Puerta de Palacio – are particularly impressive. You'll find both on calle Torrijos.

Unique Structure of the Mezquita

Córdoba boasted around 3,000 mosques during the Moorish period. Today visitors can admire what was the main mosque, used for Friday prayers, which was expanded at different times as the city's population grew. The Mezquita has a structure totally different to that found in Christian churches and could be extended without affecting the building's architectural style. Its simple structure, with parallel aisles, made it possible to build additional aisles without disturbing the building's overall unity.

CÓRDOBA

MUST SEE

Mezquita archs

© Cam/Shutterstock.com

Patio de los Naranjos

This spacious and enchanting patio, with porticoes on three sides, is named for the orange trees (*naranjos*) planted after the reconquest of Córdoba. Their allure and aroma are part of the Mezquita's charm. Muslims performed ritual ablutions here before prayer, and several Mudéjar fountains remain, along with the 10C **Al-Mansur basin**.

Interior

Color and shade interplay amid a spectacular forest of columns and arches that greets everyone who enters this building. Horseshoe-shaped arches are made up of alternate red and white blocks, while greys and pinks predominate in the columns. The doorway opens into the wide main aisle that leads to the *mihrab*. Aisles run perpendicular to the sacred walls of the *qiblah,* which unusually faces south, not toward Mecca. After the reconquest, Christians built chapels in the west nave, including the 17C marble-covered **Capilla de la Purísima Concepción**.

In 833 **Abd ar-Rahman II** removed the wall of the *qiblah* to extend the 11 aisles. The decoration was so striking that it was re-used in the extraordinary renovations carried out under **Al-Hakam II**, when all the columns and capitals were hand-carved for this part of the building. The rich ornamentation centered on the **mihrab★★★** is the jewel in the Mezquita's crown. Its octagonal niche was decorated by Byzantine artists who also created the superb mosaics in the magnificent **cupola★★**. The three ribbed domes of the **maksourah** – the Caliph's enclosure – rest on unusual multifoil arches with interwoven ribs. The ceiling of the Capilla Real (Royal Chapel) follows the same design. **Al-Mansur** was responsible for the largest expansion of the mosque, when he had an additional eight aisles added to the east.

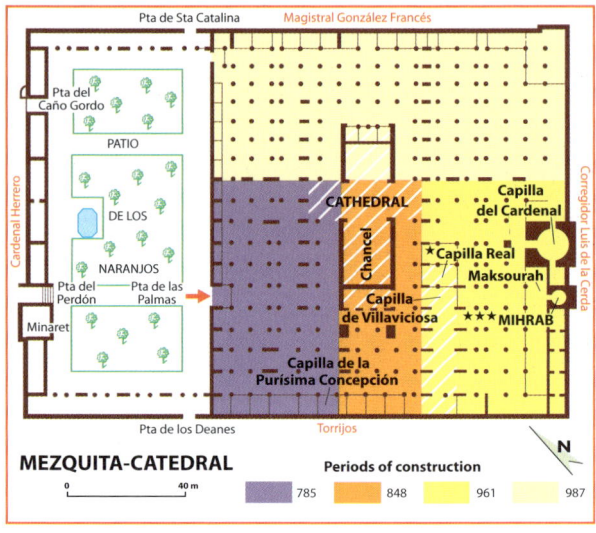

Pta de Sta Catalina — Magistral González Francés

Pta del Caño Gordo

PATIO

Cardenal Herrero

DE LOS

NARANJOS

Pta del Perdón — Pta de las Palmas

Minaret

CATHEDRAL

Chancel

Capilla del Cardenal

★Capilla Real
Maksourah

Capilla de Villaviciosa

★★★ MIHRAB

Corregidor Luis de la Cerda

Capilla de la Purísima Concepción

Pta de los Deanes — Torrijos

MEZQUITA-CATEDRAL

0 _____ 40 m

Periods of construction

| 785 | 848 | 961 | 987 |

N

Christian features

When the Mezquita was converted into a church, the aisles on the Patio de los Naranjos side were walled up, with the exception of the Puerta de las Palmas. In order to build the **first cathedral**, columns were removed and a Gothic *artesonado* ceiling supported by pointed arches was erected in their place. King Alfonso X (1221–1284) was responsible for the chancel in the **Capilla de Villaviciosa** or **Lucernario**, and built the **Capilla Real★**, decorated in the 13C with Mudéjar stucco.

Cathedral

In the 16C, despite opposition from the cathedral chapter, Bishop Don Alonso Manrique received authorization to build a cathedral in the middle of the mosque. And, despite skillful efforts by the architects Hernán Ruiz I, Hernán Ruiz II and Juan de Ochoa, and the beauty and richness of their creation, Emperor Carlos V could not hide his anger at the result: "You have destroyed something unique," he said, "to build something commonplace." Here 16C and 17C styles can be seen side-by-side in Hispano-Flemish arches and vaults, a Renaissance dome, Baroque vaulting above the choir and a Baroque high altar. Major features include two **pulpits★★** in mahogany, marble and jasper by **Michel de Verdiguier** (1706–1796). The **choir** is spectacular, in particular the Baroque **choir stalls★★** by Pedro Duque Cornejo (c. 1750). Crafted from exquisitely carved mahogany, they offer a complete iconographic program, depicting saints, scenes from the lives of Christ and Mary, and the Old and New Testaments, most notably the Ascension of Christ. Make sure you don't miss the two impressive organs (17C and 18C).

Treasury
To the left of the mihrab.
The Baroque treasury *(tesoro)*, by Francisco Hurtado Izquierdo, is in the **Capilla del Cardenal** (Cardinal's Chapel) and two adjoining rooms. A monumental 16C **monstrance★** by Enrique Arfe and an exceptional Baroque figure of Christ in ivory are of particular interest.

MEZQUITA AREA★★
Map p163.

Alongside the walls of the Mezquita, you can follow the Guadalquivir, then head into the delightful whitewashed maze of the **Judería**.

Calleja de las Flores
This narrow street in the Judería is typically Córdoban with its arches and abundance of flowers. The street ends at a small square with a fountain, where you can enjoy one of the best views of the Mezquita's tower.

Palacio de Exposiciones y Congresos
The conference center is set in the former Hospital de San Sebastián. It was once the city's orphanage and now houses the **tourist office** as well. Its **doorway★**, with fine sculptures on the tympanum and jambs, dates from the early 16C.

Triunfo de San Rafael
Dating from the second half of the 18C, this is the most impressive of all the city's monuments to St Raphael. The archangel can be seen on top of the monument, with sculptures of various allegorical figures at its base.

Puerta del Puente
This imposing monument has the appearance of a triumphal arch, having lost its original function as an entrance gateway on the north bank of the river. It was built in the 16C to a classical design with large fluted Doric columns, entablature, friezes and a curved pediment with an escutcheon supported by two warriors. The decoration can be seen on the side facing the river.

The Roman bridge

© Tupungato/Shutterstock.com

CÓRDOBA

Puente Romano

The Roman bridge rises above the Guadalquivir between the Puerta del Puente and the **Torre de la Calahorra** (which houses the **Museo Vivo de al-Andalus**, *see p 167*). First built under Emperor Hadrian, the bridge was rebuilt on several occasions, most importantly under the Moors. The river's watermills, of Moorish origin, can be seen to the right. A statue of **St Raphael** toward the middle of the bridge, on a low, altar-like wall, was erected in 1651, following an epidemic. It is usually adorned with candles and flowers, highlighting its importance as a place of devotion.

◗ *Cross the bridge, then follow calle Amador de los Ríos to the Campo Santo de los Mártires.*

Excavations at the Campo Santo de los Mártires have uncovered vestiges of **Caliphal baths**. The walls of the **Alcázar de los Reyes Cristianos**★ soon come into view on the left-hand side.

Alcázar de los Reyes Cristianos★

Open Mon–Sat 8:30am–7:30pm, Sun and holidays 9:30am–7:30pm. Light and sound shows at night. Alcázar/Museo de Julio Romero de Torres (see Museums) €4.50; €6.80 with show ticket; free Tue–Fri 8:30am–10:30am except holidays. 957 42 01 51. www.alcazardelos reyescristianos.cordoba.es.
This fortress-residence was built by Alfonso XI in the 14C and served as the headquarters for the Inquisition until 1821. On display are an exceptional 3C AD **Roman sarcophagus**★ and an interesting collection of **mosaics**★. The **baths** *(downstairs, to the right, at the end of the corridor)* are Moorish in design. Cross the Mudéjar patio to visit the delightful Moorish-style **gardens**★. At the end of the street, after the arch, enter the **San Basilio district**, famous for its charming patios. You'll find one of the most attractive at no 50, **calle San Basilio**, seat of the Córdoba Patio Association.

City walls and Puerta de Almodóvar

Calle Cairuán runs parallel to the walls of the Judería, which were just a small part of the city's defence system. Built from ashlar stone, this well-preserved section contrasts the muted green of the numerous cypress trees. The Puerta de Almodóvar (Almodóvar Gate) provides access to the **Jewish quarter**. The gate dates back to Moorish times, but was heavily restored in the early 19C, when an inner doorway was added. A statue of Seneca can be seen to the left of the gateway. If you get the chance, visit this delightful quarter by night, when illumination adds to its charms.

LA JUDERÍA★★
Map p163.

Time seems to have stood still in the old Jewish quarter characterized by whitewashed alleyways, flower-filled patios, wrought-iron grilles and typical bars and cafés.

Calle Judíos

The "Street of Jews," parallel to the walls, is one of the Judería's most famous thoroughfares.

Keep an eye out for the **Bodega Guzmán**, a charming bar at no 7 (*see For Fun*) and the **Casa Andalusí**, a 12C Moorish house at no 12, which exhibits Moorish papermaking tools.

Sinagoga

Open Tue–Sun 9am–2:45pm. Closed Mon and 18–30 Jun. €0.30 (free for EU citizens). 957 20 29 28.
This is one of only three medieval synagogues preserved in Spain (the others are in Toledo). Built in the early 14C, it consists of a small square room with a balcony on one side for women. The upper parts of the walls are covered with Mudéjar stucco and Hebrew inscriptions.

Zoco

25m/30yds further along.
Access the former Moorish **souk** beneath the brick arches of a narrow alleyway. Shops on the way to two delightful patios sell a range of Córdoban **handicrafts**.
You'll find a monument to **Maimónides**, the acclaimed Jewish philosopher and physician, in the tiny plaza Tiberiades.

Plazuela de Maimónides

This small square hosts the 16C **Casa de las Bulas**, which contains the city's bullfighting museum, the **Museo Taurino**.

CÓRDOBA

Exodus of Córdoba's Jews

The Jews arrived in Córdoba before the Moors and soon became influential, particularly in trade and teaching sciences. Following the Moorish invasion, the city's Jewish population tended to concentrate in the area now referred to as the Judería (*Jewish quarter*), mainly consisting of streets close to the Puerta de Almodóvar, where they built a fine synagogue in calle Judíos.

When Fernando III reconquered the city in 1236, the Jews maintained their influence, largely as a result of the prestige of their academies. However, as the Catholic church consolidated its power, their position in society became more complicated. In the middle of the 13C they were forced to destroy their synagogue and soon after were compelled to pay taxes for the upkeep of the Catholic Church. They were blamed for every epidemic and disaster, and in 1492 Isabel la Católica ordered their expulsion from Spain.

NORTH OF THE MEZQUITA★
Map pp156–157 (A-B-C 1-2)

Plaza del Potro

The elongated plaza del Potro takes its name from the small, 16C statue of a colt *(potro)* crowning the fountain at one end. On the opposite side is a monument to San Rafael. The square was once the site of the city's lively horse and mule fair. The **Posada del Potro**, a charming inn described by Cervantes in *Don Quixote*, faces the square. It is now a cultural center featuring temporary exhibitions. The entrance to both the **Museo de Bellas Artes** and the **Museo Julio Romero de Torres** (*see Museums*) is through a patio-garden opposite the fountain.

Plaza de la Corredera

This large, porticoed, rectangular square, accessed via vaulted passageways, recalls the main squares found in Castille. For centuries it was an important meetingplace and the setting for *autos-da-fé*, fiestas, executions, markets and bullfights.

The **calleja del Toril**, a narrow alleyway, was used as the bull enclosure.

On Saturdays, its usual tranquillity is broken by the hustle and bustle of a busy **market**.

Templo Romano
Calle Capitulares, on the corner of calle Claudio Marcelo.

The imposing columns of this 1C AD Roman temple provide a reminder of the splendor of Córdoba under Roman rule. All are fluted and crowned with Corinthian capitals.

Iglesia de San Pablo★
Calle Capitulares.

The Church of St Paul is part of the former Convento de San Pablo, built to commemorate the 1236 reconquest of Córdoba. The Baroque doorway on calle Capitulares was built in 1706. Solomonic columns flank the entrance arch, which bears an image of St Paul. The doorway leads to the atrium, which opens onto the façade. The church has a carillon instead of a bell tower. The well-proportioned interior has three wide aisles that have retained features of the transitional Romanesque-Gothic style despite subsequent restoration. The Mudéjar **artesonado ceiling★** is particularly impressive.

The chapel to the left of the presbytery contains the 18C image of **Nuestra Señora de las Angustias** (Our Lady of Anguish), by Juan de Mesa, who also carved the Christ of Great Power in Sevilla. The luxuriously dressed Virgin, her face awash with tears, holds the body of Christ in her arms. In the Epistle nave, note the 15C **Mudéjar chapel** with fine *artesonado* work, the walls of which are completely covered with stucco above a frieze of *azulejos*.

Plaza de San Andrés

Alongside this small square with orange trees and fountain is the **Casa de los Luna**, also known as the Casa de Fernán Pérez de Oliva. Built in the 16C, it has two unusual corner windows. An escutcheon and a plain window can be seen above the door, which bears a Plateresque-style orle. Another Fernandine church, the 13C **Iglesia de San Andrés**, is to the left. It was rebuilt in the 18C.

Palacio de Viana★★

Plaza de Don Gome 2. Open Tue–Sat 9am–2pm (Jul–Aug Fri–Sat 9:30pm–11pm), Sun and holidays 9:30am–2pm. Closed

Mon. €8. 957 49 67 41. www.palaciodeviana.com.
This palace is an outstanding example of 14C to 19C Córdoban civil architecture and features no fewer than 12 splendid patios. Enter from **plaza de Don Gome**, through an angled doorway. The interior is enhanced by its 16C Renaissance main staircase with magnificent Mudéjar *artesonado*. Several rooms also boast fine *artesonados*.

Iglesia de San Lorenzo★

Plaza de San Lorenzo.
Construction of this superb Fernandine church began in the late 13C and early 14C in early Gothic style. The original façade comprises a highly unusual portal which is rarely seen in this region, with three slightly pointed arches and a magnificent, finely worked **rose window★**.

The sober interior consists of three aisles with wooden ceilings and pointed arches on cruciform pillars. The chancel has Gothic vaulting. Illumination is provided by three high, narrow windows. Several 14C wall paintings remain at the apsidal end.

Plaza de las Tendillas

This spacious square is at the very heart of Córdoban life. The equestrian statue of Gonzalo Fernández de Córdoba, known as El Gran Capitán, is the work of Mateo Inurria. If you are traveling with children and the weather is hot, come here to let them play in jets of water that burst upwards from the dark paving stones.

CÓRDOBA

Iglesia de San Miguel★

Plaza de San Miguel.

This 13C church is a popular gathering place. The lovely Romanesque façade is set off by sober architectural features. The interior has three short naves, with a wooden ceiling above the central aisle; the chancel has pointed vaults with ribs set with jagged indentations. The 18C altarpiece is in red marble. Mudéjar features survive in the Capilla del Bautismo *(Epistle nave)*.

Behind the church, keep an eye out for one of Córdoba's oldest bars, the **Taberna San Miguel – Casa El Pisto** *(see For Fun)*, which makes an excellent place for a break.

Plaza de los Capuchinos★

In this austere square you'll find an impressive 18C calvary of **Christ of the Lanterns** that was once part of a *vía crucis* (Stations of the Cross) processional route.

The **Iglesia de los Capuchinos** and the church of the former 18C Hospital de San Jacinto, containing a venerated and luxuriously-dressed Virgin of Pain, also face the square.

Plaza de Colón

Named for Columbus, this square has a pretty fountain and gardens.

Palacio de la Diputación★

The provincial Parliament building began life as the 18C Convento de la Merced (Convent of Mercy). The attractive façade is painted to imitate marble.

Torre de la Malmuerta

According to legend, this magnificent 15C octagonal tower was built to imprison a knight who had killed his unfaithful wife.

Mausoleo Romano

This Roman mausoleum, discovered in 1993 during work in the Jardines de la Victoria, is a robust, circular monument from the 1C AD, the golden age of Roman Córdoba.

MUSEUMS

Museo Arqueológico Provincial★★

Plaza Jerónimo Páez.
Open Tue–Sat 9am–3:30pm,
Sun and holidays 10am–5pm.
Closed Mona. €1.50 (free for EU
citizens). 957 35 55 17.

Andalucía's foremost archaeological museum is set in the beautiful 16C Renaissance **Palacio de los Páez**. Its eroded **façade★** depicts warriors and escutcheons.

The **ground floor** exhibits prehistoric and Iberian objects – such as zoomorphic sculptures – as well as Visigothic remains.

The **Roman collection★** includes toga-clad sculptures, reliefs, sarcophagi, mosaics, capitals and column tambours.

The **first floor galleries** display Hispano-Moorish ceramics, bronzes – note the 10C **stag★** *(cervatillo)* from Medina Azahara entirely decorated with plant motifs – and a unique collection of Moorish and Mudéjar wall copings. The unusual **capital of the musicians** is decorated with human figures with mutilated heads.

Other interesting displays include a vast array of **porcelain** from different periods extending from the 17C to 20C, and the **azulejos**: 236 pieces of ceramic from the 13C to 19C. Be sure to visit the **Córdoban leather** exhibit, the best collection of its kind, comprising articles of embossed leather and cordovans from the 15C to 19C. There are also a range of impressive Flemish, French and Spanish **tapestries** on display, some of which are based on Goya. The **library** contains over 7,000 books from the 16C to 19C.

Torre de la Calahorra: Museo Vivo de al-Andalus

Open daily May–Sept 10am–2pm and 4:30pm–8:30pm; Oct–Apr 10am–6pm. The visit is a 1hr guided tour. €4.50. 957 29 39 29. www.torrecalahorra.com.
This Moorish fortress is at the southern end of the Puente Romano. It now houses a museum dedicated to the history of the Córdoba Caliphate – a period of cultural, artistic, philosophical and scientific prosperity – and includes an impressive **model**★ of the Mezquita. You can enjoy fine **views** of the city from atop the tower.

Museo de Julio Romero de Torres★

Plaza del Potro. Open Tue–Sat 8:30am–3pm, Sun and holidays 9:30am–2:30pm. Closed Mon. Alcázar (see p 162)/Museo de Julio Romero de Torres €4.50; €6.80 with show ticket; free Tue–Fri 8:30–10:30am except holidays. 957 47 03 56. museojulioromero. cordoba.es.
This mansion, the birthplace of painter **Julio Romero de Torres** (1880–1930), houses a collection of his paintings, many of which depict beautiful, dark-skinned women. The ground floor contains a number of posters advertising *ferias* of the past; the upper floor exhibits his attractive female portraits such as *La Chiquita Piconera* (The Charcoal Girl). Several canvases have religious themes, such as *The Virgin of the Lanterns*, a copy of which hangs in an altar outside the Mezquita.

Museo de Bellas Artes

Plaza del Potro. Open Tue–Sat 9am–3:30pm, Sun and holidays 10am–5pm. €1.50 (free for EU citizens). 957 10 36 59. www.museosdeandalucia.es.
The **Fine Arts Museum** displays works ranging from the 14C to the 20C, predominantly by local artists. It is housed in the former Hospital de la Caridad, founded in the 15C. The staircase, covered by a fine Mudéjar *artesonado* ceiling, has 16C and 17C murals.
Of particular interest are: *Immaculate Conception* by Juan Valdés Leal; the collection of modern Córdoban and Spanish art dating from the late 19C and early 20C (by Ramón Casas, José Gutiérrez Solana, Rusiñol, Zuloaga and others); and sculptures by the Córdoban artist Mateo Inurria.

EXCURSIONS

MEDINA AZAHARA★★

Leave Córdoba by the A 431 west. After 8km/5mi bear right onto a signposted road (follow signs to Madinat Al-Zahra). Or take the daily bus (see box).

The palace-city of Medina Azahara was built at the behest of Abd ar-Rahman III in 936. Chronicles of the day describe its amazing luxury and splendor. But no sooner was the city completed when it was razed to the ground by the Berbers in 1013 during the war with the Caliphate of Córdoba, and thereafter it became a source of construction materials. Archaeological excavations began in 1911. Although little more than 10% of the original city remains, it is still possible to imagine what this sumptuous city must have been like.

Medina Azahara is built in terraces: the upper terrace contained the Alcázar, with residences for the Caliph and other dignitaries, as well as administrative and military dependencies; gardens and the large reception room were in the middle terrace; and a mosque (excavated) and other buildings were below.

Follow the signposted itinerary. Open Tue–Sat 9am–3:30pm, Sun and holidays 10am–5pm. Closed Mon. €1.50 (free for EU citizens). 957 10 49 33. www.museosdeandalucia.es.

The tour starts outside the north wall, marked by square towers. Access is via an angled doorway, typical of Islamic defensive architecture.

Upper terrace

The **residential quarters** are to the right. The rest of the upper dwellings were built around two large square patios. To the west, at the highest point of the Alcázar, is the **Casa Real** or Royal Quarters/ *Dar al-Mulk*. The **official quarters**

Medina Azahara

MUST SEE CÓRDOBA

A daily bus to Medina Azahara takes visitors directly to the historic site. Timetable and reservations at the Tourist Information Points or online at www.reservasturismodecordoba.org. Tickets cannot be purchased in the bus. Bus stop on Paseo de la Victoria (Red Cross Hospital Roundabout) and on Paseo de la Victoria (opposite the Roman Mausoleum). €8.50.

©Turespaña

can be found to the left of the entry door. The **Casa de los Visires** (*Dar al-Wuzara*) comprises a suite of rooms. A large basilica-like hall is surrounded by dependencies and patios. The viziers held their civil audiences in the large hall. Several streets lead uphill to the impressive **portico**, the façade of a large parade ground. Only a few of the 15 magnificent arches remain; this was the monumental entrance to the Alcázar, through which ambassadors would enter.

Middle terrace

The remains of the **mosque**, which stood on the lower terrace, are to the left, along the path leading down. The middle terrace, overlooking the gardens, is dominated by the jewel of this site: the restored **Abd ar-Rahman III Room** (Salón de Abderramán III). Take a closer look at its remarkable decorations in order to get an idea of what the city's splendor must have been like when it was completed in the 10C. Beautiful horseshoe arches with alternating voussoirs are supported by grey

and blue marble, contrasting the large white marble flagstones used for the floor paving. Note the geometric and plant motif decorations on the magnificent carved stone wall panels, including stylizations of the tree of life, a common theme in Hispano-Islamic art. Opposite this room you'll find the **Pabellón Central** or central pavilion, once used as a waiting room for those granted an audience with the Caliph. It is in the center of the gardens, surrounded by four small pools.

CASTILLO DE ALMODÓVAR DEL RÍO★★

25km/15mi west of Córdoba along the A 431. Follow the road skirting the town and continue to the fortress along a dirt track. Open Mon–Fri 11am–2:30pm and 4pm–7pm (summer, 8pm), Sat–Sun and public hols, 11am–7pm (Apr–Oct, 8pm). Closed 1 Jan and 25 Dec. €6.50. 957 63 40 55. www.castillodealmodovar.com.

CÓRDOBA

The name "Almodóvar" originates from the Arabic *al-Mudawwar*, "the round one," a clear reference to the castle hill. A large fortress was established here in the 8C, under Moorish rule. Later Almódovar came under the rule of various taifa kingdoms before its reconquest by Fernando III in 1240. The present **castle** was erected in the 14C in Gothic style and is considered one of the most important in Andalucía due to its beauty and excellent condition. It was restored at the beginning of the 20C, when a neo-Gothic mansion was added. The town nestles below on the south bank of the River Guadalquivir. Climb atop the castle to enjoy magnificent **views★** of the river and the Córdoban countryside. There are two walled enclosures – one in the form of a barbican – with eight towers of varying proportions. The largest, the *torre del homenaje* (keep), is in fact a turret.

LAS ERMITAS

13km/8mi northwest of Córdoba on the El Brillante road; 10km/6mi from Medina Azahara by A 431, then left at the first crossroads (follow signs to "Ermitas").

Either way you travel this route, the **views★** of the sierra and the surrounding countryside prove delightful.
These 13 hermitages (and a solitary church), set in a wild mountainous location, date from the 18C, although hermit traditions in the area date back centuries.
In the beautiful paseo de los Cipreses (Cypress Avenue), the skull and short poem on the **Cruz del Humilladero** serve as a reminder of the transitory nature of life. Past the cross, the **Ermita de la Magdalena** is to the left, along with the hermits' cemetery and church. Entering the vestibule of the **church**, note the skull once used as a cup and plate. The rich decoration of the church – the result of donations – contrasts the hermits' austere existence. Note the attractive frieze of lustre *azulejos* behind the high altar, in the room used as a chapterhouse. Back at the entrance, a path leads to the **Balcón del Mundo**.
From this viewpoint, dominated by an enormous Sacred Heart (1929), you can enjoy a magnificent **panorama★★** of Córdoba and its surrounding countryside.
To the right, the view extends to the hilltop Castillo de Almodóvar del Río.

Guadalquivir river seen from the castle

©Vera Bogaerts/iStockphoto.com

FOR FUN

TAPAS & CAFÉS
See map pp156–157.

Córdoba does full justice to Andalucía's great tapas tradition with bars offering a huge selection of tapas and the chance to try *salmorejo* (a type of local gazpacho), *rabo de toro* (braised oxtail), *embutidos* (local sausage) and countless wines and sherries.

 Café Gaudí
Avenida del Gran Capitán 22 (A1). 957 47 17 36.
www.gaudicordoba.com.
A modern pub with a surprising U-shaped bar that "embraces" its guests, serving teas, coffees and tapas from 8am into the wee hours.

Convento de Santa Isabel
Calle Santa Isabel 13 (B1).
957 47 05 76.
The nuns in this convent are famous for their excellent pastries. Try the *almendrados* (almond dough), *coquitos* (coconut cookies), *pasteles cordobeses* (a specialty of Córdoba) and other delights.

Pastelería San Rafael
Plaza de San Miguel 6 (B1).
957 49 09 81. www.pasteleria sanrafael.com
With excellent coffees and pastries, San Rafael is perfect for a morning or late afternoon break during which you can try a local specialty: El Pastel Cordobés, a cake filled with *cabello de ángel* (a threaded jam made from Siam pumpkin pulp and white sugar). Try enjoying it the way some locals do, with Andalusian jamon.

Taberna San Miguel – Casa El Pisto
Plaza San Miguel 1 (B1).
957 47 83 28 / 47 01 66.
www.casaelpisto.com.
Founded in 1886, wallpapered with bullfight posters, this is an indispensable locale for tapas.

©Patty Orly/Shutterstock.com

See map p163 – Mezquita Area.

Bodega Guzmán
Calle Judíos 9 (opposite the synagogue). 957 29 09 60.
A traditional bar with lots of character, *azulejos* decoration, bullfighting mementos and posters advertising the local feria. Good local sausages and cheeses.

Taberna Casa Pepe de la Judería
Calle Romero 1 (between the Zoco and the Mezquita). 957 20 07 44.
www.casapepejuderia.com.
This tavern opened in 1928 and retains all its character. Tapas rooms are arranged around a patio; upstairs is a more elegant restaurant.

Taberna Casa Salinas
Puerta de Almodóvar. 957 29 08 46. www.tabernasalinas.net.
This cosy, traditional bar has a small patio, *azulejos* decoration, celebrity photos and often stages impromtu flamenco shows.

NIGHTLIFE
See map p163 – Mezquita Area.

Córdoba has a buzzing social and cultural life. During the winter, the **Gran Teatro** (*avenida Gran Capitán 3; 957 48 02 37; www. teatrocordoba.com*) hosts a regular season of concerts and theater. In addition, the **Filmoteca de Andalucía** (*calle Medina y Corella 5; www.filmotecadeandalucia.com*) organizes a varied film program. Visit www.turismodecordoba. org and click on What to Do (Qué Hacer) for listings.
Most of Córdoba's bars and nightclubs are around the **avenida del Gran Capitán** in the center and in the El Brillante residential area (5km/3mi north of the city center).

🎭 Tablao El Cardenal
Calle de Torrijos 10. Flamenco show (1hr 30 mins/2 hours) from 10:30pm. 957 48 33 20.
Guitarists, dancers and singers perform an extremely engaging flamenco show in this locale just around the corner from the Mezquita-Cathedral, in a charming patio in summer or in an historic auditorium with original wood beam ceilings in winter. Drinks are included. Given its popularity, reservations are recommended.

Sojo Ribera
Paseo de la Ribera (just beyond the Puente de Miraflores). 957 49 21 92. www.cafesojo.es.
Trendy Sojo serves from breakfast to the small hours, and stages theme parties, art exhibitions and installations.

SPAS
See map p163 – Mezquita Area.

🛁 Baños Árabes de Córdoba
Calle Almanzor 18. 957 29 58 55. www.bañosarabesdecordoba.com.
On the same site where Roman thermal baths once bubbled, take a trip back in time thanks to striking backdrops of Roman columns, palm trees, arches and Moorish motifs while you relax in baths and the hammam, or enjoy a tea out on the large patio.

🛁 Baños Árabes Hammam Al Ándalus
Calle Corregidor Luis de la Cerda 51. 957 48 47 46. www.hammamalandalus.com.
The hammam ritual is an authentic sensorial experience amid the Moorish baths located not far from the Mezquita, in a setting that will provide you a taste of what this corner of the world was like centuries ago. Enjoy traditional massages and wellbeing treatments on your way to physical nirvana!

SHOPPING

Traditional crafts in Córdoba include the famous *cordovans* (embossed leatherwork) and gold and silver filigree. The municipal market or **Zoco Municipal**, set around a small square and old lanes in the Judería, includes ceramics, leather, pottery and more (*calle Judíos 21; open Mon–Sat 10am–8pm*). **Neighborhood markets** are held almost every day. The best is held Sunday mornings and located next to the municipal stadium.

Profumeria Esencia

Calle San Basilio 50. 957 42 02 72. www.esenciadelospatios.com. Interested in bringing the essence of Córdoba's patios back home in a bottle? Visit this aromateca, set in one of the city's most beautiful patios in the San Basilio district (*see p 162*), where you can choose from various fragrances, soaps and lotions, drinking in the sunlight and flowers of the city of Mezquita…

FIESTAS & EVENTS

Semana Santa
Silent solemn processions take place against the stunning backdrop of the historic quarter.

Cruces de Mayo
In the first days of the month, flower-decked crosses dot the city in this contest involving the city's guilds and civic groups.

Concurso de Patios
Early to mid-May, patios are transformed into breathtaking floral displays. For information: www.patiosdecordoba.net, www.amigosdelospatioscordobeses.es.

Córdoba Feria
This annual fair (late May) is renowned for its *sevillanas*, feasting and drinking.

International Guitar Festival
Córdoba festival of guitar music (held the first two weeks July). www.guitarracordoba.org.

FOR KIDS

Southwest of the Mezquita, beyond the San Basilio district and the avenida del Corregidor (*off map, A2*), you'll find a vast green area that includes the **Parque Cruz Conde**, the **Ciudad de los Niños** (*Avenida de Linneo; 957 20 03 55 37/50/53. www.ciudaddelosninos. cordoba.es*) or "Children's City," a large recreation area designed specifically for kids that includes a big park area, dozens of different playground rides and games, as well as skating and skateboarding areas. There is also the **Parque Zoológico** (a wildlife center that hosts 78 different species of birds and mammals) and a **botanical garden** overlooking the River Guadalquivir.

RESTAURANTS

Blessed with coasts on both the Atlantic and the Mediterranean, and boasting some of the highest mountains in Europe, Andalucía can lay claim to a surf-n-turf cuisine unlike any other. Whether you're of a mind to sample delightful cured hams and salamis as you wind your way up through the Sierra Nevada, or feast on flavorful fish in seaside restaurants down by the coast, we've got a place for every palate.

Prices and Amenities

Restaurants were selected based on ambience, location and/or value for money, typical dishes or unusual character. Rates indicate the average cost of an appetizer, an entrée and a dessert for one person (not including tax, tips or beverages). Most restaurants are open daily and accept major credit cards. Call for information regarding reservations and opening hours.

Luxury	⊖⊖⊖⊖	>50€
Expensive	⊖⊖⊖	35€ to 50€
Moderate	⊖⊖	20€ to 35€
Inexpensive	⊖	<20€

A typical meal

Traditionally, a Spanish meal includes a first course (*primero*) or appetizer (*entremeses*), such as a salad, soup or selection of cured meats; a main course (*segundo*), consisting of meat (*carne*) or fish (*pescado*); followed by a dessert (*postre*), usually fruit (*frutas*), pastries (*pastel*) or ice cream (*helado*). Small local restaurants often offer an inexpensive *menu de la casa*, which normally includes reasonable quality house wine (*vino de la casa*).

Drinks

In restaurants, tap water (*agua del grifo*) will be provided in a carafe (*jarra*) if requested, but most people drink bottled **mineral water** (*agua mineral*), either sparkling (*con gas*) or still (*sin gas*). Most establishments will provide an excellent selection of Spanish **wines** (*vino*), including white (*blanco*), red (*tinto*) or rosé (*rosado*), available in carafes (*frasca*) as well as bottles (*botella*). **Beer** (*cerveza*) is available either draught (*caña*) or bottled; the main brands are San Miguel, Mahou, Águila and Damm. **Sangría** is normally served as an aperitif, accompanied by a selection of tapas.

Tapas

Tapas are synonymous with Spain, Andalucía and most especially Sevilla, where they originated. We have included a list of tapas bars where visitors can enjoy an aperitif or meal in several of the *Must Do* pages in the Must See section. Beware, however, that while tapas are a tempting and often very tasty treat, they are no longer the inexpensive tradition they used to be, and your tapas bill can quickly add up, sometimes even outweighing the cost of a conventional meal.

Michelin Guide

The annually updated red-cover **Michelin Guide España & Portugal** recommends a selection of restaurants recognized for the exceptional quality of their cuisine. These are highlighted by Michelin's renowned star ratings.

MUST EAT

SEVILLA AREA

*See maps p28–29 and p39
(Barrio de Santa Cruz).*

Luxury

Taberna del Alabardero
🍽🍽🍽🍽   **Modern**
*Calle Zaragoza 20, Sevilla. 954 50 27
21. www.tabernadelalabardero.es.*
The elegant, stylish dining rooms
in this 19C mansion are arranged
around a bucolic Andalusian patio,
which also serves as a tea room.

Expensive

Corral del Agua
🍽🍽🍽   **Andalusian**
*Callejón del Agua 6, Sevilla. 954
22 07 14. www.andalunet.com/
corral-agua.*
A pleasant locale serving
Andalusian cuisine, located on
a quiet alley. The terrace is filled
with leafy plants, providing a great
place to escape summer heat.

Moderate

Casa Cuesta
🍽🍽   **Spanish**
*Calle Castilla 1, Sevilla. 954 33 33
35. www.casacuesta.net.*
In the 1880's, Casa Cuesta's first
clients came here to buy wine.
Today it serves excellent food and
tapas as well. Weather permitting,
grab a table outside in the piazza
and enjoy local products like
cured hams, *gallega* meats or your
preferred *pescado*.

🍴 Az-Zait
🍽🍽   **Modern**
*Plaza San Lorenzo 1 (off map, A3),
Sevilla. 667 04 34 40.
www.az-zaitrestaurantes.com.*

Classical, elegant tables contrast
the intense red hues of the walls,
with a menu offering a blend of
international dishes that emphasize
a single basic ingredient: delicious
olive oil.

🍴 La Almazara de Carmona
🍽🍽   **Traditional**
*Calle Santa Ana 33, Carmona.
954 19 00 76.*
Located in a former olive oil mill,
this restaurant boasts a busy tapas
bar and a traditional menu, from
goat ribs and *Bacalao* (cod) to a
selection of more modern dishes.

Roche/Fotolia.com

COSTA DE HUELVA

Expensive

Casa Luciano
🍽🍽🍽   **Andalusian**
*Calle La Palma del Condado 1,
Ayamonte. 959 47 10 71.
www.casaluciano.com.*
Luciano's house has been passed
down from one generation
to the next. Behind the rustic
façade you'll find a tapas bar with
enticing display cabinets, and
two comfortable dining rooms.
Specialties include regional dishes
and above all fresh fish.

RESTAURANTS

Moderate

Acanthum
⊖⊜ **Modern**
*Calle San Salvador 17, Huelva. 959
24 51 35. www.acanthum.com.*
Located in a narrow street close to
the center, the Acanthum includes
a tapas bar and modern dining
room. Contemporary cuisine
is characterized by flavors that
change with the seasons.

Casa Cacherón
⊖⊜ **Andalusian**
*Calle Emiliano Cabot 47,
Isla Cristina. 959 33 26 82.*
Ignore the restaurant's
unpretentious appearance: you'll
eat well here. The chef has taken
over the family business to offer
traditional Andalusian cuisine with
a pleasantly modern twist.

JEREZ DE LA FRONTERA AREA
See map p72.

Luxury

Aponiente
⊖⊜⊜⊜ **Creative**
*Calle Puerto Escondido 6, El Puerto
de Santa María (14km/8.5mi
southwest of Jerez). 956 85 18 70.
www.aponiente.com.*

The chef offers creative cuisine
in this attractively restored
restaurant. The menu is based
exclusively on local seafood
dishes, reelaborated with a
modern twist, both in terms of
preparation and presentation.

Expensive

La Taberna Flamenca
⊖⊜⊜ **Traditional**
*Calle Angostillo de Santiago 3,
Jerez de la Frontera. 956 32 36 93.
www.latabernaflamenca.com.*
In addition to traditional
Andalusian and Spanish
specialties (from 8pm), this
large tavern located in a former
wine warehouse hosts exciting
flamenco performances featuring
young flamenco talents (at
approx. 10:30pm; end May–Oct,
also Tue, Wed and Sat 2:30pm).

Moderate

🍴 La Carboná
⊖⊜ **Andalusian**
*Calle San Francisco de Paula 2,
Jerez de la Frontera (off map, B2).
956 34 74 75. www.lacarbona.com.*
La Carboná occupies a former
sherry bodega in the center
of Jerez and serves traditional
Andalusian cuisine.

© fred goldstein/Shutterstock.com

Tendido 6
⊖⊛ **Andalusian**
Calle Circo 10, Jerez de la
Frontera. 956 34 48 35 35.
www.tendido6.com.
Located next to the bullring, this
is one of the best restaurants in
Jerez, serving Andalusian meat
and fish specialties on a covered
patio as full meals or as tapas.

 ### Casa Bigote
⊖⊛ **Fish and seafood**
Pórtico de Bajo de Guía 10,
Sanlúcar de Barrameda.
956 36 26 96. www.restaurante
casabigote.com.
This renowned restaurant is
decorated in a neo-rustic style
and dotted with maritime features.
The Casa Bigote's main selling
points are its fresh ingredients
and attractive prices. Highlights
include the stews and fried dishes.

CÁDIZ AREA
See map pp80–81.

Expensive

El Faro
⊖⊛⊛ **Andalusian**
Calle San Félix 15, Cádiz. 956 21
10 68. www.elfarodecadiz.com.
Nicely set up tables and
unpretentious cuisine in this
family-run restaurant, with
outstanding fish and seafood
dishes.

Ventorrillo del Chato
⊖⊛⊛ **Andalusian**
Vía Augusta Julia (carretera San
Fernando), Cádiz (off map, C2).
956 25 00 25. www.ventorrillo
elchato.com.
A well-kept and cozy
establishment located inside a

beautiful historic building near
the beach dunes.

Moderate

La Pepa
⊖⊛ **Traditional**
Paseo Maritim 14, Cádiz
(off map, C2). 956 26 38 21.
www.restaurantelapepa.es.
La Pepa's specialty is rice,
served no fewer than 41
different ways, many in dishes
featuring fish and seafood: from
Verde Pepa rice with mussels,
baby squid and shrimp to *Ciega*
de Mariscos paella or tapas.
The restaurant features a rustic,
intimate dining room and
outdoor tables.

El Duque
⊖⊛ **Traditional**
Avenida del Mar 10, Medina
Sidonia (45km/28mi east of
Cádiz). 956 41 00 40.
www.hotelelduque.com.
El Duque has a bar with an open
fireplace and several tables for
those ordering from the regular
menu, as well as a welcoming à la
carte dining room framed by large
windows. There is an extensive
traditional menu dominated
by meat dishes. A few simply
furnished guestrooms are also
available.

STRAIT OF GIBRALTAR AREA

Expensive

Mesón el Guadarnés
⊖⊛⊛ **Traditional**
Avenida Guadarranque, San Roque
(11km/7mi northwest of Gibraltar).
956 78 65 04.

RESTAURANTS

Managed by its owner, this small rustic-style restaurant offers a traditional and international menu with meat specialties.

Moderate

Trafalgar
🍽🍽 **Traditional**
Plaza de España 31, Vejer de la Frontera. 956 44 76 38. www.restaurantetrafalgar.com.
This welcoming culinary destination specializes in delicious fresh fish in minimalist and rustic dining rooms and features a glass-fronted wine cellar. Tapas are also served at the entrance.

COSTA DEL SOL
See map pp98–99 (Málaga).

Luxury

Calima
🍽🍽🍽🍽 **Creative**
Calle José Meliá, Marbella. 952 76 42 52. www.restaurantecalima.es.
This restaurant has a minimalist layout featuring an open kitchen and spacious, immaculately arranged dining room with large picture windows looking out to sea. The extensive tasting menu combines high technical ability and originality.

Expensive

Sollun
🍽🍽🍽 **Modern**
Calle Almirante Ferrándiz 53, Nerja. 653 68 94 52. www.sollunrestaurante.com.
A small, modern looking restaurant in one of Nerja's central pedestrian streets. The chef prepares

contemporary cuisine featuring some interesting innovative touches.

Moderate

Altamirano
🍽🍽 **Fish and seafood**
Plaza Altamirano 3, Marbella. 952 82 49 32. www.baraltamirano.es.
This local restaurant on a small square in the old quarter specializes in fish and seafood. Note the Azulejo decoration on the façade.

La Menorah
🍽🍽 **Traditional**
Urbanizacion Arena Beach, Estepona. 952 79 27 34.
La Menorah has a pleasant terrace and white-walled dining room, and features an extensive traditional menu, including freshly caught local fish.

Mar de Plata
🍽🍽 **Fish and seafood**
Avenida Mar de Plata 3, Almuñécar (13km/8mi west of Salobreña). 958 63 30 79. www.restaurantemardeplata.es.
A group of brothers have teamed up to run this enjoyable eatery, where you can choose from an extensive menu with a variety of delicious fish baked in salt crusts, plus rice dishes on weekends.

Restaurante María
🍽🍽 **Traditional**
Avenida Pintor Joaquín Sorolla 45, Málaga (off map, D2). 952 60 11 95.
Enjoy a drink in the bar before taking a seat in the attractively decorated dining room with its profusion of wood, arches and exposed brickwork. Traditional cuisine, including delicious stews.

Inexpensive

El Trillo
🍽 **Andalusian**
*Calle Don Juan Díaz 4, Málaga. 952
60 39 20. www.trillomalaga.com.*
A tapas bar in the entrance and a
cheerful dining room attest to this
restaurant's rustic style, underlined
by its choice of delightful
traditional dishes.

RONDA AND PUEBLOS BLANCOS

Expensive

Casa Santa Pola
🍽🍽🍽 **Andalusian**
*Calle Santo Domingo 3, Ronda. 952
87 92 08. www.casasantapola.com.*
This charming restaurant has
several Moorish-style rooms
overlooking the ravine, and
provides gourmet regional cuisine.

Moderate

Cádiz el Chico
🍽🍽 **Andalusian**
*Plaza de España 8, Grazalema.
956 13 20 67.*
A simple restaurant with two rustic
dining rooms featuring gabled
wood ceilings and large menu of
traditional fare that focuses on
lamb, roast meats and game.

Asador La Trapería
🍽🍽 **Meats and grills**
*Calle Doctor Manuel Elkin
Patarroyo 36, Osuna. 954 81 24 57.
www.asadorlatraperia.es.*
Run by a local couple, this rustic-
style restaurant specializes in
roast and grilled meats, and offers
an extensive à la carte menu of
traditional dishes.

GRANADA AREA
See map pp118–119.

Luxury

Ruta del Veleta
🍽🍽🍽🍽 **Traditional**
*Avenida de Sierra Nevada,
Cenes de la Vega (6.5km/4mi east
of Granada). 958 48 61 34.
www.rutadelveleta.com.*
Ruta del Veleta's appealing *à la
carte* menu, regional décor
and position inside a luxurious
building have earned it
widespread recognition.

Expensive

Alacena de las Monjas
🍽🍽🍽 **Modern**
*Plaza Padre Suárez 5,
Granada. 958 22 95 19.
www. alacenadelasmonjas.com.*
This somewhat unusual restaurant
is located in the heart of Granada
and boasts both a tapas bar and
an attractive dining room in the
basement, formerly a vaulted
water cistern. The menu features
contemporary, seasonally-inspired
cuisine.

I.Pompe/Hemis.fr

RESTAURANTS

Moderate

Mariquilla
⊖⊜ **Traditional**
Calle Lope de Vega 2, Granada.
958 52 16 32.
A family-run restaurant serving
adventurous "market" cuisine. Cozy,
with paintings of Granada hanging
on the walls.

SIERRA NEVADA

Moderate

Alcadima
⊖⊜ **Traditional**
Calle Francisco Tárrega 3,
Lanjarón. 958 77 08 09.
www.alcadima.com.
This restaurant boasts panoramic
views of the Alpujarras region,
and overlooks the ruins of a
14C-Moorish castle. The menu
blends Mediterranean flavors with
typical Andalusian cuisine.

El Rincón de Yegen
⊖⊜ **Traditional**
Camino de las Eras 2, Yegen
(32km/20mi east of Trevélez).
667 96 40 10. www.elrincon
deyegen.com.
A series of small houses on the
edge of town with a bar and two
regionally inspired dining rooms,
serving traditional dishes and
local specialties.

COSTA DE ALMERÍA

Expensive

Alejandro
⊖⊜⊜ **Creative**
Avenida Antonio Machado 32,
Roquetas de Mar. 950 32 24 08.
www.restaurantealejandro.es.

Located in the port area, this
modern restaurant has comfy sofas
in the entrance, a meticulously
arranged dining room with views
of the open kitchen, as well as two
private dining areas. It serves light,
well-presented contemporary
dishes, showcased on two enticing
tasting menus.

La Gruta
⊖⊜⊜ **Meats and grills**
Carretera Nacional 340, Km 436,
Almería (5km/3mi west of the city
center toward Aguadulce). 950 23
93 35. www.asadorlagruta.com.
The huge caves of this ex-quarry
are a unique setting for a menu of
prime grilled meats prepared in
simple, time-honored fashion.

Moderate

Terraza Carmona
⊖⊜ **Andalusian**
Calle del Mar 1, Vera (19km/12mi
north of Mojácar). 950 39 07 60.
www.terrazacarmona.com.
A family-run business with a
welcoming, charming atmosphere,
particularly in the main dining
room. Regionally inspired menu
and local dishes. The property also
offers a few pleasant guestrooms.

NORTHEAST ANDALUCÍA

Moderate

Amaranto
⊖⊜ **Modern**
Calle Hortelanos 6, Úbeda.
953 75 21 00. www.restaurante
amaranto.es.
This restaurant is run by a couple,
with the husband managing the
kitchen and the wife seating clients.

Foodpictures/Shutterstock.com

The menu features cuisine with a modern twist, served in a simple, contemporary dining room.

La Sarga
◎◎ **Traditional**
*Plaza del mercado 11, **Cazorla**. 953 72 15 07.*
This cheerful, welcoming locale features detailed modern décor and a variety of regional dishes.

Mesón Río Chico
◎◎ **Traditional**
*Calle Nueva 12, **Jaén**. 953 24 08 02. www.mesonriochico.com.*
Designed as an inn along modern lines, the restaurant features a daily menu, tapas and snacks. The upper floor hosts a classical-style dining room and various private spaces.

CÓRDOBA AREA
See maps pp156–157 and p163.

Expensive

Almudaina
◎◎◎ **Traditional**
*Plaza Campo Santo de los Mártires 1, **Córdoba**. 957 47 43 42. www.restaurantealmudaina.com.*

An attractive restaurant near the Alcázar with exquisite regional decor, serving the city's specialties, like artichokes *a la Cordobesa*.

El Churrasco
◎◎◎ **Traditional**
*Calle Romero 16, **Córdoba**. 957 29 08 19. www.elchurrasco.com.*
Old Jewish houses with a bar at the entrance and a cosy Cordovan patio. Visit the wine cellar-museum in an annex. The house specialties are grilled meats.

Moderate

Taberna Salinas
◎◎ **Andalusian**
*Calle Tundidores 3 (plaza de la Corredera), **Córdoba**. 957 48 01 35. www.tabernasalinas.com.*
Among the specialties of this traditional 19C Córdoba tavern are *gazpacho*, Cordobesian tomato salad, eggs with asparagus, prawns and spanish ham, fried aubergine and fired homemade *chorizo* (spicy pork sausage).

🍴 La Taberna
◎◎ **Andalusian**
*Calle Antonio Machado 24, **Almodóvar del Río**. 957 71 36 84. www.latabernadealmodovar delrio.com.*
This family-run, centrally located restaurant in Almodóvar del Río has a bar at the entrance and a number of classical-style dining rooms. Enjoy regional home cooking, including tasty specialties like the *carrillada* of veal meat in its sauce and potatoes.

HOTELS

Whether you're looking to hole up in a countryside parador and relax, or sample luxurious pampering and Moorish baths in an elegant urban setting, you'll find a wide range of accomodations to choose from here. Try spending a night underground in a grotto in the Sierra Nevada, or drift asleep to the sounds of seawater rolling onto a nearby beach in the Costa del Sol. Andalucía is all this and more.

Prices and Amenities

Properties were selected based on ambience, location and/or value for money, and in some cases for their intrinsic charm.

Price categories reflect the average cost for a standard double room for two people in high season, not including taxes or surcharges. There can be a significant difference in rates between high and low season, so always ask for written confirmation of prices when booking. Summer is high season along the coasts and islands, but not in the cities further inland, where visitors usually venture during cooler months in the spring and autumn.

Luxury	🛏🛏🛏🛏	>150€
Expensive	🛏🛏🛏	100€ to 150€
Moderate	🛏🛏	60€ to 100€
Inexpensive	🛏	<60€

Reservations

Book as far in advance as possible to ensure the best rooms at the lowest prices. Reservations can generally be made online with a credit card, either at the individual property's website or on specialized travel websites like **www.viamichelin. com**. Bear in mind that off-season specials are often available on websites. Offers of this kind or low season prices can often reduce a hotel indicated here as "Expensive" to the "Moderate" category.

Michelin Guide

Updated annually, the red-cover **Michelin Guide España & Portugal** is an indispensable complement to this guide, providing hotel recommendations based on category, price, level of comfort, setting and facilities

The roof terrace bar of Hotel Doña María

© Hotel Doña María

MUST STAY

(swimming pool, tennis court, golf course, garden, etc.).

SEVILLA AREA

See maps pp28–29 and p39 (Barrio de Santa Cruz).

If you're planning to stay for Holy Week or the Feria, book months ahead and beware the room rate, as prices can double, triple or more during these periods.

Luxury

Hotel Doña María

⊖⊖⊖⊖   **64 Rooms**
Calle Don Remondo 19, Sevilla. 954 22 49 90. www.hdmaria.com.
This hotel boasts arguably the finest location in town, with spectacular views of the Giralda from its delightful roof terrace bar (open to outsiders, see picture on the opposite page) and a small swimming pool (clients only). The bedrooms are a bit bland and formal, however.

Hotel Las Casas de la Judería

⊖⊖⊖⊖   **119 Rooms**
Callejón Dos Hermanas 7, Sevilla. 954 41 51 50. www.casasypalacios.com.
Modern luxury meets old-world charm in this former mansion of the Duke of Béjar, located in the old Jewish quarter. Swimming pool.

Expensive

Casa de Carmona

⊖⊖⊖   **31 Rooms**
Plaza de Lasso 1, Carmona. 954 19 10 00. www.casadecarmona.com.
This historic 16C palace of Lasso de la Vega (once Governor of Chile) is located in the old quarter and boasts impressive salons, a Moorish garden and fine dining.

🛏 Hotel Amadeus Sevilla/La Música

⊖⊖⊖   **20 Rooms**
Calle Farnesio 6, Sevilla. 954 50 14 43. www.hotel amadeussevilla.com.
A family of musicians transformed this magnificent 18C house in Santa Cruz. Musical instruments are available to guests, including a grand piano on the patio!

Hotel Simón

⊖⊖⊖   **29 Rooms**
Calle García Vinuesa 19, Sevilla. 954 22 66 60. www.hotelsimonsevilla.com.
This historic white mansion by the cathedral, arranged around a cool patio, is filled with antiques and large mirrors. Rooms are comfortable, and the best are decorated with colorful *azulejos*.

Moderate

Hostería del Laurel

⊖⊖   **20 Rooms**
Plaza de los Venerables 5, Sevilla. 954 22 02 95. www.hosteriadellaurel.com.
Blessed with an unbeatable location on one of Sevilla's most charming plazas, this hosteria has comfortable rooms, Provençal furniture and a restaurant serving regional dishes.

Hotel Doña Blanca

⊖⊖   **19 Rooms**
Plaza Jerónimo de Córdoba 14, Sevilla. 954 50 13 73. www.donablanca.com.
A newly built mansion with distinctive red façade, very reasonably priced given the decor and comfort. Located in the busy area by Santa Catalina.

HOTELS

Hotel Londres

⬒⬒ **7 Rooms**

*Calle San Pedro Mártir 1, **Sevilla**. 954 21 28 96. www.londreshotel.com.*
This charming Sevillian house has basic, clean rooms. Those with a balcony are generally more pleasant and, despite the central location, relatively quiet.

Posada de Cortegana

⬒⬒ **40 Rooms**

*Carretera El Repilado-La Corte, Km2.5, **Cortegana**. 959 50 33 17. www.posadadecortegana.es.*
Pleasant wooden bungalows, all with air-cond. The complex enjoys a shady rural setting in the Parque Natural de la Sierra de Aracena y Picos de Aroche, with fine views, a pool and a good rustic restaurant.
The hotel organizes various activities, including horseback rides, hiking, lessons in local crafts and various sports.

COSTA DE HUELVA

Luxury

🏛 Parador de Mazagón

⬒⬒⬒⬒ **63 Rooms**

*Playa del Parador, **Mazagón**. 959 53 63 00. www.parador.es/en/parador-de-mazagon.*
Located in the privileged setting of Doñana National Park, near the sea and surrounded by green, this parador is synonymous with serenity. Comfortable rooms, a large garden and pool, and a restaurant with views of the surrounding pine forest.

Paradores

Expensive

Monte Conquero

⬒⬒⬒ **162 Rooms**

*Calle Pablo Rada 10, **Huelva**. 959 28 55 00. www.hotelesmonte.com.*
Extremely courteous personnel add to this hotel's value, where you'll find a panoramic elevator and small but quite comfortable rooms.

Moderate

Hotel & Apartments Paraíso Playa

⬒⬒ **39 Rooms**

*Avenida de la Playa, **Isla Cristina**. 959 33 02 35. www.hotelparaisoplaya.com.*
Beachfront ambiance and family-oriented organization for this hotel. Rooms are decorated in classical and Castilian styles. Apartments are also available in a building nearby.

Hotel La Malvasía

⬒⬒ **16 Rooms**

*Calle Sanlúcar 38, **El Rocío**. 959 44 38 70. www.lamalvasiahotel.com.*
Behind this hotel's wonderful façade you'll discover rooms decorated with classical and rustic details. The hotel's restaurant offers traditional local dishes.

JEREZ DE LA FRONTERA AREA
See map p72.

Luxury

Hotel Jerez & Spa
😑😑😑😑 **126 Rooms**
Avenida Alcalde Álvaro Domecq 35 (1.5km/1m from city center), Jerez de la Frontera. 902 41 84 28. www.hace.es/hoteljerezspa.
This luxury hotel and spa has rooms overlooking the garden or the swimming pool.

Expensive

Hotel Doña Blanca
😑😑😑 **30 Rooms**
Calle Bodegas 11, Jerez de la Frontera. 956 34 87 61. www.hoteldonablanca.com.
Set in a typically Andalusian building, the hotel is located in the heart of the town and offers large, comfortable rooms.

Moderate

Hotel Chancillería
😑😑 **14 Rooms**
Calle Chancillería 21, Jerez de la Frontera. 956 30 10 38. www.hotelchancilleria.com.
The hotel is set in two 17C houses divided by a courtyard, and has sober, functional rooms. The rooftop terrace provides views of the historic center.

Nuevo Hotel
😑😑 **27 Rooms**
Calle Caballeros 23, Jerez de la Frontera. 956 33 16 00. www.nuevohotel.com.
This 19C mansion was one of the first hotels in Jerez. Rooms are modestly furnished but large, laid out around a central patio; no. 208 displays fine, Moorish-inspired plasterwork.

CÁDIZ AREA
See map pp80–81.

Expensive

Hotel Argantonio
😑😑😑 **17 Rooms**
Calle Argantonio 3, Cádiz. 956 21 16 40. www.hotelargantonio.es.
Antique brick paving and personalized rooms characterize this 19C building turned hotel, located in a narrow street in the historic district.

Hospedería Las Cortes de Cádiz
😑😑😑 **36 Rooms**
Calle San Francisco 9, Cádiz. 956 22 04 89. www.hotellascortes.com.
A charming 19C house in the old quarter that has been equipped with modern facilities including a gym and jacuzzi. Rooms around the patio have been decorated in historical themes, and the restaurant is a treat.

Moderate

Hostal Bahía
😑😑 **14 Rooms**
Calle Plocia 5, Cádiz. 956 25 91 10 / 90 61. www.hostalbahiacadiz.com.
You'll find modern rooms in this small hostel in the old quarter. The location can be quite noisy, but the hostel is clean and one of the least expensive in Cádiz.

STRAIT OF GIBRALTAR AREA

Moderate

Mesón de Sancho
⌂⌂ **40 Rooms**
Carretera N 340, km 94, Tarifa. 956 68 49 00. www.meson desancho.com.
Strategically-located on the Strait of Gibraltar, this establishment has large, luminous rooms and a nice pool surrounded by trees. The rustic restaurant has an interesting collection of whiskies.

Hotel La Casa del Califa
⌂⌂ **20 Rooms**
Plaza de España 16, Vejer de la Frontera. 956 44 77 30. www.lacasadelcalifa.com.
This unusual hotel is spread out across various small houses in the center of Vejer. Rooms are minimalist, but decorated with antique furniture and brightly-colored bathrooms. The layout can feel labyrinthine… but entirely intriguing!

COSTA DEL SOL
See map pp98–99 (Málaga).

Luxury

🏨 La Villa Marbella
⌂⌂⌂⌂ **29 Rooms**
Calle Principe 10, Marbella. 952 76 62 20. www.lavillamarbella.com.
Three houses in the historic center provide luxuriously-decorated rooms and a carefully crafted and fascinating Oriental ambiance.

Expensive

Hotel Monte Victoria
⌂⌂⌂ **8 Rooms**
Conde de Ureña 58, Málaga (off map, C1). 952 65 65 25. www.hotel-montevictoria.com.
Impeccable rooms in a family villa hotel, with a garden-terrace that boasts fine city views. The hotel is set on a narrow, inclined street (hard to park). 15min walk to the historic center.

Hotel La Morada Más Hermosa
⌂⌂⌂ **6 Rooms**
Calle Montenebros 16, Marbella. 952 92 44 67. www.lamoradamashermosa.com.
A delightful little boutique hotel personalized with arts and crafts on a lane bursting with plants. Charming rooms are individually decorated in Andalusian style. Room no. 2 has a pleasant terrace.

Moderate

Hotel California
⌂⌂ **24 Rooms**
Paseo de Sancha 17, Málaga (off map, D2). 952 21 51 64. www.hotelcalifornianet.com.
A stone's throw from the sea and ten minutes from the old city, the hotel is old-fashioned, but with cozy rooms.

Hostal Guadalup
⌂⌂ **10 Rooms**
Calle Peligro 15, Torremolinos. 952 38 19 37. www.hostal guadalupe.com.
A pensión in a narrow street just 50m/55yd from the beach. Rooms are Spartan but spotless.

MUST STAY

Inexpensive

Hostal El Pilar
🛏 **20 Rooms**
Plaza de las Flores 10, Estepona.
952 80 00 18. www.hostalelpilar.es.
Time seems to have stood still
in this pretty Andalusian house
on Estepona's main square, with
black and white family photos
on the walls and an imposing
staircase leading to basic but
pleasant bedrooms.

RONDA AND PUEBLOS BLANCOS

Luxury

Parador de Arcos de la Frontera
🛏🍴🛎🛎 **24 Rooms**
Plaza del Cabildo, Arcos de la
Frontera. 956 70 05 00.
www.parador.es.
Andalusian light plays with vibrant
colors and carefully selected
furnishings in this magnificent
parador. Guests enjoy five-star
views and wonderful regional
Cádiz cuisine in the restaurant.

Moderate

Hotel San Gabriel
🛏🛎 **22 Rooms**
Calle Marqués de Moctezuma 19,
Ronda. 952 19 03 92.
www.hotelsangabriel.com.
A magnificently decorated if
somewhat formal mansion dating
from 1736. Ask for a room with a
view over the charming patio.

Hotel Real de Veas
🛏🛎 **12 Rooms**
Calle de la Corredera 12 , Arcos
de la Frontera. 956 71 73 70.
A typical historical house with a
central patio and rooms equipped
with jacuzzi baths.

GRANADA AREA
See map pp118–119.

Luxury

🏛 Hotel Casa Morisca
🛏🍴🛎🛎 **14 Rooms**
Cuesta de la Victoria 9,
Granada. 958 22 11 00.
www.hotelcasamorisca.com.
A quiet, yesteryear ambiance
pervades this hotel set in a 15C
house. Staying here is a delight,
as much for the rooms as for the
portico under which you can relax,
close your eyes and listen to the
sounds of running water and
wind in the leaves.

Expensive

Hotel América
🛏🍴🛎 **16 Rooms**
Calle Real de la Alhambra 53,
Granada. 958 22 74 71.
www.hotelamericagranada.com.
A small, charming family hotel
superbly located within the
Alhambra. Cosy, welcoming and
full of character. The restaurant
serves traditional dishes from the
Granada region.

Moderate

Hotel Anacapri
🛏🛎 **49 Rooms**
Calle Costa 7, Granada. 958 22
74 77. www.hotelanacapri.com.
This hotel has comfortable rooms,
almost all of which are decorated
in colonial style, and a covered
internal courtyard.

HOTELS

🏨 Villa Sur
🛏🍽 **11 Rooms**
Avenida Andalucía 57, Huétor Vega (8.5km/5mi southeast of Granada). 958 30 22 83. www.hotelvillasur.com.
Elegance, warm welcomes and Andalusian flavors distinguish this exquisitely-decorated villa. Note the luminous breakfast area looking out over the garden.

SIERRA NEVADA

Luxury

Hotel Meliá Sierra Nevada
🛏🍽🍽🛏 **221 Rooms**
Plaza de Pradollano, Pradollano. 958 48 04 00. www.melia.com.
Located within the ski station in the Sierra Nevada, this hotel includes a ski school and spa with views of the mountains. Rooms are quite comfortable and the restaurant serves hearty mountain fare.

Moderate

🏨 Cuevas La Granja
🛏🍽 **19 Rooms**
Camino de la Granja, Benalúa de Guadix (8.5km/5mi northwest of Guadix). 958 67 60 00. www.cuevas.org.
The grottoes typical of this area, not far from Guadix, have been transformed into rustic apartments where you can enjoy a truly unique night's stay. One grotto hosts a restaurant serving Andalusian cuisine.

Hotel Finca los Llanos
🛏🍽 **45 Rooms**
Carretera Sierra Nevada, Capiléira (5km/3mi north of Pampaneira). 958 76 30 71. www.hotelfincalosllanos.com.

Sober rooms are spread out across three buildings bearing the names of writers connected with Andalucía: Gerald Brenan, Washington Irving and Federico García Lorca. The pool has mountain views.

COSTA DE ALMERÍA

Expensive

Hotel Plaza Vieja
🛏🍽🛏 **10 Rooms**
Plaza de la Constitución 4, Almería. 950 28 20 96. www.plazaviejahl.com.
Arab details appear amid the modernity of this hotel set in a building on the town square. Rooms have murals depicting various local scenes.

Moderate

Hotel Blanca Brisa
🛏🍽 **34 Rooms**
Calle Isla de Santa Elena 1, Cabo de Gata. 950 37 00 01. www.blancabrisa.com.
A family-run hotel with spacious, modern rooms, all with balconies. The restaurant serves local cuisine.

Inexpensive

Hotel Costasol
🛏 **50 Rooms**
Paseo de Almería 58, Almería. 950 23 40 11. www.hotelcostasol.com.
A smart, comfortable hotel on the busiest street in Almería. Rooms are large, some with balconies.

NORTHEAST ANDALUCÍA

Luxury

Parador de Jaén

⊖⊕⊖⊕ **45 Rooms**

Carretera del Castillo de Santa Catalina, Jaén (4.5km/2.8mi west of the city center). 953 23 00 00. www.paradores-spain.com.
Welcoming rooms laid out in a 13C castle that has an imposing hall and provides exceptional views of the city and surrounding territory. The stone-vaulted restaurant serves traditional regional fare.

Expensive

Palacio de la Rambla

⊖⊕⊖ **8 Rooms**

Plaza del Marqués 1, Úbeda. 953 75 01 96. www.palaciodela rambla.com.
This glorious 16C palace is now a splendid hotel where guests are treated like family friends in refined yet relaxed atmosphere. Its most impressive features are the magnificent Renaissance patio and life-size warrior figures.

Inexpensive

Hotel Guadalquivir

⊖ **12 Rooms**

Calle Nueva 6, Cazorla. 953 72 02 68. www.hguadalquivir.com.
A family-run hotel with extremely clean rooms, decorated in country style with pine wood furniture.

CÓRDOBA AREA
See maps pp156–157 and p163.

Expensive

Hotel Lola

⊖⊕⊖ **8 Rooms**

Calle Romero 3, Córdoba. 957 20 03 05. www.hotellola.es.
Lola, Yasmina, Zulema and Aida are just a few of the seductive lady's names given to the carefully decorated rooms in this hotel, located in the Jewish quarter. Wonderful terrace on the top floor.

Moderate

🏛 Hotel Casa de los Azulejos

⊖⊕ **8 Rooms**

Calle Fernando Colón 5, Córdoba. 957 47 00 00. www.casadelosazulejos.com.
Charming hotel in a traditional house with plant-filled patio, large rooms, wrought-iron bedsteads and designer baths. Good value.

Hotel González

⊖⊕ **16 Rooms**

Calle Manríquez 3, Córdoba. 957 47 98 19. www.hotel-gonzalez.com.
Rooms off the patio in this 16C palace, between the Mezquita and the Judería, are spacious and well decorated.

Inexpensive

Hostal La Milagrosa

⊖ **8 Rooms**

Calle Rey Heredia 12, Córdoba. 957 47 33 17. www.lamilagrosahostal.es.
This attractive hostel is located in the old city near the Mezquita, with a patio and airy rooms.

Hotel & Hostal Maestre

⊖ **26 & 8 Rooms**

Calle Romero Barros 4–6, Córdoba. 957 47 24 10. www.hotelmaestre.com.
One of Córdoba's better value accommodations, near the plaza del Potro, with spacious if plain rooms. The owners also run a less expensive hostel and apartments nearby.

ANDALUCÍA

List of Maps

Photo Credits (page Icons)

INDEX